THE SEARCH FOR JUSTICE

THE SEARCH FOR JUSTICE
Trócaire: A History

Brian Maye

VERITAS

Published 2010 by
Veritas Publications
7–8 Lower Abbey Street
Dublin 1
Ireland

publications@veritas.ie
www.veritas.ie

ISBN 978-1-84730-167-3

10 9 8 7 6 5 4 3 2 1   2502 9541

A catalogue record for this book is available from the British Library.

Designed by Lir Mac Cárthaigh
Printed in Ireland by Hudson Killeen, Dublin

Veritas books are printed on paper made from the wood pulp of managed forests. For every tree felled, at least one tree is planted, thereby renewing natural resources.

Front cover printed on Cyclus Offset, a 100% recycled board manufactured using post consumer waste.

To the memory of Brian McKeown,
Director of Trócaire 1973–1993

FOREWORD

When I was appointed a bishop I always had a hope at the back of my mind that I would be involved in the work of Trócaire. The first intimation of possible involvement was an invitation to go on a Trócaire-organised exposure trip to South Africa in November 1991 at the invitation of Bishop Eamon Casey, who was chairman of the agency at the time.

I little expected that, within six months, Bishop Casey would have resigned. I was then nominated as a member of the Board of Trócaire. Bishop Michael Murphy succeeded Bishop Casey from 1992–1993. I then succeeded Bishop Murphy as chairman of Trócaire in June 1993.

Bishop Casey, who had been chairman for almost twenty years, would be a hard act to follow. He had been a dynamic character with a marvellous ability to get work done and was blessed with genuine leadership qualities. He also had a genuine feel for people's sufferings and deprivation and was a most articulate spokesman. In addition, of course, he had been the founding father, as it were, of Trócaire and its driving force, along with Brian McKeown, for its first two decades. Sadly, Brian died in July 2009. We have dedicated this book to his memory.

Looking back over my almost seventeen years as Trócaire chairman, some memories stand out. An abiding memory is of that first South African trip. Nelson Mandela had been released from prison but it would be nearly another three years before he became leader of his country.

I stayed in the house of Archbishop Denis Hurley in Durban. He was one of the most remarkable people I have ever met. He was born in South Africa of Irish parents and partially educated by the Oblate Fathers in Inchicore in Dublin. While we were in his house, he spoke of cycling to the Phoenix Park for the Eucharistic Congress in 1932 as a seventeen-year-old.

He was named a bishop in December 1946 and consecrated early the following year. To his eternal credit, he condemned apartheid before it went onto the statute book and contested the policies of the white National Party before it came to power. It ruled South Africa from 1948–1994 and he opposed it fearlessly during that time. He combined a fierce anti-apartheid commitment with a very gentle per - sonality. That meeting with him is one of the highlights of my involvement with Trócaire.

The other memory I have of that South African visit also relates to Durban. We were taken to visit a men's hostel where black mineworkers lived. The showers consisted of a few spouts coming out of walls, with no privacy or protection; the floors were caked with rotting food; the beds stank of urine – yet human beings were meant to live amid such degradation. It made my blood boil to see the horror of what human beings were capable of doing to others.

In November 1996, I was in Rwanda to witness the hundreds of thousands of refugees who had been forced to leave Mugunga camp in Zaire and were flooding back into Rwanda (see chapter 12).

The sheer size of the throng on that occasion has stayed with me. People moved in regular formation, three or four wide, carrying their belongings with them, the women carrying their bundles on their heads. One woman's bundle became untied and she stooped down to reassemble it. But the crowd continued moving forward in its regimental way and she was of no importance as she strove to get her few pots and pans together.

The crisis in East Timor, now Timor Leste, is another issue in which I became personally involved. In July 1999 I paid Bishop Carlos Belo of Dili a solidarity visit, one month before the referendum on independence from Indonesia. I recall clearly his sense of foreboding about the referendum. He was sure that his countrymen would vote for independence but he was equally certain that widespread violence would follow that vote. His foreboding proved justified, and in that violence that he had predicted, his own house was burned. I spoke out strongly against that violence and particularly against the slowness of the United Nations to get involved to stop it.

Trócaire's commitment to campaigning and advocacy is a most important part of our work. I was in Cologne in June 1999 for the demonstration that the Jubilee 2000 campaign (of which Trócaire was part) had organised to coincide with the G8 summit that was taking place at the time there (see chapter 17). The Make Poverty History campaign was a natural follow-on from Jubilee 2000 and, at the end of June 2005, I had the privilege of being one of the leaders of a rally in Dublin, which up to 20,000 people attended, proof that the issue of putting an end to world poverty means a lot to the Irish people.

Each January, The Holy Land Coordination of the Holy See sends an international delegation of Catholic churchmen to visit the Holy Land and Trócaire has funded that visit for the past three years. Ireland's first involvement occurred in January 2007, when Bishop Ray Field and I participated in the delegation.

I found it frightening and disturbing to see the so-called 'separation wall' the Israelis are building around the West Bank Palestinian territory. It is eight metres high and enormously imposing. We saw one house where, on three sides, the 'wall' was less than two metres away, which meant one could just about walk around the house. The land belonging to that house was on the far side of the 'wall' but the access point to the land was five kilometres away. This meant a round trip of twenty kilometres for the man who owned that land. It is hardly difficult to see how hostility and resentment would build up in that type of situation.

Trócaire's work in providing humanitarian relief while supporting local Palestinian and Israeli NGOs shows that work for justice and human rights is an important part of our response to the current crisis in that region.

I have had the privilege of meeting many outstanding individuals in my time in Trócaire. One is Fr Jon Sobrino, a Jesuit who was fortunate to escape being murdered when six of his fellow Jesuits were killed, along with their housekeeper and her daughter, in the University of Central America in San Salvador on 16 November 1989. He was in Asia at the time of the atrocity. I was impressed by his skill as a lecturer and theologian. On my first day as chairman of Trócaire, 1 June 1993, I met Mother Teresa of Calcutta. She had been invited to Ireland to give the annual Maynooth College/Trócaire lecture. No words of mine could add anything to her deservedly legendary stature.

In my travels I have witnessed the extraordinary work of Trócaire staff and our many partners throughout the developing world. I have seen their courage and commitment as they stand up for justice and the rights of the people we serve, often in the face of great oppression and intimidation. This book tells many of their stories, and of Trócaire's commitment to continue to work for a just world.

BISHOP JOHN KIRBY
Former Chairman of Trócaire
April 2010

CONTENTS

LIST OF ABBREVIATIONS

AfrI: Action from Ireland
APSO: Agency for Personal Service Overseas
CAFOD: Catholic Fund for Overseas Development
CI: Caritas Internationalis
CIDSE: Coopération Internationale pour le
            Développement et la Solidarité
CRS: Catholic Relief Services
DDCI: Debt and Development Coalition of Ireland
EEC: European Economic Community (1957–1993)
EU: European Union (1993–)
FAO: Food and Agriculture Organisation (UN)
GDP: Gross Domestic Product
GNP: Gross National Product
ICJP: Irish Commission for Justice and Peace
IMF: International Monetary Fund
MDGs: Millennium Development Goals
MOSOP: Movement for the Survival of the Ogoni People
NGO: Non-Governmental Organisation
ODA: Overseas Development Aid
OECD: Organisation for Economic Cooperation and
            Development
RCJP: Rhodesian Commission for Justice and Peace
UNESCO: United Nations Educational, Scientific and

	Cultural Organisation
UNHCR:	United Nations High Commissioner for Refugees
UNICEF:	United Nations International Children's Emergency Fund
WFP:	World Food Programme (UN)
WHO:	World Health Organisation (UN)

INTRODUCTION

When visiting Trócaire's southern Africa regional office in Mozambique in 2007 I was asked over a meal one evening by our staff there to tell them something of the history of Trócaire's involvement in southern Africa. That involvement predates my own time in Trócaire, but I had heard the stories about Rhodesia, now Zimbabwe, in the 1970s, and the work of the Rhodesian Committee for Justice and Peace. I told them of the request to Trócaire for funds to buy a typewriter for the South African journalist, Donald Woods, on which he wrote his story, *Cry Freedom*, about the life of Steve Biko.

My young colleagues were fascinated. I realised that all of these things happened when most of them were in primary school, or for some, before they were born. So on the flight home from that visit I resolved that it was time to capture the stories from the past. This book, *The Search for Justice*, is the product of that resolve.

This is not a formal history of the organisation – that is another day's work. It is an attempt to capture, for the benefit of a new generation of supporters, partners and staff, the inspiring stories of Trócaire's work over almost forty years. Knowing these will reaffirm Trócaire's radical roots and illustrate why 'courage' is one of our organisational values. In a crowded space, with so many development agencies competing for attention and support, it will help define that elusive issue of what differentiates Trócaire from the others. It will challenge us to stay close to our roots and our legacy in an ever-changing world.

The main sources for this book, worked on so diligently by author Brian Maye, have been press cuttings accumulated since the beginning of the organisation in 1973 and a series of interviews with key people involved as staff and board members over the years.

As such the focus is on the stories that made the news, such as Zimbabwe's independence, the struggle against apartheid, the famine and oppression in Cambodia and North Korea. The work in Central America, still so central to the organisation, is a major feature. Here our founding chairman, Bishop Eamon Casey, our first director, Brian McKeown, and Sally O'Neill (currently Latin America regional director) played a crusading role in bringing the struggle for justice and human rights of the peoples of Central America to the fore.

Crises and disasters in Timor Leste, Somalia and the 2004 tsunami-affected countries also feature. However it is important to recognise that our initial response to these events outlined here is only a small part of the work that Trócaire has carried out over the years. Long after the cameras have gone, the famine has ended, the political crisis has been resolved, the painstaking work of long-term development continues. For instance, eighteen years after the Somali famine of 1992, Trócaire remains in Gedo district working with local communities to provide health and education services.

Not all the stories could be told in one volume. Notably absent is an account of our involvement in Kenya, Sierra Leone and Zambia in Africa; Pakistan and Bangladesh in Asia; Colombia and Peru in South America. What brought Trócaire to many of these countries, and others, was the Irish missionary presence there. In Trócaire's early days there was some confusion, and even tension, as to what exactly would be the relationship between this new agency of the Irish

Catholic Church and the Irish missionaries. Trócaire was defined in one of its founding documents as 'a further contribution' of the Irish Church to the developing world. If in the early days there was a need to create a space for this further effort, Trócaire's work must be seen now, with the benefit of historical perspective, as very clearly built on the missionary tradition. The stories in this book bear testimony to this, in larger than life figures such as Bishop Donal Lamont and Fr Niall O'Brien, amongst others. Trócaire's work throughout Africa, in Brazil, Pakistan and many other countries was done in partnership with missionaries and was built upon their legacy. The relationship with the Irish missionary congregations – the Holy Rosary Sisters and the Medical Missionaries of Mary, the Kiltegan Fathers and Columban Fathers – has been central to Trócaire's develop-ment, as has been the relationship with so many missionaries from other orders.

What we share with the missionaries, of course, is our faith, which manifests itself in the work of development and justice through Catholic Social Teaching. The opening chapter illustrates this very comprehensively. Catholic Social Teaching, however, is not just the historical basis underlying Trócaire's work. It is at the heart of it today, as the church's teaching has evolved to address current global issues. Pope Benedict XVI's recent encyclical, *Caritas in Veritate* (Charity in Truth), published in 2009, is yet a further challenging develop-ment in that teaching.

All of Trócaire's work is underpinned by the main principles set out in Catholic Social Teaching. From the outset the founders recognised that the work of justice lay at the heart of good development work; that the beneficiaries of development projects must be the main authors of their own development, participating in the design and implemen-tation of projects, not simply the objects of projects designed elsewhere by others. We have built up an extensive network of partners over many years, both church-based and secular, and worked with them to develop programmes that promote sustainable development, help communities overcome poverty, and allow each person to fulfil their potential as human beings. Our key approach has been the development of local leadership, called leadership training in our earlier days, now referred to as strengthening civil society. It is this aspect of our work that shines through in the stories that follow. The real heroes of the struggle for justice are the local leaders who have challenged vested interests, stood up to oppressive governments and put their lives on the line, and in many cases tragically lost them, as a result of their courage and leadership.

Trócaire is bound together with the social action arm of the universal Catholic Church as a member of Caritas Internationalis the humanitarian confederation of 165 Catholic development agencies from around the world. Caritas is organised from the national to the parish level throughout the developing world, giving access to the poorest countries and providing a network for support in times of crisis. It is an extraordinary strength for Trócaire to be part of this network with such a global reach.

The other network which has been central to our work is Coopération Internationale pour le Développement et la Solidarité, the working group of Lenten Campaign organisations across Europe and North America. Increasingly we have focused our joint work on advocacy and lobbying, pooling our expertise and resources to advocate for pro-poor policies at the United Nations, the World Bank, the International Monetary Fund, the European Union and with national governments. The results of some of this work are illustrated in the chapters dealing with the Jubilee Campaign and Make Poverty History Campaign.

The relationship between Trócaire and successive Irish governments has been something of a rollercoaster ride over nearly four decades. The Irish Overseas Development Aid programme was set up the same year that Trócaire was founded, 1973, which was also the year of Ireland's accession to the European Economic Community.

In Trócaire's founding document, the bishops called for a commitment on Ireland's part to reach the target of spending 0.7% of Gross National Product as development assistance. This call has remained a constant refrain in the dialogue between government and Trócaire ever since. However, that dialogue is now at a much more sophisticated level. The Irish development aid policy has evolved to the extent that Ireland's aid programme is widely recognised for its poverty focus, its commitment to resolving the problem of world hunger, its eschewing of tied aid and, most importantly, its renewed commitment to increase the volume of aid to reach the UN target. The 'White Paper on Irish Aid', published in 2006, stated: 'For some, political and strategic motives may influence decisions on the allocation of development assistance. That is not the case for Ireland. For Ireland, the provision of assistance and our cooperation with developing countries is a reflection of our responsibility to others and of our vision of a fair global society.' This vision has been shaped in part by the tremendous work of Irish missionaries and Non-Governmental Organisations over many decades. The recognition by Irish Aid of the role that both the Irish NGOs and missionaries can play, working in partnership with them, in delivering our aid commitment is a distinguishing feature of Ireland's aid programme. Trócaire is proud to have played our part in establishing the political understanding and commitment to this vital issue and enjoys a solid partnership with Irish Aid in delivering on our national commitments.

In establishing Trócaire in 1973, the bishops of Ireland in their pastoral letter spoke of our duties as Christians towards the poorest countries and said: 'These duties are no longer a matter of charity but of simple justice.' Trócaire's approach to the work of development, based on that principle, took many by surprise. On the tenth anniversary of Trócaire's founding, Cardinal Cahal Daly, then Bishop of Down and Connor, gave the keynote address. He said: 'If Trócaire were to be criticised for concerning itself with political issues in Third World countries in cases where political policies and institutions manifestly violate justice and human rights ... or were to be criticised for exerting pressure on Irish governments and politicians to increase a niggardly state contribution to world development, then Trócaire must invoke the charter given to it by the Hierarchy at its foundation.' The courage and steadfastness of the church in safeguarding Trócaire's mandate has borne much fruit. The history of our work, which you are about to read, bears testimony to that. Let us hope that this volume will inspire this generation, and generations to come, to continue the struggle for justice, for at the heart of justice lie true peace and development for all.

JUSTIN KILCULLEN
Director of Trócaire
April 2010

CHAPTER 1:
The Development of Peoples:
Establishing Trócaire

Inspiration

To discover the inspiration behind the founding of Trócaire, one must go back to the Second Vatican Council (1962–1965) and particularly to the social teachings of the Catholic Church as enunciated at the council.

Of particular importance is the encyclical issued by Pope Paul VI on 26 March 1967, *Populorum Progressio* (On the Development of Peoples). In addressing issues of trade, debt, the limits of capitalism, oppressive regimes and the temptation to violent revolt, superfluous wealth and the need for generous development aid, Paul VI set out issues that would become Trócaire's mandate from the bishops of Ireland in their pastoral letter establishing the Irish Catholic Church's development agency six years later.

The 1960s could be referred to as the first development decade. It was a period of decolonisation, with the emergence of newly independent states throughout the developing world. It was a time of great optimism in developing countries. But it was also a period of great naivety as regards development. The 'trickle-down theory' (the politico-economic argument that an increase in the wealth of the rich is good for the poor because some of that additional wealth will eventually trickle its way down to the poor) was very much in vogue and development was characterised by large infrastructural projects. There was very little attention paid at this time to human development.

From the outset, the Catholic Church could see the dangers and limitations in this approach. Pope Paul VI published his encyclical to highlight these limitations and to offer a different vision of development. His opening sentence set the tone: 'The development of peoples has the church's close attention, particularly the development of those peoples striving to escape from hunger, misery, endemic diseases and ignorance; of those who are looking for a wider share in the benefits of civilisation and a more active improvement of their human qualities; of those who are aiming purposefully at their complete fulfilment.'

Pope Paul warned of the dangers and evils of uneven economic growth, in contrast to proponents of the trickle-down theory. 'Rich and poor alike – be they individuals, families or nations – can fall prey to avarice and soul-stifling materialism,' he wrote.

A key passage of the encyclical stated: 'The development we speak of here cannot be restricted to economic growth alone. To be authentic, it must be well rounded; it must foster the development of each man and of the whole man.' Central to this sentiment was the recognition that sustainable development requires the participation of communities and peoples in the development process, and that basic human needs must take precedence in development planning.

The mandate for Trócaire was outlined in the Irish Bishops' pastoral letter on development of February 1973 and that letter drew heavily on *Populorum Progressio*. The political and economic analysis in both documents is very similar and the issues raised continued to be dealt with by Trócaire over the next thirty-seven years and beyond. The agency continued to apply the teachings of the encyclical as it planned its responses to the modern world.

Asking why they are poor

Two events occurred in the early 1970s that were to prove defining in the foundation of Trócaire. Serious flooding, war and famine devastated Bangladesh and the country's plight received widespread media coverage. The Irish Catholic Church decided to hold a special collection to fund aid to the stricken country and the Irish people responded generously, donating some £250,000. This led some in the Irish hierarchy, and particularly Cardinal William Conway, to contemplate the need for an Irish Catholic Church agency to channel such generosity. The second event – and it strengthened this train of thought on the cardinal's part – was a visit he and Monsignor Tomás Ó Fiaich paid to Mother Teresa's community in Calcutta. The grinding poverty they witnessed left a lasting impression on them.

Into this evolving situation came a man named Brian McKeown. He had trained as an engineer in his native Belfast but his first job was as a lay missionary with the Legion of Mary in the Congo for four years in the 1960s. He then went to Queen's University Belfast to study sociology and his next job was as assistant secretary-general of Coopération Internationale pour le Développement et la Solidarité (CIDSE), a Brussels-based coordinating group for Catholic development agencies around the world.

He was aware that in a number of countries the Catholic Church had set up development agencies for the Third World, but that this had not yet happened in Ireland. He made contact with Cardinal Conway and found him very interested in development issues and in what was going on within these other countries. He also found the cardinal very anxious that the Irish Church would do something, but uncertain that he would have the support of the majority of Irish bishops. Gorta was already in existence and Bishop Michael Harty's brother was chairman of that organisation (Bishop Harty was Bishop of Killaloe). The Concern agency had also been operating in Ireland since 1968.

Cardinal Conway suggested to Brian McKeown that he sound out a few of the Irish bishops informally, which he did. The cardinal then contacted Mr McKeown in Brussels to inform him of the collection that had been made by the church for Bangladesh. Cardinal Conway was astounded by the amount that had been donated and said he would like advice on how the money should be spent. He also said that he was going to go ahead with promoting the idea of an Irish Church development agency among the hierarchy and that Bishop Eamon Casey of Kerry would be getting in touch with Mr McKeown.

Before his appointment as bishop of Kerry in 1969, Bishop Casey had spent ten years ministering to the Irish in Britain. There he had set up the Shelter organisation to help Irish emigrants (and others) to acquire housing. As a result of this work, he was invited to join the board of the Catholic Fund for Overseas Development (CAFOD), which had been set up by the Catholic bishops of England and Wales in 1962. In a recent interview for this book, he stated that part of the impetus towards the establishment of Trócaire was his awareness that CAFOD was interested in setting up a branch in Ireland.

Bishop Casey met Brian McKeown shortly afterwards and asked him how they should go about advancing the idea of setting up a development agency of the Irish Catholic bishops. Mr McKeown suggested that there would be a general agreement among the bishops on the broad outlines of the policy of the new organisation and that this policy be agreed by the Irish Bishops' Conference. The next step would be to put this agreement into a pastoral letter that would be issued by the bishops announcing the new organisation.

Brian McKeown was asked to go ahead and draft a pastoral letter on development for the bishops' approval and to return to Dublin to assist in the setting up of the new agency. He returned in December 1972 and laid the groundwork for the first Lenten collection in March 1973 – from then on the Lenten Campaign became the cornerstone of Trócaire's fund-raising. The idea for the Lenten collection was Mr McKeown's; he had seen how many of the other Catholic Church development agencies in Europe raised their funds by means of such a collection.

In the meantime he had also set up a structure of sub-committees to work through a set of policy recommendations which would be made to the bishops. One of the subcommittees concerned itself with how the funds collected should be distributed, another with how best to organise and carry through a policy of development education. These policy recommendations were presented in the Progress Report to the Hierarchy at a conference of the Irish bishops at Maynooth in October 1973 at which Trócaire was formally launched. It was Cardinal Conway who came up with the very effective and resonant title for the organisation, which means 'compassion' in Irish.

Brian McKeown was appointed the first director of Trócaire and Bishop Casey became its first chairman. There was a board of trustees consisting of the four archbishops of Ireland and three other bishops, one of whom was the chairman. In addition, the new agency had an executive committee which comprised two bishops and five lay people. The role of the committee was to review requests for funding and to recommend projects for acceptance to the trustees.

In their pastoral letter on development, which is the foundation document of Trócaire, the Irish bishops had set out the following two-fold aim for the organisation: 'Abroad, it will give whatever help lies within its resources to the areas of greatest need among the developing countries. At home, it will try to make us all more aware of the needs of those countries and of our duties towards them. These duties are no longer a matter of charity but of simple justice.' To generate a greater awareness within Ireland of the problems of underdevelopment and its causes, Trócaire went on to implement a development education programme jointly with the Irish Commission for Justice and Peace (ICJP), which was also an Irish Catholic Church body (national commis -

sions for justice and peace were specifically provided for by Vatican II).

Development education, informed by 'the universal purpose of all created things' to use the great Vatican II phrase, was aimed at creating an informed public opinion in rich countries which would demand changes in the economic, social and political structures that maintained the gap between rich and poor countries. Such changes, which were necessary for the development of the Third World, could be undertaken only at governmental or inter-governmental level. But Trócaire believed governments would act only where there was an informed public opinion demanding such changes.

Development education was a long-term process. Part of Trócaire's programme involved the research, compilation and dissemination of information to individuals, groups, schools, organisations and so on by means of a wide variety of material which Trócaire produced on development issues and problems.

Trócaire announced it was to devote 20 per cent of its core income to development education, one of the most innovative aspects of its approach and one which differentiated it from agencies already existing. In addition, 10 per cent was to go to emergency aid and 70 per cent to development cooperation programmes. Bishop Dominic Conway of Elphin told a press conference in mid-December 1973 that the main part of Trócaire's effort would be devoted to tackling the basic problems of underdevelopment that made disasters in Third World countries such catastrophes. He also said that development education was not just a matter of giving statistics about underdevelopment but was concerned with helping to form the attitudes of people in the West, which would eventually lead to a change in outlook towards problems in Third World countries.

Bishop Conway stressed Trócaire's aim of transferring responsibility for decision-making about development co-operation programmes to competent and representative groups within the developing countries themselves. The aim was to help, as far as possible, the efforts of those working towards their own development and to arrive at a real partnership with those they were trying to help.

Mary Sutton worked as research coordinator for Trócaire for more than ten years. In a recent interview for this book, she said that from the outset she would have been aware that Trócaire was different in a number of respects from existing Irish Non-Governmental Organisations (NGOs) at the time, especially in its decision from the beginning to spend 20 per cent of core income on development education. Research was to be part of the development education process – the part for which she was to be responsible.

She regarded this approach as very far-sighted in that Trócaire was always keen to have a strong evidence base for what it was saying on the issues of the day. It was also far-sighted, she believed, because it indicated that the new agency was not content to take a superficial perspective on the question of world poverty. For Trócaire, she said, it was not just about feeding hungry people but about questioning why they were hungry, and analysing the causes and underlying structural determinants of poverty.

Tackling the causes rather than treating the symptoms
A few months after Trócaire's establishment, the *Catholic Standard* newspaper had the following to say about the organisation (in early January 1974): 'It embodies in its activities the principles of accepting the cultural differences of the world, of self-determination in policy-making for individual people, of awareness of the dangers of paternalism, and of helping those in need, irrespective of creed and the possibility of making converts.' The article said that in many ways Trócaire had to be ranked as 'one of the most advanced of the church's development agencies in the world'. The *Catholic Standard* saw it as a matter of 'extreme relief' that the Irish hierarchy had not only not blocked Brian McKeown's plans but had actually welcomed and defended them.

In an interview he did for *Africa*, the magazine of St Patrick's Missionary Society, Kiltegan, Co. Wicklow, in June/July 1974, Trócaire's director stressed the new agency's commitment to tackling the underlying causes of poverty in the Third World:

Trócaire could collect much more money if we adopted a different policy of fund-raising. But this would not be in the interest of the Third World. You can put up the image of a starving child, which will evoke sentiments of pity and fill collection boxes, without telling the people why the child is starving, without attacking the causes of the problem. The starving child may be a good fund-raising gimmick, if your aim as an agency is the collection of the largest amount of money, irrespective of the underlying needs of the Third World or the feelings of people whose dignity is continually hurt by being shown on posters and appeals as wretched and starving. Such gimmicks can wound international relations irreparably.

During the first full year of Trócaire's existence various papers, both local and national, reported on the amounts of money that the agency was allocating to projects in developing countries. The *Irish News*, for example, in October 1974 said that Trócaire had allocated almost £440,000 towards Third World projects since the previous December. 'The latest grants are for medium- and long-term development programmes aimed at tackling the causes of underdevelopment rather than treating the symptoms,' the paper made clear. It went on to say that funds were given to people and groups working on the ground, 'in keeping with Trócaire's policy of encouraging local participation and initiative'.

From the outset, Trócaire effectively conveyed to the Irish public, via the media, what it was really about. In doing so, it also managed to get across that it was not just about providing disaster relief. Nor was it about converting people to the faith or building churches in the developing world because there were already other organisations in existence providing support and funding in those areas.

However, not everyone in the media was convinced that it was all sweetness and light in the new agency. An article in *Hibernia* (8 November 1974) suggested that tension existed between the director of Trócaire and the bishops, the legal trustees. The article asserted that Brian McKeown was too radical for them, that they wanted Trócaire to send money to help missionaries and to repair damage after disasters anywhere in the world, while Mr McKeown wanted to channel funds to people on the ground who best knew how they should be spent. His actions, the article argued, made it obvious that he wanted 'to help create an anti-imperialist consciousness in the Third World, rather than merely giving money to local disaster cases'. The article went on to declare that Mr McKeown had fallen foul of a number of Irish bishops and it expressed doubt that he would be able to continue on his independent course for long.

A fortnight later, Bishop Casey had a letter published by *Hibernia* in which he described the article as 'mischievous and misinformed'. The bishop said that all proposals for funding for projects were submitted to the executive committee of Trócaire for recommendation to the trustees, who made the final decision, and that Mr McKeown did not make independent decisions on projects. Bishop Casey made it clear that it was the trustees, i.e. the bishops, who controlled funding for projects.

When asked about this *Hibernia* article in a recent interview, Mr McKeown said that the best evidence for refuting it lies in the fact that it was the bishops who employed him. They knew what they were getting when they did so and they also knew very well what the policy of the new development agency was going to be since, he said, they approved of that policy in their February 1973 pastoral letter on development which established Trócaire.

CHAPTER 2:
The Struggle for Zimbabwe's Independence

Striving to bring about social justice

The British established the colony of Southern Rhodesia in the late nineteenth century. When the colony unilaterally declared itself independent of British rule in 1965 and called itself Rhodesia, it was ruled by a minority white government led by Ian Smith, which frustrated attempts to establish a majority democratic system of government in the country. A resistance campaign against the minority white government began in the early 1970s.

In June 1974, Bishop Donal Lamont, the Irish-born Bishop of Umtali (known as Mutare since 1982), submitted documentation to Trócaire about violence by Rhodesian security forces. The documentation included testimonies from people who had been brutally treated by the soldiers. The Justice and Peace Commission of the Rhodesian Catholic Bishops' Conference (RCJP) had compiled the documentation and had called on the Smith regime to conduct an inquiry into the allegations. The Rhodesian Minister for Justice denied there was any need for an inquiry and accused the bishops of trying to undermine lawful authority.

Bishop Lamont demanded an apology from the minister for his remark that the Catholic Church was opposed to the law. Earlier in June, on a visit to New York, the bishop had told congressmen that the terror and intimidation used by the Rhodesian government 'differs, not in essence, but only in degree, from the persecutions of the Jews by the Nazis'.

In response to a request for assistance from the RCJP, Trócaire had given a grant of £3,000. In making the request, the president of the RCJP, the Rt Rev. Alois Heane, had written: 'Our position is such in Rhodesia that due to sanctions, political tensions and fear of losing one's privileges, the white population is not prepared to support financially or otherwise a commission whose aims are to bring about social justice.'

As president of the commission, Bishop Lamont was anxious to make known as widely as possible the denials of human rights to the black population. For years, he had been an outspoken critic of racism and had often complained that Irish people living in Rhodesia were lukewarm in their support of racial equality. The official policy of the Irish hierarchy, through its agencies Trócaire and the ICJP, was that any involvement in development programmes implied working for social justice.

One witness cited in the RCJP documentation told of being arrested on a bus by an African policeman and handed over to a group of armed soldiers who forced him to carry a suitcase and a cardboard box, while handcuffed to a lorry, in which he was taken away to a temporary interrogation camp. There he was asked for information about 'a meeting of terrorists' that had taken place in a local mission. He knew nothing of the meeting but was tortured and beaten. Five sticks were broken during this period of torture, by which time he was unable to stand up or walk by himself, and he eventually passed out.

The following day, four corpses were taken into the camp and detainees were forced to undress them completely; one had part of his head blown off, another his bowels protruding. Afterwards the bodies were wrapped in plastic and taken away, probably to be burned.

At the time of the giving of the grant to the RCJP, Brian McKeown told the *Catholic Standard* (4 January 1974) that

31 THE STRUGGLE FOR ZIMBABWE'S INDEPENDENCE

Trócaire would welcome requests for aid from liberation movements. He pointed out that a grant already approved by the Irish hierarchy was specifically anti-racist, that grant being the £3,000 given to a long-term programme of education run by the RCJP. 'This is a back-up to a commission which has clashed with the Smith regime and which is a multi-racial, anti-racist organisation,' he said.

In 1976, Bishop Lamont addressed an open letter to the Rhodesian government in which he was deeply critical of their policies. Not long afterwards, he was arrested and accused of inciting disaffection against the state. In September of that year, Bishop Casey, as chairman of Trócaire, sent a telegram of solidarity to Bishop Lamont who was due to appear in court at the time. The telegram read: 'Profoundly shocked at recent events in Rhodesia and South Africa. Trócaire expresses full support for courageous stand taken by Your Lordship and the Bishops' Conference on issues of justice in Rhodesia. Appalled by charges brought against you by Rhodesian authorities in the exercise of your pastoral duties and denunciation of injustices. Pledge continued solidarity and prayers.'

Trócaire gave a grant of £5,000 to help black Rhodesians who had been forced by the authorities to move from their homes along the borders of Zambia and Mozambique into so-called 'protected villages'. The churches in Rhodesia had established and coordinated a programme to relieve the hardships people in these villages were suffering. An estimated half-million had been affected by the enforced-movement policy of the Rhodesian government.

At the beginning of October 1976, Trócaire financed and jointly published (along with the ICJP and the Catholic Institute for International Relations in London) 'Civil War in Rhodesia', a report compiled by the RCJP. It contained details of the abduction, torture and killing of innocent Africans by the Rhodesian security forces. Brian McKeown said that the document had to be smuggled out of Rhodesia in bits and pieces to be printed abroad because it would probably have been seized by the authorities after publication in that country.

The report contained photos of tortured black civilians, and corpses with holes blown in their heads and bodies. It detailed a campaign of terror against rural Africans. It contained harrowing accounts by victims of how they had been tortured by the Rhodesian security forces – punched, kicked, beaten with belts, given electric shocks to the genitals and having heads pushed and held under water. The report gave the example of the unprovoked, brutal attack by security forces on Karima village, in June 1975, where twenty villagers were killed and fifteen badly injured; nine of those killed were children and babies. The government refused requests from the RCJP for an independent inquiry into the atrocity.

The following year, Trócaire began to support adult education and leadership schemes to help combat the discriminatory and racist Rhodesian regime. The agency continued to fund legal-assistance projects and research-and-documentation projects on the Rhodesian situation.

Late in 1978, Trócaire gave a total of £52,000 to provide health, education and housing assistance to Africans who continued to be forcibly moved from their homes into 'protected villages' for so-called security reasons, and to fund a leadership-training programme designed to generate awareness among black Africans of their rights and to help them assume their responsibilities. A grant of £15,000 was also given to help the RCJP set up an information service.

Trócaire published 'Rhodesia at War: A Story of Mounting Suffering' in September 1979, which had been prepared by the RCJP. This report said that malnutrition, starvation, torture and the use of napalm and phosphorous grenades had all become familiar features of a war that was resulting, according to official figures, in an average of more than 1,000 deaths a month. However, RCJP estimates put the number of deaths considerably higher.

In rural areas, many now lacked a permanent supply of food. More lacked basic services such as stores, grinding mills, clinics, schools and transport. Malnutrition was wide-spread and potentially killer diseases such as measles were rife. Even when food and basic services were available, people were living in continual fear as they were drawn into an increasingly vicious war between security forces and guerrillas, who each demanded total allegiance.

Hundreds of thousands had fled from their rural homes and, as a result of the government policy of creating 'no-go' areas, hundreds of square miles of rural Rhodesia lay empty. The chairman of the RCJP, John Deary, warned of the danger of famine. He said that earlier in the year government forces had destroyed crops in large areas in a 'starve-the-terrorists policy'. From a military point of view, the policy had been a success but it had been disastrous for the ordinary people who were forced to leave their homes.

Transition to majority rule

By 1980, Trócaire had been providing much-needed support and assistance for the majority for more than five years, as the minority white government tried to prevent change. Bishop Lamont had been imprisoned and charged with treason for his support of black activists. Trócaire funded a legal team for his defence and he was eventually released after a year but was deported.

In a recent interview for this book, Mary Sutton described Bishop Lamont as 'a most unlikely oppositionist'. An urbane, erudite and very composed man, he found himself in a set of circumstances in which he simply had to speak out against the injustice and wrongs that were being inflicted on the majority in the country in which he ministered. She said that during her years in Trócaire she was impressed by a number of people and that she would certainly count Bishop Lamont as one of these. One could not but admire his courage in speaking out, she said, and his stance often proved less than popular with his white Catholic Rhodesian flock.

Trócaire was invited as an observer to the Lancaster House talks in London from September to December 1979, which eventually resulted in the establishment of a majority-led government in the new Zimbabwe. (During the brief colonial interregnum from September 1979 until the formation of the new government in April 1980, the country was known as Zimbabwe-Rhodesia.) Ms Sutton recalled Brian McKeown telling a meeting at Trócaire headquarters at the time how the agency provided the funding for the suits the Zimbabwean delegation wore to the talks at Lancaster House.

Trócaire became involved in the major programme of resettling 216,000 refugees in Zimbabwe-Rhodesia in January 1980, and allocated £50,000 to help finance the massive movement of refugees from Botswana, Zambia and Mozambique back to their own country. The operation was orchestrated by the United Nations High Commissioner for Refugees (UNHCR) in cooperation with the Rhodesian Catholic Commission on Social Service and Development (CCSSD). Trócaire's grant went directly to the CCSSD. The British government, which was overseeing the Lancaster House talks and the interim period until the establishment of a majority government, wanted the refugees to be returned in time for the 27 February elections.

The UNHCR was responsible for the refugees only until they reached their homes, at which point the churches provided for the people until the government's relief programme was set up and the 1981 harvest was in. The huge operation got under way on 21 January and the hope was that 60,000 would return each week until the programme was completed. Trócaire expressed serious concern about the British election stipulation and argued that the entire oper - ation was being carried out in too much haste. The agency warned: 'There appears to be little consideration for the dignity or problems of the refugees. Many, for example, will find that their former homes no longer exist and are expected to return to holding camps and remain until the rains are over.'

It also pointed out that no provision had been made in the plan for those caught up in the war and removed from their homes – people still living within Zimbabwe-Rhodesia in 'protected villages'. The repatriation of the refugees was a slow process and the election stipulation was not met, nor was it likely that it could have been.

At the end of June 1980, Trócaire urged the Irish govern - ment not to put any obstacle in the way of Zimbabwe's accession to the Lomé Convention – a trade and aid agree- ment between the European Economic Community (EEC) and African, Caribbean and Pacific countries first signed in February 1975. Brian McKeown said at the time that to object would deprive the newly independent country of the EEC aid which flowed with such membership. He said that Zimbabwe had come through a long period of dislocation of its agriculture and industry, and if it were to solve its problems it had to receive all the help the developed world could give. He added that, unfortunately, the assistance that had been promised at the time of independence had not materialised in nearly sufficient quantities and it did not appear that it would.

What Zimbabwe sought was a concession on beef and sugar imports into the EEC; in terms of total EEC production, this concession did not amount to much, but in terms of Zimbabwe, it was vital to survival. Mr McKeown appealed to the Irish ministers for Agriculture and Foreign Affairs to acknowledge their duty in justice to the struggling people of the new state and to be aware that a hard-faced attitude on the part of the Irish government would likely mean refusals from the governments of the other nine EEC states.

He said that in a year when the Irish government had cut its Overseas Development Aid (ODA) allocation drastically, not one project submitted to the government by Trócaire for co-financing that year had up to that time been approved. This made a concession in favour of Zimbabwe all the more vital. The following day, a delegation from the Zimbabwean government, led by the Prime Minister, Robert Mugabe, came to Dublin to meet Irish ministers to discuss the Lomé Convention.

In the event, Zimbabwe was admitted to Lomé but some limitations were imposed on its sugar and beef exports to the EEC.

In December 1980, Trócaire announced it was sending £50,000 to help promote preventive medicine and agriculture programmes in Zimbabwe. The funds were channelled through the CCSSD to support its rehabilitation programme already under way. Food shortages were being reported in different parts of the country and the following harvest was one of the most important in the country's history. The immediate needs of small farmers were seeds, fertilisers, farm implements and vital agricultural advice.

A deteriorating situation in the early twenty-first century

All in all, over the next decade the quality of life for ordinary Zimbabweans could be said to have improved. According to a World Bank report of 1990, the country had a lower infant mortality rate and higher adult literacy and school enrolment rates than average for developing countries. But the government was short on hard currency and the International Monetary Fund (IMF) prescribed an austerity programme. Throughout the 1990s, this put pressure on Zimbabwe's large population of smallholders who had limited access to natural, technical and financial resources. The country's involvement in the war in the Democratic Republic of the Congo from 1998–2002 was a severe drain on an economy that was already struggling.

The Lancaster House agreement had blocked significant land redistribution from the white minority to the black majority for ten years. The British government had funded a 'willing buyer, willing seller' land-reform programme to the tune of £44 million but this ended in 1997 on the basis that the money was used to buy land for members of the ruling elite rather than for landless peasants. In 2000, the Mugabe government began the expropriation of white-owned farms without the payment of any compensation. This policy set the economy on a serious downward spiral.

In July 2002, Trócaire launched an appeal for €1.5 million to fund its relief activities in a number of countries in southern Africa, including Zimbabwe. The agency was distributing seeds and tools through local partner organisations and church structures at the time to hundreds of thousands of vulnerable people. The Irish government gave Trócaire €650,000 for its relief and rehabilitation programme in the region.

Some six million Zimbabweans were in need of emergency food aid. Eamonn Meehan, deputy director of Trócaire, said that many were already hungry and far more would need assistance later in 2002. He warned that unless urgent and adequate action was taken, there was a risk of serious famine and loss of life. The international community had to improve its response if millions of southern Africans were to enjoy their fundamental right to food, he said.

Across Zimbabwe, a chronic shortage of maize, exacerbated by stubbornly destructive government policies, was pushing a once plentiful country to the verge of famine. The UN appealed for $285 million to stave off what it called the 'largest food crisis in fifty years'.

President Mugabe's rule was not entirely to blame for the crisis. A severe drought at the beginning of 2002 seriously damaged the country's maize crop. The scourge of HIV/AIDS made a bad situation worse; it was estimated that one in three Zimbabwean adults was infected with HIV, and a growing orphan population of 600,000 gave an indication of the numbers that had died. But Mugabe's policies turned a manageable crisis into a full-blown disaster. At best, he did nothing; at worst, he used the food crisis as a tool of political power.

The seizure of white-owned commercial farms threw the vital agricultural sector into disarray when Zimbabweans needed it most. Commercial farming accounted for almost half the national maize requirements – its disappearance coupled with drought reduced maize production by 70 per cent. The farm seizures also hit the tobacco business, a key foreign-currency earner. As the government struggled to import food stocks, it discovered it had precious little hard cash with which to buy them.

Aid agencies such as Trócaire said that it was not too late, in July 2002, to prevent a famine, but early signs of starvation were already starting to show. In thousands of villages, people had been reduced to having one meal a day. In schools, hungry children started to faint in class and absentee rates soared as parents sent their children to search for food, often wild berries and fruit. Some died from eating poisonous roots.

In western Zimbabwe, war veterans shut down a food project run by the Catholic Commission for Justice and Peace (CCJP), claiming that the project, which fed 40,000 and was funded by Trócaire, was controlled by the Movement for Democratic Change (MDC), the main opposition to Mugabe's ruling ZANU-PF party. Following negotiations with the local governor, the project restarted under a different Catholic body.

While widespread disaster was avoided at that particular time, the overall situation remained volatile. At the beginning of August 2005, Trócaire launched an Africa-wide, €3 million emergency appeal to help many countries across the continent where people faced hunger and food insecurity. One of those countries was Zimbabwe where some four million were in need of food aid. Drought at the beginning of that year had caused significant damage to crops. The high HIV/AIDS rate was causing serious labour shortages, while the government, which had halted food operations the year before and assumed responsibility for food relief, now following the elections stopped food distributions completely. Combined with all this, inflation was over 600 per cent in 2004, reducing purchasing power considerably and pre - venting the importation of various commodities.

During the previous few years, Trócaire had provided emergency food relief to the most vulnerable communities throughout Zimbabwe, while also funding much-needed agricultural recovery projects. Following its successful 2005 appeal, it continued to do so.

According to an *Irish Times* report, President Mugabe used the twenty-seventh anniversary of his country's independence (18 April 2007) to smear and threaten his country's pro-democracy movement. In his address, Mugabe accused opponents of 'fomenting anarchy' at the behest of alleged Western masters. He described the main opposition leader, Morgan Tsvangirai, as a 'pathetic puppet' of Britain and the US and warned that he would not hesitate to deal firmly with elements that were engaged in what he termed 'criminal activities'.

The new threat followed a decision by his government to de-register all NGOs and aid agencies in Zimbabwe in an attempt to weed out political opponents. It had been ann - ounced that all NGOs would have to submit new applications to remain in the country – Mugabe's government claimed some were using relief activities as a cover for supporting opposition groups.

Trócaire, which supported a number of outspoken human rights groups in Zimbabwe, told the *Irish Times* that it would not be immediately affected by the clampdown because it operated from outside the country, channelling funds through local partners. But its southern Africa programme officer, Niall O'Keefe, expressed concern that some Zimbabwean NGOs would spend the following six months 'troubled by their own survival' rather than being able to concentrate on the parliamentary and presidential elections proposed for 2008.

Traditionally, African leaders marked Zimbabwe's independence anniversary with messages of unqualified support for President Mugabe, but not so in 2007. President Thabo Mbeki of South Africa, who was appointed by regional governments to act as a facilitator in the Zimbabwean crisis, was seeking a solution.

In late June 2007, the Irish Catholic bishops joined Catholic Bishops' Conferences worldwide to express deep concern and dismay at the worsening political and humanitarian situation in Zimbabwe. They called on the government of that country to provide urgently needed shelter and food for its population and to facilitate the efforts of the aid agencies, including those sponsored by the churches, to provide humanitarian and development assistance to the dispossessed. The Irish bishops urged the Irish people to continue supporting Trócaire and such agencies in Zimbabwe.

A few months before, in April 2007, the Zimbabwean Catholic bishops had issued a pastoral, 'God Hears the Cry of the Oppressed', which condemned the suffering of the people; suffering which caused boycotts, strikes, demonstrations and uprisings to which the state responded with ever harsher repression through arrests, beatings, detentions, banning orders and torture. The Irish bishops' statement in June called on the Zimbabwean government to address the crisis of leadership as outlined in that pastoral.

Archbishop Pius Ncube, the Catholic Archbishop of Bulawayo, has been one of the most consistent critics of the Mugabe regime. Before the 2005 elections, he called for a non-violent popular uprising to overthrow President Mugabe. The latter's ZANU-PF party dubbed the archbishop 'a mad inveterate liar' and Mugabe himself called him 'a half-wit'. Archbishop Ncube twice visited Ireland in 2004 at the invitation of Trócaire. On one of those visits, he said he had no fear for his personal safety and vowed that whatever the threats against him, he would continue to stand up to Mugabe.

As inflation in Zimbabwe reached 14,000 per cent in August 2007, many hoped that southern Africa's leaders would take decisive action to halt the country's freefall but, as Justin Kilcullen, director of Trócaire, wrote in the *Irish Catholic* at the end of that month, their hopes were dashed.

He explained how Trócaire had been working in Zimbabwe, supporting projects to improve access to food and develop civil society. The agency had spent €1,471,947 in the country in 2006 on programmes to alleviate the worsening humanit - arian crisis and to promote peace and justice, working with local and national organisations to document the situation in Zimbabwe and to raise awareness among policy makers there and internationally. That work continues.

CHAPTER 3:
The Anti-Apartheid Campaign

The struggle against apartheid: the early stages

Shortly after its foundation, Trócaire became involved in the struggle against the apartheid system in South Africa. The agency gave £2,000 for the relocation of a carpentry school that had to be closed when the white minority government of South Africa declared, over night, that the area in which the school was located was a white residential zone. The school was for black people and had to be either moved or disbanded. Dr Kader Asmal, a leading spokesman for the Irish Anti-Apartheid Movement, told the *Catholic Standard* (4 January 1974) that he intended to arrange for contact concerning aid between liberation movements and Trócaire and said he was delighted with Trócaire's open-minded attitude.

The following year, as part of its 1975 initiative to support workers' rights around the world, Trócaire provided funding for the education and training of black trade union workers in South Africa. It also provided funds for literacy courses in the Lumko Institute.

In early 1976, Trócaire set out a detailed, clear analysis of the unjust situation existing in South Africa. The analysis detailed how, under the apartheid system, Africans (68 per cent of the population) owned only 12 per cent of the land, and whites earned six times the amount earned by African workers. Yet, whites paid less tax, had a higher tax allowance and got relief for dependents while Africans got none of these things. The cruel, evil and barbaric apartheid laws were being supported, upheld and enforced by Christians.

Forced removal was a basic pattern of life in South Africa under the Group Areas Act, and the analysis reported an estimate that more than two million Africans had been resettled in the province of Natal alone. Trócaire committed itself to fighting such racism.

In 1977, it began to support adult education and leadership schemes to help combat the discriminatory and racist regime. The black human rights activist, Steve Biko, died in police custody in September that year.

The following month, Trócaire director Brian McKeown expressed the agency's shock at the banning of South African black-consciousness movements and the arrest of their leaders and of the acting secretary of the South African Bishops' Conference, Fr Smangaliso Mkhatshwa. Trócaire had been grant-aiding the work of the black-consciousness organisations that had been banned. The banning and arrests were proof of the effectiveness of these non-violent movements, which were making blacks aware of their own dignity and potential to bring about change in the whole system of apartheid by peaceful means.

Brian McKeown said that the arrest of Fr Mkhatshwa showed the great pressure the government was exerting not only on black opposition groups but also on all institutions opposed to apartheid.

In 1978, Trócaire supported a survey of church facilities in South Africa to promote their alternative use in times of crisis. Following disturbances in Soweto and other black townships, a committee started to examine ways of making church buildings and land near Durban available for use by communities and organisations which had nowhere else to turn. Church properties proved very useful as refugee centres and as housing for homeless squatters.

THE ANTI-APARTHEID CAMPAIGN

In July that year, Trócaire gave £4,000 towards an adult-education programme in a black township in Pretoria, in an area suffering from chronic unemployment. Local people had got together to provide education and vocational training for themselves so that they could find work. The Trócaire grant enabled them to set up literacy training programmes and to organise training seminars and workshops within their own community.

At the beginning of 1981, Trócaire called on the Irish Rugby Football Union (IRFU) to cancel a proposed rugby tour of South Africa in response to calls from justice and human rights groups inside the country. 'Many of the people involved in the projects which Trócaire supports in South Africa have been tortured and jailed by the regime which the Irish rugby players now intend to support with their presence,' Bishop Casey pointed out. He went on to urge the Irish government to impose an Irish trade embargo on South Africa and suggested a lead could come from the trade union movement by denying facilities to South African produce reaching Irish ports.

Ireland's largest trade union at the time, the Irish Transport and General Workers Union (ITGWU) supported Dr Casey's call on the IRFU and also called on the Irish Congress of Trade Unions (ICTU) to look at the possibility of a trade boycott. In February 1981, the IRFU announced the tour would go ahead but the Federated Workers Union of Ireland threatened to refuse travel facilities for members of the rugby party at Dublin Airport. Gradually, some players let it be known that they did not wish to be considered for the tour.

At the end of that month, Trócaire published a special bulletin explaining the working of the apartheid system, which it described as 'an immoral social, economic and political system designed to perpetuate exclusive white control of South Africa's wealth and resources'. The bulletin showed that there was one doctor for every 400 whites as against one for every 44,000 blacks; in education, R654 was spent annually on each white child and R48 on each black child.

In March 1981, Archbishop Denis Hurley of Durban, president of the South African Bishops' Conference, joined those calling on the IRFU to cancel their proposed tour. He said he was appalled that any group of Irishmen would propose to do what the IRFU intended. In a message he sent to Trócaire, he said, 'Be quite clear about it. Both the white South Africans and the oppressed majority of the people of South Africa clearly interpret the tour as an acceptance of the policy of apartheid'. Unfortunately, his words went unheard as far as the IRFU was concerned and the tour went ahead.

Donald Woods, a white South African journalist, anti-apartheid activist and friend of Steve Biko, addressed a Trócaire press conference in Dublin in October 1982, at which a comprehensive information pack about South Africa was launched. He said governments of small countries like Ireland could act more effectively against apartheid. They could be more effective by being more consistent and outspoken in their opposition. He agreed that Ireland had a good record in opposing racial oppression but he believed it could be more forthright.

He argued that Ireland should oppose an application made by the South African government for a loan from the IMF. He said other South African loan applications to the IMF had been made, not because the money was needed but to ensure that other governments would have an interest in wishing that there would be reasonable stability in the country, so that it could repay its debts. Brian McKeown promised that Trócaire would make representations to the Irish government to see that it would exercise its influence to have the loan application rejected.

At the same press conference, Donald Woods said he thought the Irish rugby team's tour of South Africa the previous year had done a lot of harm and he expressed the hope that no similar tour would take place again. The IRFU's claim that the tour had contributed to racial integration in sports in South Africa was totally without foundation, he said. He also said that the main thrust of official South

African propaganda was to ensure that proposals for sanctions were opposed at the UN, and as long as Britain and the US vetoed sanctions in the Security Council, the South African government was safe.

He denied that black South Africans had a better living standard than people of other African countries – in fact they came in twelfth in the league table of Gross National Product (GNP) per capita for the continent. He also denied the propaganda that the apartheid system was being reformed; perhaps it was being tinkered with at the peripheries but it was being strengthened at the core, he contended.

In June 1983, Trócaire held a major international seminar in University College Galway to mark the tenth anniversary of its founding. Archbishop Denis Hurley was one of the speakers. While he was in Ireland, he gave an interview to the *Irish Times* (20 June 1983) in which he expressed a wish for Pope John Paul II to visit South Africa. He said he and his fellow South African bishops believed that, far from giving papal blessing to the separation of races, such a visit would give a big boost to the efforts of the Catholic Church to promote racial and social justice there.

As an outspoken critic of apartheid, he said he understood that violence against the system was inevitable but that he would prefer a non-violent approach. He was strongly against visits to South Africa by European sports teams, arguing that they were very demoralising to blacks who saw the sports boycott as their one, if not their only, weapon against apartheid.

The following month, Trócaire condemned the plan by five Irish international rugby players to travel to South Africa on a trip, believed to be financed by the South African government, to mark 100 years of rugby in the country's Western Province. A Trócaire spokesperson said the organisation had spent £400,000 in the previous decade trying to deal with some of the unfortunate effects of apartheid on the country's black population, and that the Irish people and government had made it plain in the past that they did not support apartheid.

The spokesperson went on to say that Irish athletes should take whatever opportunity they had to let the South African government know that they could not expect their country to be treated as a normal friendly nation, while they mistreated almost 80 per cent of their own population.

The anti-apartheid struggle intensifies

Near the end of 1983, Trócaire announced it was to step up its campaign against apartheid. Already it had launched a poster campaign aimed at increasing awareness among the Irish public, under the slogan 'Apartheid Hurts'. A priority of the agency would be supporting the development of a strong trade union movement inside South Africa where, at the time, less than 10 per cent of the workforce was unionised. 'The entire political and economic system is geared to the concept of slave labour, which has been institutionalised in the homelands' system, leaving black workers with virtually no rights,' said Justin Kilcullen, Trócaire's Africa Project Officer at the time.

In late May 1984, Brian McKeown called for the blocking of the secretive efforts by the South African Prime Minister, P.W. Botha, to be received officially by the European Commission during his visit to Europe. Mr McKeown made representations against any sort of EEC recognition of Botha and sought support for his stance from the Irish Minister for Foreign Affairs, the Irish European Commissioner and the president of the European Commission. He said that development agencies were deeply shocked at the possibility of the commission receiving under any circumstances the prime minister of a country condemned internationally for its racist and oppressive policies. (On his European tour, Botha was officially received by Prime Minister Margaret Thatcher of Britain and unofficially by the leaders of West Germany, Belgium, Portugal and Italy, as well as by Pope John Paul II, but not by the European Commission.)

In February 1985, Bishop Casey said that the striking Dunnes Stores workers in Dublin, who were refusing to handle South African produce, should receive the support of the community. But he did not urge other workers to follow suit, saying that it had to be an individual decision. Speaking at the launch of Trócaire's 1985 annual Lenten Campaign, he said the boycott technique was a significant and valid means people had to express their rejection of apartheid and their solidarity with those who suffered under it.

The bishop said that as a community we must be edified by the sight of thirteen young people suffering for months because of their conscientious objection to trading with a racist country. He called on all concerned in the dispute to recognise that they were not faced with an ordinary industrial relations problem about wages and conditions but with a serious issue of moral conscience.

In August 1985, reporting on Trócaire's Lenten Campaign having raised more than £3 million (a 33 per cent increase on the 1984 figure), and in a reference to the Dunnes Stores strike, then in its second year, Bishop Casey called on the Irish government to introduce trade sanctions against South Africa and thereby 'give a lead to a largely cynical world'. He also pointed out that since the declaration of a state of emergency in South Africa, a number of people working on Trócaire projects, many of them lay church workers, had been detained by police.

Shortly afterwards, Brian McKeown commented in public on a much-heralded address to a National Party congress (the National Party was the ruling white party in South Africa) that President Botha had just given. He said that rather than signifying any change, the address reinforced the determin - ation on the part of the white minority community in South Africa not to bring about any radical transformation in the apartheid system. While it was obvious that the international pressure exercised by Western governments had forced a reaction from South Africa, this reaction was inadequate, he said, and he went on to argue that Botha's speech showed very clearly that the US administration's policy of con- structive dialogue had not and could not work.

It was now crucial to step up economic and political sanctions on South Africa, Mr McKeown said, and he expressed the belief that the Irish government was in a particularly good position to take the moral lead on this issue at the level of the EEC Council of Ministers.

Trócaire's anti-apartheid work continued in 1986. It supported on-the-ground projects in South Africa, campaigned on the international stage for an end to apartheid and engaged in education work with schools, youth organisations and other groups in Ireland. Trócaire was the only Irish organisation working at that time in South Africa. In addition to giving financial support, it sponsored fact-finding missions to the country by Irish Catholic Church personnel, trade unionists and parliamentarians. Trócaire also brought South African leaders – including Archbishop Hurley, Donald Woods and Archbishop Desmond Tutu, Anglican Archbishop of Cape Town and Nobel Peace Prize winner – to Ireland.

Along with a handful of other European agencies, Trócaire was successful in persuading the EEC to set up the largest ever special fund to cope with an emergency situation. This fund channelled more than ECU150 million to black organisations inside South Africa. Following the recommendations of the South African Bishops' Conference, Trócaire put pressure on the Irish government and the EEC to impose sanctions on South African produce. The highly publicised Dunnes Stores strike increased this pressure.

In late March 1986, the Irish government announced a ban on imports of fruit and vegetables from South Africa. Trócaire welcomed the ban, saying the decision was all the more significant because it gave a lead to Ireland's EEC partners on the important issue of economic sanctions against South Africa. Bishop Casey said it was the first step towards the progressive sanctions which Trócaire and the ICJP had sought when a joint delegation had met the Taoiseach the previous October. He also said the principled and moral position taken by the Dunnes Stores strikers had undoubtedly been a major factor in securing 'this historic step'.

The following June, at the launch of a major apartheid-awareness campaign, Brian McKeown asked the Irish Minister for Foreign Affairs to press for stricter trade sanctions against South Africa at an upcoming meeting of EEC foreign ministers. He said the existing EEC sanctions had 'failed miserably'. He also urged the Irish government to reconsider its trade links with South Africa and ban all trade, not just imports of South African fruit and vegetables. The awareness campaign was being funded by the EEC and the Irish Department of Foreign Affairs and was the second such campaign organised by Trócaire on South Africa.

In August 1986, Trócaire protested at the torture of Fr Smangaliso Mkhatshwa, who had been arrested in the early stages of the state of emergency declared the previous June. When his assistant visited him, she found he was unable to stand without the support of a broom handle and that his feet were badly swollen. An affidavit filed by him alleged he was interrogated while handcuffed and blindfolded for at least thirty hours. In a telegram to the South African government, Bishop Casey objected to 'this unwarranted treatment of a priest and leader who has played an important role in supporting peaceful change in your country'.

He said that Trócaire protested at the unjust and inhuman treatment of Fr Mkhatshwa and called on the South African government to cease such acts and to release him. Trócaire was concerned that the mistreatment of a person as prominent as the secretary of the Catholic Bishops' Conference indicated that the treatment of the mass of black South Africans arrested under the emergency declaration must be even worse.

The following November/December, Bishop Wilfrid Napier of Kokstad, Natal, who was vice-president of the South African Bishops' Conference, and another bishop, Dr Hugh Slattery, visited several European countries to explain the South African Catholic bishops' view. At a press conference given by Trócaire in Dublin in late November, Bishop Napier called for economic pressures on South Africa that would bite and make the white community change its position.

In August 1987, Bishop Casey and Brian McKeown paid an eight-day visit to South Africa. When they returned, they announced the donation of £10,000 towards the support of the families of 360,000 striking South African mineworkers. Brian McKeown said that the strike was not just an attempt to get a better wage deal but a blow against the whole apartheid system. For that reason, it was extremely important that it should be supported by the Irish trade union movement, morally and financially. Trócaire made the decision to give the grant following discussions he and Bishop Casey held in South Africa with Cyril Ramaphosa, secretary-general of the National Union of Mineworkers in that country.

Mr McKeown said that six mineworkers had already been killed and 200 injured by a combination of mine security forces and police, that intimidation and violence had been used against strikers and that more than 200 had lost their jobs, with thousands of others facing dismissal. He pointed out that the minimum wage for black South African miners was £78, and £71 in coalmines. To survive, they generally worked a 96-hour week, and some put in even longer hours. He concluded by saying that Trócaire had allocated £300,000 over the previous year to a wide variety of projects in South Africa.

'Front-line states' and *Cry Freedom*

In August 1988, Bishop Casey went to Mozambique on a fact-finding mission. When he returned he said that South Africa was supporting a campaign of murder and brutality in that country and that there would be no peace there for as long as apartheid continued. He compared the so-called Mozambique National Resistance (MNR), the South African-backed rebel army, to the Khmer Rouge in Cambodia and said that its campaign cried out to the world for intervention.

Mozambique, he said, had been singled out by South Africa as a principal target for aggression in its ongoing campaign to wreck the economies of its neighbouring states (these neighbouring states formed the organisation known as 'the front-line states' – Angola, Botswana, Mozambique, Tanzania, Zambia and Zimbabwe – to fight the white minority regime in South Africa). He said South Africa was using the MNR to terrorise the population of Mozambique and to cause as much economic and social disruption in that country as possible.

He explained that vital rail links to the Indian Ocean crossed Mozambique from Zambia, Tanzania, Malawi, Botswana and Zimbabwe. The only alternative routes were through South Africa, and the strategy of that country's government was to cut rail links through Mozambique, forcing the land-locked states to become totally dependent on South Africa for their imports and exports.

Bishop Casey said there was 'unbelievable fear and terror' in Mozambique because of the MNR. He had met a twelve-year-old boy who had been forced by MNR soldiers to help them kill his parents with axes and then burn their bodies. Another boy of the same age had been taken to a camp for forced training, made to shoot one of his friends and was then put in charge of a unit which murdered many people before he was captured and sent to a rehabilitation centre.

In Mozambique, some six million had become dependent on food aid because of the war, over one million were displaced persons in their own country and there were a further 700,000 refugees in neighbouring states, the bishop said. The solution to the problems of the region lay in dismantling the apartheid system, he believed. Trócaire had provided £1 million in development aid to Mozambique since 1984 and was involved in farming and food projects and in an education scheme there.

In January 1988, Trócaire had sponsored the Irish film premiere of *Cry Freedom*, based on Donald Woods's book of the same name about his friendship with Steve Biko. The premiere was used as a celebrity charity event, all of the proceeds of which went to Trócaire. The film's director, Sir Richard Attenborough, attended the event, as did Donald Woods himself.

In September that year, Trócaire invited Woods to address, as principal guest, a public meeting in Galway on apartheid. Until he was silenced by South African government banning orders in October 1977, shortly after the death in police custody of his friend Steve Biko, Woods was editor of the *Daily Dispatch*, the leading anti-apartheid newspaper in South Africa. He escaped from South Africa disguised as an Irish missionary priest. His family joined him and they went to live in London where he worked as a writer, broadcaster and lecturer on South African affairs.

Brian McKeown remarked in a recent interview that someone had given Donald Woods his name, shortly after he got out of South Africa, and that he contacted him and came over to Dublin to meet him. He explained what he had been through to Mr McKeown and told him he was trying to set up a small organisation to continue the work that he had been carrying out in South Africa. He said he needed some basic help to buy an electronic typewriter – something as slight as that! Trócaire gave him a grant which enabled him to restart his great work and, as Brian McKeown put it, he remained a very loyal friend of Trócaire from then on. When *Cry Freedom* was to be premiered, Donald Woods insisted it would be done in Dublin and that the proceeds would go to Trócaire.

On the occasion of Trócaire's twenty-fifth anniversary in 1998, Donald Woods paid tribute to the agency in these words:

> You were with us in the dark days of the struggle. Now you continue to support us in redressing the injustices that remain after apartheid; we are grateful for Trócaire support in training the new African journalists that are essential for the continuation of the present transition process and for the future development of a healthy civil society in our new democracy.

The transition to majority rule
In September 1989, F.W. de Klerk replaced P.W. Botha as president of South Africa. Early the following year, he

announced that anti-apartheid groups were no longer illegal and that Nelson Mandela would shortly be freed. A few days before Mr Mandela's release in February 1990, Brian McKeown expressed cautious optimism that the changes announced by President de Klerk would in the long term lead to a democratic, non-racial South Africa. 'The news that groups which have been working for years for change are to be legalised is a welcome development. Some of Trócaire's major partners in the country, including church groups and trade unions, will once again be in a position to continue their efforts towards achieving a peaceful end to apartheid.'

He said international pressure, and especially the application of sanctions, had finally begun to have results, and that the South African government recognised it could not effectively maintain apartheid in the face of massive opposition from within and without. But he believed there was still a need to keep up the pressure. While President de Klerk had made a statement of intent, the repressive machinery of the apartheid system remained in place and the state of emergency had not been lifted, he pointed out. Trócaire had allocated almost £1 million to a variety of programmes to help combat apartheid during 1989.

In April 1991, Marist Brother Jude Pieterse, secretary-general of the South African Bishops' Conference, visited Dublin. At a press conference held by Trócaire, he urged the Irish government to emphasise to President de Klerk, on the occasion of his forthcoming visit to Ireland, the absolute necessity of initiating talks to bring about a just and equitable solution to the land issue in South Africa. He said he believed the land issue was crucial to any long-term solution to the social and political problems of South Africa.

Since the coming to power of the National Party in 1948, some 3.5 million black South Africans had been forcibly dispossessed of their lands, Brother Pieterse said. This represented a 'running sore' in South African politics, an injustice of such enormous magnitude that there was little chance of political progress until the government committed itself to restoring lands confiscated by force. He pointed to how important land was in the Irish national question for centuries and said that, as a result, the Irish were better placed than most Europeans to bring home to President de Klerk the need to rectify this blatant injustice.

He urged the Irish government to remind the president that no political progress had been possible in Ireland until the land issue was resolved. The government should also impress on him that the resolution of the Irish land issue was achieved by direct government action, the very opposite of what President de Klerk was then proposing for South Africa – 'passive reliance on market forces to rectify what is a terrible injustice against millions of dispossessed people'.

Brother Pieterse was back in Dublin in September 1992 where he launched a report by Trócaire, which outlined proposals for further development and human rights work by the agency in South Africa. He said the refusal by President de Klerk to accept majority rule remained the real stumbling-block to a resolution of the political impasse in South Africa. He also said the white government was trying to entrench its control over the future administration by pushing strongly for a federal system, to which the African National Congress (ANC) was firmly opposed. He urged that the remaining sanctions not be dropped and that external pressure be kept on the de Klerk government.

In December 1992, Trócaire joined other European develop - ment agencies in calling on the European Commission to operate openly and transparently in relation to the EEC Special Programme for Victims of Apartheid. In a statement issued to mark the visit of a delegation of prominent South African churchmen to the EEC, Brian McKeown said the vital role played by European NGOs since the EEC Special Programme was established in 1986 had to be maintained and strengthened. He said the NGOs had played a crucial role at both an operational level and in promoting debate in Europe on policy issues relating to South Africa.

He argued that they assumed an important role in supporting many community, non-governmental and church organisations working in the development field within South Africa. The long-term partnership with these organisations was widely regarded as a way of overcoming the effects of apartheid and of sustaining the process of healing and reconciliation in the country.

He went on to say that large, externally directed development-assistance programmes, such as those envisaged by the EEC, were liable to fail if they were not closely attuned to the priorities and capacities of responsible South African organisations. As the only Irish agency to have received support for its programmes in South Africa under the EEC Special Programme, Trócaire strongly urged that it be implemented in cooperation with representative European and South African NGOs.

The slow, gradual progress towards democracy continued throughout 1992 and into 1993 as the ANC, the National Party and nineteen other parties agreed a new constitution, a bill of rights and a transition executive council. In 1993, Nelson Mandela and F.W. de Klerk won the Nobel Peace Prize, and the following year Mr Mandela became the democratically elected leader of South Africa.

Five years later, on the twenty-fifth anniversary of Trócaire's founding, Mr Mandela, President of South Africa from 1994–1999, sent the following message to the agency:

It is with great pleasure that I congratulate Trócaire on its twenty-fifth anniversary. South Africans have had a long association with Trócaire, who have not only been staunch opponents of apartheid but have also initiated and supported several projects within South Africa since 1977. The new and democratic South Africa shares the commitment of Trócaire, and, indeed, the people of Ireland, to the alleviation of poverty and the development of a human rights culture.

Looking back

In his interview for this book, Brian McKeown said the South African campaign was extremely important in the development of Trócaire, as the organisation played a central and dynamic role in the long struggle against the apartheid system. Part of Trócaire's very vigorous approach was to display posters relating to the situation in South Africa all around Ireland on a regular basis. In fact, he said, its South African campaign drew a lot of criticism on the agency, particularly along the lines that Trócaire should be giving money to feed the hungry and not getting involved in politics.

As part of its campaign, he said, Trócaire worked closely with the Irish trade union movement and sponsored visits by Irish trade union delegations to highlight the injustices being faced by workers in South Africa every day. In addition, Trócaire channelled significant funds during the 1980s to black trade unions active in South Africa.

Also in a recent interview, Eamonn Meehan, deputy director of Trócaire, referred to 'the significant but often unrecognised role' that the Catholic Church played in the anti-apartheid struggle. The solidarity of the clergy at grassroots, parish level with local communities was of enormous importance, he said. He gave the example of how the church in many cases had opened up its schools to the children of all races in South Africa at a time when the country's laws actually made it illegal to do so. At the level of the Bishops' Conference, he believed the political engagement undertaken and the relationships established and sustained both inside and outside the country, while not having a high profile in the media, were none the less of huge significance. And this important work was carried over into the transition period from 1992–1994, he said.

Mr Meehan explained that, after the transition to and establishment of black majority rule, Trócaire began to look to other countries in the southern African region that had also, in a sense, been victims of the apartheid regime in South Africa. He mentioned in particular Mozambique and Angola,

THE ANTI-APARTHEID CAMPAIGN

where there were high levels of poverty. Over a number of years, Trócaire began to transfer its financial and human resources from South Africa to those countries and to set up offices there. The agency has continued to be involved in South Africa but that involvement is now at a very low level in comparison to what it once was.

CHAPTER 4:
The Marcos Regime in the Philippines

Providing basic medical care

In 1975, Trócaire began to support workers' rights around the world. One of the projects, which was an example of this activity, was the provision of leadership training for the National Federation of Sugar Workers in the Philippines.

In November 1976, Bishop Fernando Capalla, the auxiliary Bishop of Davao City in Mindanao, led a delegation from the National Social Action Secretariat of the Philippines Bishops' Conference to Ireland. The previous August, an earthquake and tidal wave had killed thousands in the southern Philippines and Trócaire had sent aid to the victims.

The island of Mindanao was populated mainly by fishermen and subsistence farmers for whom life was already a daily struggle, and Trócaire had been supporting, through the Asia Fund for Human Development programmes, to improve the conditions of the fishing and agriculture communities there. Brian McKeown had visited the area earlier in 1976.

Economic life in the Philippines was ultimately controlled by foreign multinationals – mainly American and Japanese – and local big businessmen, top government officials, high-ranking military officers and wealthy landlords, i.e. a tiny percentage of the population. Some 83 per cent of the people lived on or below the poverty line. Strikes were illegal and torture was used as an instrument of oppression.

Despite the mass poverty, the administration's policy was to invest in promoting tourism. Multi-storeyed modern hotels along the sea front in the capital, Manila, were in sharp contrast to the numerous shantytowns that existed there as well.

In a recent interview for this book, Marian Cadogan, who was Trócaire projects officer for Asia and the Pacific Regions from 1981–1987, said that it is important to remember that this was still very much the era of the Cold War. The American military bases in the Philippines were of great strategic importance to that superpower and that was why the Americans were so engaged there, and were so supportive of the existing status quo.

However, Ms Cadogan said that it was also an era of great hope. Trócaire and other development agencies sought a new international economic order, a more equitable world where poverty could be eradicated and human rights upheld.

Constant conflict because of the oppressive regime of President Ferdinand Marcos had led to the imposition of martial law in 1972, and this ushered in a climate of fear and oppression against which the Catholic Bishops' Conference spoke out. The conference wrote to President Marcos in 1975 deprecating the climate of fear and urging him to take bold steps to lift martial law. The Archbishop of Manila, Cardinal Jaime Sin, called a press conference to inform foreign media correspondents of the many violations of human rights. The Bishops' Conference pointed out that in Manila alone, one million squatters lived in shantytowns.

Bishop Capalla's delegation mentioned above was the guest of Trócaire and visited a number of places around the country. It went to Derry to thank the people of that diocese for the huge amount they contributed to Trócaire every Lent. (The Derry diocese was the largest single contributor, per capita, to Trócaire's Lenten collection for many years.)

Bishop Capalla praised Trócaire for its partnership approach and its emphasis on development education. He said its information programme tended to influence the policy of governments and decision makers. He also said that development in the Philippines was not just a matter of building schools and hospitals but of making people aware of the causes of poverty and helping them to organise themselves and claim their rights. Trócaire was contributing in the Philippines in the areas of leadership training, credit unions, cooperatives, adult-education programmes and rural-health programmes.

Its work in the Philippines brought Trócaire into contact with Karl Gaspar (a widely respected lay Church leader and community development expert, who, a number of years later, became a Redemptorist brother) and Fr Niall O'Brien, a Columban priest from Blackrock, Co. Dublin. Both of these men were imprisoned on false charges by the Marcos regime as a result of their defence of the poor. Trócaire campaigned vigorously for their release.

In April 1983, the agency reported that a recent national survey showed that sixty-two in every 100 Filipinos died without receiving any kind of medical care. Everyday illnesses, such as TB, whooping cough and gastroenteritis, diseases that had known effective treatment for years, were still claiming the lives of many in the Philippines.

For the previous ten years, Trócaire had contributed regularly to schemes designed to provide the poorest Filipinos with basic medical care. The schemes provided basic health training for selected people from rural villages who then returned to their communities and taught the people there the importance of healthcare, including the importance of clean water and sanitation. They also provided the cheapest medicines and treatments that even the poor could afford.

These people were known as 'barefoot doctors' and one of the most successful schemes was set up by Fr Niall O'Brien, who by this time had been persecuted for months by the military and the elite on the island of Negros, where he had spent over ten years living and working among the poorest.

His scheme began in the early 1970s and had trained dozens of highly motivated barefoot doctors who had succeeded in greatly improving basic healthcare in sixty communities in his parish.

Since its foundation, Trócaire had consistently contributed to Fr O'Brien's healthcare schemes. The agency had also helped him to set up a small-scale answer to the single biggest health problem in the Philippines: hunger. He set up a communal farm from which destitute farm workers and their families had succeeded in making a living.

However, Trócaire and Fr O'Brien had long recognised that the problems of the Philippines were far greater than the lack of food or medicine. As with many repressive societies, the problems of the Philippines were a matter of justice. The rich land and abundant coastal waters over which President Marcos ruled were more than capable of feeding the Filipino people. That they did not was due to the greedy and brutal system of government, backed by military might, that forced the rural poor from the land so that it could be used by rich landowners and multinational corporations, and that held down the wages of the hungry workers at the point of a bayonet.

While 5 per cent of the Filipino people were amazingly rich, living behind armed sentry posts, 90 per cent had seen their standard of living slide from subsistence level to well below it in the previous decade. During that time, thanks to the generosity of the Irish people, Trócaire had been able to help at least some of the poor of the Philippines to improve their own lot.

The ESB in the Philippines

At a Trócaire press conference in October 1977, a Jesuit Filipino bishop, Francisco Claver, said that the $1 million consultancy contract the Irish Electricity Supply Board (ESB) had recently signed with the Philippine National Power Corporation would not benefit the ordinary people of the Philippines. The bishop had spent a week in Ireland as a guest of Trócaire. He had intended to come the previous February but had been refused an exit visa from the Philippines. Because he had taken a strong stand on human rights issues against the Marcos regime, his diocesan radio station had been closed down and his movements restricted.

He was critical of several World Bank projects in the Philippines, especially the Chico River Basin hydroelectric scheme that threatened to uproot thousands from their homes. Bishop Claver, who was of the Igorot tribe, said that 100,000 Igorots would be displaced.

The ESB denied the consultancy contract had anything to do with the Chico River project. A spokesperson said the ESB had been invited by the World Bank to provide a management consultancy service. Bishop Claver met members of the ESB Officers Association (ESBOA) trade union on the issue. Afterwards he said he got a 'fairly mixed reception'.

The bishop also said that after five years of martial law in the Philippines, the rich were becoming richer and the poor were getting poorer. A poor family of six had to live on 10 pesos (the equivalent of 85 cent in our modern currency) a day, and half of that money had to go on rice. The official attitude of the Catholic Church (in a country where 85 per cent of the population was Catholic) to the regime was one of what he called 'critical collaboration'. He believed the stance of the Marcos regime was akin to a communist attitude – prepared to sacrifice a generation of people for greater economic gain.

Following Bishop Claver's visit to Ireland, Bishop Casey went to the Philippines to see for himself the situation in which the ESB had become involved. In a recent interview for this book, he told an amusing story about a meeting he attended with representatives of some of the people affected by the hydroelectric scheme. There were few English speakers at the meeting and among them was a dog chasing in and out and around the room. The bishop found this a distraction; he was working through a translator and needed all his concentration to make sure he understood the points the people there were making to him.

Others had tried but failed to catch the playful dog but Bishop Casey managed to get hold of it and hand it over to someone so that it could be taken out of the room. What he did not know at the time was that one of the customs in the Philippines is to serve dog meat to special visiting dignitaries, and that this particular dog that had distracted him was to end up on his plate.

He regarded the situation in the Philippines of sufficient gravity to request, when he returned to Ireland, representatives of the board of the ESB and of the company's trade unions to return with him to the Philippines to form a judgement for themselves. In interviews he gave at the time, the bishop said that the issue of ESB involvement raised serious questions about human rights abuses and Ireland's role in the developing world.

In March 1979, Trócaire, the ICJP and two trade unions, the ESBOA and the Amalgamated Union of Engineering Workers (Technical, Administrative and Supervisory Section), produced a joint report, written by Mary Sutton of Trócaire and the ICJP, urging the ESB to reassess the consultancy contract it had with the National Power Corporation of the Philippines since 1977. The report asserted that the ESB involvement may have been helping to entrench the repressive Marcos regime. It also urged unions in the ESB not to cooperate with the consultancy contract, and Trócaire called on the ESB to re-examine its role in the Philippines 'as a matter of urgency'.

One of the most controversial projects the World Bank was funding was the building of dams on the Chico River, which led to the eviction of thousands of people. At a press conference, Bishop Casey said they were not imputing blame to the ESB but that responsibility lay with the Irish govern-ment to produce guidelines for the involvement of Irish semi-state bodies with developing countries. He also said that several Filipino bishops had requested that the report be carried out; they said they would not have objected so much to the ESB presence under normal democratic conditions but because of martial law and the denial of the rights of a free press and free assembly, they had no power to correct the situation themselves.

The Columban Fathers, who had 220 missionaries in the Philippines, wrote to Trócaire to endorse the report. They pointed out that the benefits of ESB involvement were outweighed by the cost in human rights.

Thanks in part to the pressure exerted by Trócaire, which attracted enormous publicity in Ireland at the time, the ESB withdrew from its contract with the Philippine National Power Corporation. At the seminar in June 1983 in UCG, which marked Trócaire's tenth anniversary, Mildred Nevile of the Catholic Institute for International Relations in London questioned the role of the ESB in the Philippines and said that national and multinational companies were quite willing to do business with repressive governments in the interests of profit. The *Sunday Press* (19 June 1983) carried a report on her article and the ESB wrote to that paper to ask it to point out that the company had had no involvement in the Philippines for more than five years, and that whatever involvement it had before that was at the behest of the World Bank.

In a recent interview for this book, and looking back from the vantage point of twenty years later, Mary Sutton expressed the view that the ESB was unfortunate to have attracted the negative publicity that it did at the time. She believed the management consultancy contract it had with the World Bank had no direct involvement with the controversial Chico River project. However, part of the problem was that there was quite an amount of confusion about what exactly the ESB was doing in the Philippines.

Ms Sutton said that the point Trócaire was making at the time was a simple one. With Ireland developing a foreign aid programme, with all the principles that went with that, and especially a programme that was not a commercial, strategic, geopolitical exercise but a genuinely altruistic one, there was an inconsistency in Irish semi-state companies engaging with regimes that had appalling records of abuse of human rights.

Supporting sugar-plantation workers

In an article in the *Catholic Standard* (29 August 1980) Trócaire singled out the sugar-plantation workers in the Philippines as one of the many groups it was supporting in developing countries. The sugar workers' struggle against injustice, the agency said, was not to be seen in isolation from our own experiences nor from the rest of the Third World's because it encapsulated many of the problems of the Third World as well as relating to the responsibilities of rich countries towards poor nations.

The Philippine Islands were still suffering from the legacy of colonialism, during which vast acreages of prime land were given to settlers, the article explained. During that period, a market for sugar in Europe led to the establishment of sugar plantations in the Philippines, employing virtual slave labour from among the displaced smallholders. The Marcos martial-law government in power in the country continued to condone this system of plantation labour at minimal wages. On Negros, the main sugar-producing island, very rich land-owners owned most of the land. The poor – the vast majority – were forced to work cutting cane and processing sugar for western markets for pitifully low wages.

The Catholic Church in the Philippines, the *Standard* article continued, was taking a stand on behalf of the poor by protesting to the government about the abuses of human rights as well as supporting the action of the oppressed to better their living conditions. On Negros, the sugar workers were uniting to try to set up a free trade union with which they hoped to negotiate for better wages and conditions. Their struggle was not easy because union members in the Philipp-ines were subject to arrest and imprisonment if they went on strike, and any attempts to hold meetings for the purpose of joint initiatives were considered subversive by the authorities.

Trócaire supported the efforts of the Negros workers through its partners in the Philippines, the church agency known as NASSA, which was the development wing of the Catholic Bishops' Conference in the country. Its funds went towards the training of sugar workers in leadership skills.

The situation of the sugar workers was the key to an understanding of the whole problem of world poverty and of Western responsibilities in this area, the *Catholic Standard* article argued. The effects of colonialism, the violation of human rights in the name of law and order by an oppressive government, the prices of primary commodities such as sugar on the world market and how this affected the wages of the poor, and the necessity of supporting the actions of the oppressed to gain justice – all of these were vital aspects of the complex causes of Third World poverty and injustice, the article concluded.

Resisting military oppression
In December 1981, Trócaire allocated £10,000 to help resettle 2,000 villagers on the island of Samar, who had been removed from their homes by the army to create a free-fire zone. During the removal, forty-five villagers – men, women and children – were massacred by the army.

In the spring of 1981, Pope John Paul II, on his visit to the Philippines, had appealed to President Marcos to stop using his vast military machine to murder and to brutalise the poor. Instead, he asked him to ensure the poor received enough of the country's considerable wealth to live with dignity. But his plea went unheard. Instead, church workers continued to be locked in a confrontation with the Marcos military machine, which cracked down on their efforts to help the country's increasingly desperate poor.

The mounting tension between church and state led in late 1982 to an international incident when the regime accused the Irish Columban, Fr Niall O'Brien, and the Australian missionary, Fr Brian Gore, of plotting murder. It was only after an outcry that the regime said it would take no further action on the charges.

Fr O'Brien pledged that he and other church workers would not be intimidated from helping the poor. He told

Trócaire their attempt to be a voice for the voiceless had called up a violent reaction on the part of some with vested interests, and that the allegations made against him and his co-workers were totally baseless. They had been active in organising poor labourers and sugar workers who had suffered a dramatic fall in their living standards in the previous year and who were subject to growing military abuse. They had also been involved in cooperative farming ventures and in the monitoring of military brutality, and were accused of committing 'murder by inducement' of a former mayor of the island town of Kabankalan.

Trócaire published a major investigation detailing the abuses by the military: bombing, strafing, torturing and kidnapping more people than ever, with around half a million smallholders forced off their land without proper compensation – usually to make way for big business. The Trócaire report disclosed that, with urban unemployment passing 40 per cent, the government had launched a new wave of repression, jailing the most effective trade union leaders on flimsy subversive charges. The real value of wages fell by one-third between 1975 and 1980 and was falling again.

A total of 157 political killings and disappearances for the first six months of 1982 had been documented by human rights groups. More and more Filipinos had been forced to do without food, clothes and freedom from arrest and faced torture and death, while the one item that expenditure was increased on was weapons. Military assist-ance from the US had risen to seven times its 1970 rates, which was protecting the increasing private US investment. Government economic policies had led to increased wealth for (mainly US) investors, and to growing disaster for the Filipinos. The natural resources of the country were being squandered.

In late March 1983, Karl Gaspar was imprisoned in the Philippines. He had been invited to Trócaire's tenth anniversary seminar in UCG but languished in prison instead, and in a symbolic gesture his chair was kept vacant at the seminar. His links with Ireland had begun around six years before when he came here with Bishop Labayen (Bishop of Infanta), the chairman of NASSA, at the invitation of Trócaire. He returned several times in the intervening period. In the spring of 1983, having prepared the first week of a recent three-week tour by a Trócaire-sponsored Irish delegation, he attended a meeting of Third World lay theologians in Geneva.

Afterwards he returned to Mindanao – a flashpoint in the Philippine conflict. 'Strategic hamletting' – forcing people off their land and resettling them in militarised hamlets or zones – was taking place on a large scale. The tactic had been used by the Americans in Vietnam to control populations and prevent them from becoming involved in guerrilla activity; 80 per cent of the entire Philippine army was based on Mindanao.

Vincent Tucker, a University College Cork anthropologist who had been part of the Irish delegation that visited the Philippines, said there was a concerted campaign by the military to prevent any information leaking out about what was really happening on Mindanao. They had compiled lists of church workers whom they considered 'subversives', with Karl Gaspar being regarded as a leading church worker because of his background and experience.

Having at first kept silent, under intense international pressure the Philippine authorities admitted holding him in the national military and police headquarters on the outskirts of Manila. Church sources said he was badly tortured and his family and lawyers were denied access to him. Trócaire expressed gratitude to Jim O'Keefe, the Irish Minister of State for Foreign Affairs, for the pressure the Irish government had brought to bear internationally on Mr Gaspar's behalf.

Fr Niall O'Brien and the 'Negros Nine'

In May 1983, Fr Niall O'Brien and two other priests, together with six lay workers, were arrested on trumped-up murder charges. They were kept under house arrest for eight months but 'escaped' to prison in Bacolod City, where they felt they would be safer. They became known internationally as 'the Negros Nine'.

The Redemptorists, who were based in Negros, alerted Trócaire to the arrests and Marian Cadogan facilitated contact with RTÉ so that as much media attention as possible would be focused on the prisoners' plight. RTÉ managed to get a phone-mic into Fr O'Brien in Bacolod Jail and in this way kept up regular contact with him. The station also sent a young reporter, Charlie Bird, who interviewed him for Irish television directly from the prison itself.

The plight of the Negros Nine became a huge media event in Ireland. This was due in part to Niall O'Brien himself, because he was highly articulate and media friendly. His mother also played a leading part in the public campaign waged in Ireland to free her son and his co-accused. The fate of the prisoners was followed on an almost daily basis on radio and television in Irish homes, and the Negros Nine spent six months in jail before the case was dropped. Fr O'Brien afterwards told Marian Cadogan that when he was released and returned to Ireland, he was known and greeted everywhere he went.

In February 1984, Bishop Casey visited Fr O'Brien in Bacolod. He described the prison conditions there as 'sub-human' and called on the Irish government to condemn publicly the Philippine record, not just over the false evidence against Fr O'Brien but over the many cases of injustice in the country. At their meeting with him, a group of Filipino priests urged Bishop Casey to condemn the US foreign policy that supported the oppressive Marcos regime. The bishop then went on to Mindanao to visit Karl Gaspar, who was still being detained.

Bishop Casey (together with an Australian bishop, Dr Myles McKeown) then went to the US to make represen-tations to the US Catholic hierarchy about the pending trial of Fr O'Brien (one of the other priests arrested with him, Fr Brian Gore, was Australian). They also met with US officials to raise the issue of human rights in the Philippines. As a result of their visit, the US bishops urged the Reagan administration to put pressure on President Marcos.

On his return to Dublin, the bishop made a report to the Department of Foreign Affairs and suggested it should raise concern through international bodies about the arrests and impending trial and the denial of human rights in the Philippines. He said the arrests were seen in the Philippines as an attack on the Catholic Church. The detainees were in good spirits, he said, but prison conditions were bad, with few if any medical services: some 600 men and boys confined there were suffering from TB.

In early July 1984, the charges against Fr O'Brien and his eight co-accused were dropped, and they were released from prison. He was exiled and returned to Ireland but went back to the Philippines two years later after the fall of the Marcos regime. On the occasion of Trócaire's twenty-fifth anniversary in 1998, he sent the following message to the agency:

> Trócaire is one of the things that makes me proud to be Irish. It is a church organisation that both feeds the poor and asks the difficult question: 'Why are they poor?' This takes courage and Trócaire has always had that courage. I have had dealings with Trócaire for many years now. I have always been impressed by their careful analysis of the situation, helping us to ask the difficult questions.

On 11 July 1985, Fr Rudy Romano, a Redemptorist and a member of the Irish Redemptorist Province, disappeared in Cebu City. He had worked selflessly on behalf of the poor and had taken part in many anti-Marcos marches. It is believed that he was abducted by elements of the Military Intelligence Group of the Philippine army. Bishop Casey contacted the Filipino government to express Trócaire's concern over his disappearance.

A 'Save Fr Romano Group' was organised in Ireland. It held daily vigils outside the US embassy in Dublin and petitioned the US government to use its influence with the Philippine authorities, but neither Fr Romano's fate nor his whereabouts was ever divulged by his abductors. He left a legacy of service to the marginalised sectors of Philippine society and inspired many to continue his work.

The end of Marcos rule
After twenty years of corrupt rule, Ferdinand Marcos lost the 1986 presidential election to Corazon Aquino. He tried to quash the result by falsifying the election returns but was forced to resign because of the enormous opposition within the country. Trócaire continued its support of the people of the Philippines that year. It allocated £14,000 to strengthen the people-based organisations and communities on Mindanao and set up alternative education and training programmes.

During the Marcos era, Marian Cadogan frequently visited the Philippines in the course of her work for Trócaire. She described the period of Marcos's rule as one of extensive human rights abuses, with no normal rule of law in the sense of ordinary people having the right to defend themselves. There was a pervasive climate of fear accompanied by widespread poverty.

She recalled spending a day on a sugar plantation in Negros. The nearest approximation she could think of to describe the scenes she witnessed was the period of feudalism that existed in Europe during the Middle Ages. People were working in the hot sun for long hours for what amounted to no more than a pittance. Yet, she found that despite the hardship of their lives, the ordinary Filipinos displayed a strong sense of humour. They were always ready to make a joke and laugh at the world – however harshly it might be treating them.

One of the staunchest supports these unfortunate people had in their lives, according to Ms Cadogan, was the Catholic Church. She believed that men such as Bishop Labayen, whom she regarded as heroic, were fearless and inspiring figures, who spoke out on behalf of the poor, calling attention to the injustices being perpetrated on them, urging the government to grant them fair play and a share in the wealth that the country was palpably producing.

The end of the Marcos era did not see an end to all problems in the Philippines and Trócaire continued its vital work there. That work has included providing relief after typhoons, earthquakes and volcanic eruptions, defending the rights of women workers, supporting shantytown dwellers and those made landless, promoting ecological awareness and a wide range of other development projects.

CHAPTER 5:
'Communists Need To Be Loved As Well': Breaking the Vietnam Aid Embargo

The Vietnam War

One of the first projects Trócaire was involved in and financed was in North Vietnam, during the Vietnam War. The finance went to a hospital in Hanoi, capital of what was then North Vietnam, which was treating children who had been deafened by US bombing of the city. In an interview for this book, Brian McKeown said the project helped to highlight what was going on in that country and how innocent people were suffering as a result.

Trócaire also aided a refugee settlement on the south-east coast of Vietnam that was destroyed by a typhoon in November 1973. The US-based Catholic Relief Services (CRS) contacted Trócaire for help. The CRS programme director, Fr John McVeigh, afterwards thanked the agency for its help. 'Without this timely support from Trócaire, we would not have been able to furnish such a diversity of assistance to so many genuinely needy people,' he said.

The people living in the refugee settlement in question, at Son Tinh, had been there since 1968, when their village was taken over by the Viet Cong, one of the main communist forces fighting the Americans and the South Vietnamese. The land in the settlement was not arable and the men there could make only a marginal livelihood as labourers. In

November 1973, a typhoon struck, drowning twenty-five people, destroying 400 houses, sweeping away all food reserves and destroying the village well. When the villagers returned, they found that only a few pieces of furniture had survived the flood.

CRS did a survey of the area and then approached Trócaire and other development agencies for assistance. Trócaire allocated £2,000 from emergency relief funds towards the project, which was used to help 795 families with food supplies and equipment and to construct a drinking well to replace the one ruined by the flood.

The grant helped the villagers build up small cash reserves by freeing them from the need of having to spend all their daily earnings on food. Trócaire money was used to provide a wage for unemployed heads of families who worked on building the new well. The refugees' final request was for paper and pencils for their children to use at school, so Trócaire provided 450 school kits as well.

Aiding reconstruction after the war

The Vietnam War ended in early 1975. In April that year, Trócaire gave a grant of £4,000 to Cooperation for the Reconstruction in Vietnam (COREV), a church agency set up to coordinate and plan relief and development programmes. Reports, which Trócaire had received, indicated that almost the whole population of Quang Tri province, hundreds of thousands, had fled southwards to Hue and, joined by most of Hue's civilian population, made their way towards Da Nang, where a massive air and sea evacuation programme was planned. Altogether, about a million refugees fled their homes with nothing except what they could carry on their backs.

The initial Trócaire grant was quickly exhausted and the agency appealed to the Irish public for more help. Reports reaching the agency said that there were close to two million refugees in Vietnam and the number was increasing daily. A serious problem for aid agencies in the country was the inaccessibility of many refugees. CRS in Saigon (capital of South Vietnam from 1954–1975, and later renamed Ho Chi Minh City) told Trócaire it was increasingly difficult to determine the needs that had to be met and they were regularly learning of new groups of refugees needing urgent assistance.

Caritas Internationalis (CI), the humanitarian confederation of 165 Catholic development agencies from around the world, also appealed to Trócaire. It said the population of Vietnam had been the victim of almost uncontrolled panic. CI's resources were rapidly depleted because of the large influx of refugees arriving in the areas around Saigon from the plateaux and more northerly regions.

The Vietnamese refugee problem would take many years to work itself out and was really only beginning in 1975. Over the next twenty-five years, nearly two million people left their homes in Vietnam, taking into account land refugees and those unfortunates who became known as 'the boat people'. They found resettlement mainly in Western countries, including a small number in Ireland, and in Australia. Countless thousands more lost their lives while leaving Vietnam in rickety boats, only to be preyed upon by pirates, battered by rough seas and, at times, denied access to land in what should have been friendly territory.

In October 1978, Trócaire gave an emergency grant of £10,000 to help victims of severe floods in Vietnam. The floods, which followed torrential monsoon rains, affected more than two million people, with more than a million in need of urgent relief. In addition, 200,000 houses were destroyed or damaged and 218,000 livestock perished. One of the worst affected areas was around the Mekong Delta – the 'rice bowl of Vietnam' – where almost two million acres were under water and the rice crop destroyed.

Brian McKeown, who made a ten-day visit to the country the following December, said that Vietnam faced one of its worst crises since the ending of the war. It was threatened with the loss of two rice harvests because the floods were preventing the planting of the following year's crop. It is difficult, if not impossible, to ascertain how many perished as a consequence of the flooding of 1978 but the number is most likely upwards of 700. A far greater number would have died from starvation due to the damage the floods caused but for the intervention of international agencies, Trócaire among them.

In February 1981, Trócaire allocated £20,000 to help in the relief of those affected by four typhoons which had struck the northern and north-central provinces of Vietnam the previous year. In the fourth and final typhoon, which struck the previous December, an estimated 300,000 tons of rice were lost, hundreds of thousands were made homeless and more than 100 were killed.

Mary Cole paid a fact-finding visit to Vietnam on behalf of Trócaire in the spring of 1981. In her report, she said she found a country struggling to rebuild itself after years of devastation. A vicious circle of a sinking economy and a rising black market was directly traceable to the years of the American occupation of the south. The potentially large yields of the Mekong Delta still had not materialised owing to a combination of natural disasters, the unfamiliarity of half a generation with the wiles of the rice plant and the reluctance of southerners to join the cooperatives that were compulsorily organised by zealous communist cadres.

The attitude in the north was very different. There people were used to the communist system, and although the land was poorer, it was intensively cultivated. The medical and educational systems were better in the north as well. However, droughts, flooding and major typhoons had damaged harvests in the previous five years and malnutrition was rising.

China was a constant threat and had backed Khmer Rouge (the ruling regime in Cambodia) attacks across the Cambodian border between 1976 and 1978. As a result of Chinese and American hostility, Vietnam was being thrown ever closer into the arms of the Soviet Union. The fiercely independent Vietnamese strongly resented this dependence. However, continued isolation from international support in aid, trade and diplomatic relations was eroding that independence.

In a recent interview for this book, Mary Cole said that what struck her on this visit was that the war was still, in effect, going on, in terms of human casualties. She pointed out that at the formal end of hostilities, 300,000 tons of the fifty million tons of bombs dropped on Vietnam still lay unexploded in the fields. Despite massive clean-up operations, devices the size of golf balls still littered the countryside, as insidious a reminder of US warfare as the escalating instances of liver and skin cancer and of strange deformities among the offspring of thousands contaminated by the defoliant, Agent Orange.

Ms Cole recalled being struck by the sheer amount of work that was going on all over the country in the effort to rebuild after the long years of devastating warfare. She found the Vietnamese to be a very proud, hard-working and dynamic people, in contrast with the more laid-back Cambodians, whose country she had just toured. Despite the deprivation the Vietnamese were experiencing in their lives, despite the added problems caused by the typhoons and despite the fact that so little aid was being made available to them, those who chose to remain in the country were determined to press on with the reconstruction, she said.

A number of impressive people's projects, encompassing metalwork, food production and health, stood out in her memory. She recalled visiting a hospital in Ho Chi Minh City where a concentrated campaign aimed at reducing the incidence of TB had yielded good results. In addition, and although Vietnam was a land of rice paddy fields where mosquitoes were plentiful and big – twice as big as those she had seen in Africa – malaria had been brought within manageable levels thanks to the disciplined approach of the authorities and their emphasis on primary healthcare as opposed to expensive hospitalisation.

North Vietnam had had such programmes in place for some time before Ms Cole visited the united country in 1981.

They were then extended to the south of the country following the end of the war with the Americans. She remarked that there might not have been much emphasis on wealth creation by the authorities but that they certainly looked after the people in terms of primary healthcare and a cooperative approach to agriculture and industry. It might have been a case of poverty, rather than wealth, being distributed equally but at least everyone was expected to share the burden, Ms Cole observed.

Following her visit to Vietnam, Mary Cole wrote the following in an *Irish Times* article (2 March 1981): 'The US failed to provide the promised reconstruction funds that might have helped refloat the shattered economy and keep Vietnam out of the Sino-Soviet power game. Western countries follow US policy with economic blockades that make neither geopolitical nor humanitarian sense. The cutting off of EEC food aid in 1979, with Ireland's backing, is a particular case in point. Now, when food shortages reach alarming proportions, no moves have been made to resume it.'

In December 1981, Trócaire allocated £10,000 for the relief of typhoon victims. The grant helped fund the provision of food, medicines, school materials and construction materials for the people of Phukhanh province, which had been struck by the worst typhoon in sixty years.

Marian Cadogan, who was later to play an important role for Trócaire in Vietnam, first visited the country in 1983. In a recent interview for this book, she recalled the extraordinary impact her first impressions of Vietnam made on her. At that time, the country was what she called 'a pariah nation'. All of the neighbouring countries, Thailand in particular, were very afraid of it because it had the largest standing army in Asia. It had already invaded and taken control of Cambodia, and Thailand feared it would be next.

Ms Cadogan described the kind of society that existed in Vietnam at that time as 'Dickensian'. Almost all Vietnamese women wore plain black suits and conical-style hats and practically all the men wore old faded green army uniforms and green pith helmets. Hanoi, she said, was 'a city of bicycles'. She considered it a beautiful jewel of a city, with the fading colonial grandeur of its French-style villas and the striking Hoan Kiem Lake at its centre. There was little street lighting so at night darkness suffused the city. The countryside was almost entirely without electricity. When she landed in Ho Chi Minh City, what struck her was how quiet it was – a quietness that would be inconceivable to anyone who knows the city today.

Ms Cadogan subsequently spent up to twelve years of her life in Vietnam and she described its people as the most heroic she has every encountered. In those early days that she was there, she witnessed thousands working together digging canals, for example, doing what they could to shape nature to meet human needs, and doing that with only the most primitive of equipment.

Trócaire and other voluntary agencies continued to do what they could to help Vietnam but there was a limit to what they could achieve. In July 1984, Brian McKeown paid, what he found, a harrowing visit to the country. On his return, he said living standards in Vietnam, which received virtually no post-war aid from anybody except the distant Soviets who were not allowed transport through China, were very low indeed. There was a desperate need for more aid at all costs, he said. He had spent time in both Hanoi and Ho Chi Minh City and reported that the black market still thrived in the latter and that dollars were still in circulation there.

In October of the same year, he appealed to the European Commission to lift an embargo that prevented humanitarian aid being sent to Vietnam from the EEC. He said he wanted the Commission to endorse an opinion of the European Parliament that emergency food and medical aid could be routed from EEC countries to Vietnam via NGOs such as Trócaire. Aid to Vietnam had been suspended by the EEC in 1979 because of that country's involvement in Cambodia, but Trócaire believed people in need should not suffer because of political considerations or because of the type of government they had.

Working to end the aid embargo
In the following years, Trócaire continued to campaign to have the embargo against Vietnam lifted. This involved lobbying politicians and officials in Ireland and in other EEC countries.

At the beginning of 1984, Trócaire was asked to become the lead agency of the CIDSE programme for Vietnam, Cambodia and Laos, and agreed to do so. Justin Kilcullen, who had been Trócaire's African project officer, became the new coordinator. In a recent interview for this book, he said that there was a political dimension to Trócaire's interest in the CIDSE programme in that the agency was campaigning strongly to bring about an end to the US/EEC embargo. The challenge for the agency, he said, was to see if it could also incorporate the issue of the aid embargo into its work.

Brian McKeown was keen to engage in the new responsibility at a political level. In June 1984, Trócaire organised a high-level delegation, comprising Mr McKeown and Justin Kilcullen, the director of their French counterpart (CCFD) and the secretary-general of CIDSE, to go on a mission to meet with the Vietnamese political authorities to discuss how they, as NGOs, could make a contribution in terms of getting around the embargo. They met the Vietnamese Foreign Minister, Nguyen Co Thach. Brian McKeown made a compre - hensive presentation to him on how CIDSE saw the situation and how they could try to bring American NGOs, particularly CRS, into the picture and perhaps get them to join the consortium and use them as a way of opening up American assistance.

Justin Kilcullen expressed the belief, in his recent inter - view, that the Vietnamese recognised that, politically, CIDSE had something to offer. However, he said that at the same time CIDSE was very careful not to become just a tool or puppet of the Vietnamese government. The delegation made

'COMMUNISTS NEED TO BE LOVED AS WELL'

what he called 'a very strong statement' about human rights in Vietnam and about the position of the Catholic Church, which was under persecution in the country at the time – and still is up to the present.

As well as meeting with the political authorities, the CIDSE delegation insisted on meeting with the church authorities. They met with Cardinal Trinh Van Can of Hanoi. Mr Kilcullen himself had already met with Archbishop Binh of Ho Chi Minh City. When the latter and other Vietnamese bishops travelled to France in April 1984, Mr Kilcullen and other CIDSE representatives met with them to explain the work they were doing in Vietnam and to ensure the church there was happy with the work in which they were engaged.

Mr Kilcullen recalls a conversation with Archbishop Binh, who was very elderly (the Vietnamese government would not agree on who would replace him and he could not retire until a successor was agreed). He said to the archbishop that CIDSE could be criticised for funding, or being seen to fund, the communist government in Vietnam, at a time when the church was under persecution there. The archbishop's response was: 'Well, you know, communists need to be loved as well.' Mr Kilcullen thought that response to the existing situation a very Christian one.

There was some division within the Catholic Church in Vietnam at the time. The Association of Patriotic Catholics had taken root in the country – the Vietnamese attempt to have a Chinese-style patriotic church. Some bishops allowed the association to operate in their dioceses and assigned priests to work with the organisation. Other bishops would have nothing to do with them. Mr Kilcullen had the opportunity to visit one of the latter category of bishops in 1986 when he went to Hue and met Archbishop Philippe Nguyen Kim Dien, who was under house arrest.

Mr Kilcullen was in Hue looking at irrigation projects that CIDSE was likely to fund. He said to the authorities who were showing him around that whenever CIDSE representatives visited an area, they liked, as a matter of courtesy, to call on the local bishop, and so asked if it would be possible to see the archbishop; a request that provoked some rather startled looks on the faces of the officials. However, the following morning he was taken to the archbishop's house and there followed a meeting of the archbishop, himself and a cast of some forty 'minders'.

The archbishop really appreciated the visit, Mr Kilcullen recalled. He also remarked that the archbishop was a lively character who was not in any way intimidated by all the officials surrounding them or by the circumstances of his house arrest. Mr Kilcullen presented him with a 'Penal' cross made of bog oak, a present, he informed him, from the bishops of Ireland.

It was certainly an interesting time in Vietnam. On one side was the government, out in the cold as it were, isolated from much of the international community; on the other was the Catholic Church, under persecution. Then there was CIDSE somewhere in the middle, representing Catholic agencies working their way delicately between the two. Mr Kilcullen expressed the opinion that Brian McKeown showed great skill in the way he handled a situation fraught with pitfalls.

In late August 1985, Brian McKeown welcomed the Irish government's decision to allocate £40,000 to a Trócaire-sponsored programme in Vietnam for the eradication of TB. The previous year, Trócaire's attempts, on behalf of a group of Catholic development agencies, to secure EEC humanit - arian aid for Vietnam failed when proposed programmes were rejected by the outgoing European Commission.

Brian McKeown said Trócaire's efforts to end the embargo on humanitarian aid to Vietnam had received the full support of the Irish Minister of State at the Department of Foreign Affairs, Jim O'Keefe. He said that Trócaire and other European voluntary agencies would continue to press for the lifting of the EEC embargo. The people of both Vietnam and Cambodia desperately needed European help to fight off famine and rebuild their lives after so many years of war, he added.

The Vietnamese ambassador to Britain paid a three-day visit to Ireland in late October 1985. He said that TB, malaria and a type of polio were still serious problems in the south of his country, and he spent a day meeting Trócaire officials as the agency coordinated several health programmes in Vietnam.

Shortly afterwards, Trócaire was nominated to coordinate the first allocation of emergency aid to Vietnam through NGO sources. The EEC allocated £700,000 – the embargo was finally broken – to help victims of the recent typhoon that had devastated ten provinces, leaving more than 1,000 dead and many more thousands homeless, while CIDSE contributed a further £100,000. More than two million were affected by the disaster and an estimated one million tons of rice harvest were destroyed. Vietnam desperately needed food, medical supplies, blankets and clothing. Trócaire was nominated to coordinate the response of a three-agency consortium, which included Secours Populaire of France and Oxfam Belgium.

In early December 1986, the first shipload of relief supplies from Trócaire arrived in Vietnam to help victims of Typhoon Wayne, which had devastated four areas of the country the previous September, leaving 400 people dead and 2,500 seriously injured. The shipload of clothing, blankets, rice, medical supplies, supplementary foods and agricultural equipment was distributed in Thai Binh and Ha Nam Nimh provinces through the local authorities there. The supplies, part of a £700,000 aid package, helped 10,000 families in areas where hundreds of thousands were homeless.

Brian McKeown welcomed the aid package and said that though development assistance to Vietnam had been blocked for a number of years, over the previous year the commission had shown an increased willingness to provide humanitarian assistance to Vietnam through NGOs.

A different kind of aid
In July 1987, the medical director of Ho Chi Minh City's centre for fighting TB, Pham Ngoc Thach Hospital, called Trócaire's aid 'very precious help'. It provided new medication that had

increased the cure rate from 45 per cent before 1985 to 80 per cent in 1987. Trócaire and CIDSE funding provided the most effective anti-TB drug, pyrazinamide, which made all the difference. Irish money also helped to build a new emergency ward at the TB hospital.

Unlike Soviet aid, which focused on grandiose power stations, steel mills and infrastructural projects, Catholic aid carefully selected small-scale projects that produced quicker human benefits. For example, the Van Phuc silk cooperative in Hanoi was provided with new machinery parts which increased productivity. Wages rose as a result by 30 per cent and living standards improved. One of the biggest CIDSE projects was a water-supply system in the port of Haiphong. The pumping station there provided much-needed drinking water for the 1.3 million inhabitants.

Justin Kilcullen's recent interview gives an insight into the difference between the two types of aid. He recalled travelling to villages in the south of Vietnam with Dr Quynh Hoa who ran one of the paediatric hospitals in Ho Chi Minh City. They went to visit very poor communities, tribal minorities living in long houses – as many as five or six families in one long building. Mr Kilcullen said he had not witnessed poverty quite like this anywhere, including the years he had spent in Africa.

When he dined with his Vietnamese hosts in the evening, he found them very critical of Soviet aid administrators who came to the country. They seldom left the hotels they were staying in; if they were brought out of the hotel, they took their own knives and forks with them, and they would not eat local food. They were there on official missions and they had no interest in meeting ordinary local people. In an informal moment, one Vietnamese official remarked to Justin Kilcullen that they called the Soviets 'the Yanks with no dollars'.

There were just a small number of Catholic NGOs working in Vietnam and their workers went out into the villages, mixed with the people and ate their local food. Mr Kilcullen

'COMMUNISTS NEED TO BE LOVED AS WELL'

said they saw it as part of the solidarity and the witness that they were giving as church agencies there and that the local church was very happy to see it that way. (About 7 per cent of the population of Vietnam was Catholic, i.e. four and a half million people, with many concentrated in specific areas.)

In August 1987, the *Irish Times* ran a series of articles on Vietnam. Justin Kilcullen wrote to the paper to congratulate its correspondent on the articles. He thought the *Irish Times* might well have been surprised to read of the extent of Trócaire's involvement in Vietnam and said that the country, along with its neighbours Cambodia and Laos, remained one of the poorest and most neglected countries in the world. Despite the terrible hardship suffered by those Indo-Chinese people through thirty years of war, he continued, the governments of the West had chosen to deny practically all development assistance to the region.

He went on to say that as a result of the abandonment of the peoples of Indo-China by the West, Trócaire and other Catholic development agencies in Europe and North America felt compelled to undertake a major programme of development assistance in Vietnam, Cambodia and Laos. The fact was, he continued, that voluntary development agencies had had thrust upon them a role that went far beyond the mandate of a voluntary agency because Western governments had reneged on their duty to the peoples of those countries. It placed a heavy strain on the financial resources of the agencies who had no option but to continue to work in that way.

The people of Vietnam, Cambodia and Laos had not chosen to isolate themselves from the West; it was the other way round, he said. However, he assured the newspaper's readers that while their political leaders might have chosen to ignore the claims of the Indo-Chinese people to the right to a means of furthering their own development, Trócaire would continue to bring to them the support of the peoples of their countries. Archbishop Binh of Ho Chi Minh City underlined the importance of this when he told the *Irish Times* correspondent that the assistance gave them 'not only more aid but also more contact and communication and shows that the rest of the world has not forgotten us'.

Trócaire runs the new CIDSE office in Hanoi

In July 1988, Trócaire opened a field office in Vietnam on behalf of CIDSE. The move followed talks with the Vietnamese government in which Brian McKeown played a central role. He succeeded in persuading the Vietnamese Foreign Minister of the necessity for and value of such an office.

This was the first time since the end of the war that any NGO development agency had been permitted to set up a field office in the country, and so was a measure of the trust the Vietnamese government had in the work of Trócaire and CIDSE. The new office was responsible for monitoring humanitarian and development assistance. Marian Cadogan was appointed country representative for the CIDSE programme in Vietnam in 1988 and was in charge of the new office, which opened in Hanoi in the north of the country. She fulfilled the role for two years, working initially out of a hotel bedroom, which constituted her 'office'.

Her role was a very pioneering one, as she afterwards described it. A few other NGOs occasionally visited but were not permitted, for some time, to establish their offices in Vietnam. She said the foreign community in Vietnam at the time was tiny: the staff of the communist bloc countries' embassies, the staff of a handful of Western embassies and the members of a few UN agencies, mainly the United Nations International Children's Emergency Fund (UNICEF) and the UN Food and Agriculture Organisation. She recalled that there was a social club in the Australian embassy to which the foreigners used to go on Friday nights and she would know everyone there – so small were their numbers. As Ms Cadogan was the only NGO representative in Hanoi at the time, representatives from other NGOs around the world who visited the country would tend to visit her to discuss programming and to share insights on the ever evolving socio-political situation.

       'COMMUNISTS NEED TO BE LOVED AS WELL'

Because of the widespread bureaucratic constraints that existed in the country, it was some time before CIDSE could arrange for a car to be shipped to Hanoi for Ms Cadogan's use. There was no taxi service available in the city, so she made her way around on a bicycle. She recalled going to the Ministry of Foreign Affairs on one occasion for an important meeting with Phan Thi Minh, who had responsibility for the activities of aid agencies in Vietnam. It was very important in such a society to show due respect, so Ms Cadogan dressed up in her best and cycled to the Foreign Ministry building. She gave herself plenty of time, parked her bicycle well out of sight, brushed herself down and went to the impressive old building which housed the ministry. Phan Thi Minh herself was waiting at the gate of the ministry. She enquired how Ms Cadogan had travelled there, a question the Irishwoman had hoped she would not be asked. When Ms Phan heard the means of transport, she spontaneously embraced Ms Cadogan, describing her as 'one of ourselves'. Phan Thi Minh, it turned out, cycled to work every day.

During Marian Cadogan's second year in Vietnam, a representative from Oxfam and another from the Mennonite Central Committee became based in Hanoi. Gradually representatives of a few more NGOs began to locate themselves in the city and the first coordinating meeting of NGOs in Vietnam took place in Ms Cadogan's room. Subsequently, the NGO Forum in Vietnam became enormously important and a very powerful lobbying group.

But CIDSE was the trailblazer, and because the programme, and Ms Cadogan's work there, was so effective, the way was prepared for others to come in and begin to operate.

Justin Kilcullen went to Hanoi in 1998 to celebrate the tenth anniversary of the opening of the CIDSE office, a reception that was 'packed with NGOs', as he put it. He took the opportunity to tell the gathering how CIDSE and Trócaire had blazed a trail ten years before. None of the NGO repre-sentatives present was aware of how pioneering CIDSE and the Irish agency had been – a typical illustration of how little those who come afterwards wondered about what went before them. As far as they were concerned, things had always been the way they were when they arrived.

Back in 1988, Brian McKeown said that the opening of the office represented a significant political decision to facilitate the work of the Catholic agencies that had been assisting in humanitarian and development aid in Vietnam since the end of the war. He also said that Vietnam was at that time facing the most serious crisis since the end of the war in 1975, with seven million at risk of famine and three million already facing food shortages. He pointed out that at that critical time in Vietnam's history, Western governments were doing little to avert what could become a major famine in a matter of months.

Though Vietnam had by that time succeeded in increasing its agricultural production since 1975 to levels of seventeen million tons a year, it had not managed to become self-sufficient, so that poor harvests had an immediate and serious effect on its vulnerable supply systems. The overall shortfall in supply for 1988 was around 1.7 million tons, up one million tons since the previous year, when the harvest was markedly better.

The efforts of the UN World Food Programme (WFP) and of the voluntary relief agencies succeeded in averting widespread famine at the time. Following this period of emergency aid, Trócaire worked with a talented young Dutch agronomist, Siep Littooy, setting up small-scale, farmer-focused agricultural projects. These were done in close coordination with the local government extension service of the Vietnamese provinces in many of the communes, with which the agency had become familiar during the 1988 emergency.

All the farms were state owned and going through a transition period as part of the Doi Moi (Renovation) programme – begun in 1988, gathering pace over the next two years and bringing about significant change. As a result, Vietnam went from being a place of famine in 1988 to one of the premier rice-exporting countries of the world by about

1991. The state leased the land to the people and Trócaire engaged in small-scale irrigation programmes, working closely with the farmers, helping them to set up and manage their own irrigation schemes. They also worked in land management and rehabilitation programmes, experimentation with new seeds, new crop patterns, infrastructure to get produce to markets and so on.

Continuing aid and gradual normalisation
The British government's decision to repatriate forcibly 40,000 'boat people' from Hong Kong to Vietnam was strongly condemned by Trócaire in November 1989. The agency made a strong plea to the Irish government to press for a coordinated response on the part of the EEC and other Western nations to the plight of the Vietnamese in Hong Kong. Brian McKeown said their plight was closely linked to the failure of the West to provide development assistance to Vietnam. The flow of refugees, most of whom had been living in subhuman conditions in Hong Kong, could be significantly reduced, he said, by helping Vietnam on a scale which would enable it to become self-sufficient.

He referred to the crisis when he announced the allocation of £107,000 from the EEC to victims of three devastating storms in Vietnam the previous month. He said the disaster highlighted the country's acute need for adequate international aid to enable it to develop its economy, increase food production and rebuild a shattered infrastructure.

The following month, he urged that Ireland and other Western countries should give sanctuary to those refugees in Hong Kong who did not wish to return to Vietnam. He said that for 1989, a total of £1.3 million in aid would be channelled towards Vietnamese development. The Chief of Mission for the UNHCR, the UN's refugee agency, also condemned the expulsion of the boat people from Hong Kong.

In early January 1990, RTÉ's *Today Tonight* did a special programme on Vietnam, the making of which was facilitated by CIDSE. The producer/reporter, Michael Heney of RTÉ, said that the people of Vietnam were in dire circumstances, having had a dreadful time since the Americans left; farming families were on the breadline and an estimated 7.5 million out of sixty-two million were hungry, almost all living in the mountainous region bordering China. The Vietnamese people felt that they had been relentlessly punished by the West for centuries and that the process of punishment still had not stopped. But, he said, they were deeply grateful to Trócaire and to CIDSE, and as a result every door was open to him and his crew in the making of the programme.

The situation in Vietnam slowly but gradually improved. In April 1992, Trócaire announced that in the course of the previous year, it had received £500,000 of EEC money for aid projects in Vietnam. And at the beginning of the following year, Justin Kilcullen, Trócaire head of the CIDSE programme, welcomed President George Bush's announcement the month before of a relaxation of the US economic embargo against Vietnam. Because of the economic strides the hard-working Vietnamese people had made, he said, the US business community saw possibilities there and put pressure on the Bush administration to allow them access to the country.

Mr Kilcullen now called on the US to go the full mile and remove the embargo completely. He quoted the words of Pope Paul VI: 'Peace is not just the absence of war … peace is another name for development.' It was time for the Americans to conclude a 'sad chapter in human relations' and let real peace begin in Vietnam, he said.

At the beginning of December 1993, Trócaire announced the sending of £50,000 – half of it donated by the Irish government – to aid the victims of the typhoon that had just struck southern Vietnam. Bishop John Kirby, the new chairman of Trócaire who had succeeded Bishop Casey in June that year, was visiting the country at the time and said that the money would be used immediately to buy food, medicines, cooking utensils and shelter for the worst affected by the storm, which had caused widespread damage in Phu Yen province, south of Ho Chi Minh City.

Bishop Kirby and Justin Kilcullen, the new director of Trócaire who had just taken over from Brian McKeown in 1993, met Le Mai, the Vietnamese Deputy Foreign Minister. Le Mai paid tribute to the development work of Trócaire in Vietnam. He recalled that the agency's first project had been during the Vietnam War when medical treatment was funded for children deafened by the US bombing of Hanoi in 1973.

A Trócaire health worker from Vietnam, Ms Nguyen Than My, visited Dublin in February 1994. She said that poor people in her country were still experiencing very great difficulties, with women in particular suffering. She described how the increasingly harsh economic climate had caused rising rates of malnutrition, disease and serious social problems such as drug abuse, prostitution and corruption. An indication of the extreme poverty in the north of Vietnam was the large number of Vietnamese women who secretly married Chinese men from across the border, where life for rural women was not as harsh as in Vietnam.

Ms My, a programme officer in charge of health projects in the Vietnamese province of Bac Thai, had been working for Trócaire for nearly two years. She pointed out that women in Vietnam bore almost total responsibility for the welfare of their children, so that any deterioration in the economic situation inevitably meant greater suffering for women. More and more they had to care for their families alone because their husbands were being forced to leave rural communities to look for work in cities.

Also in February 1994, the Clinton administration lifted the US economic embargo on Vietnam, a move that the Vietnamese government welcomed as a step towards full diplomatic relations with the US. Trócaire also welcomed the move, saying it would mean that at last Vietnam would have access to the aid it so urgently needed. Justin Kilcullen said that the harsh economic measures taken by the Vietnamese government in the previous year had brought much hardship to many poor Vietnamese. The prospect of significant inter -

national aid brought with it the hope that the country's severe economic difficulties could be reversed, he added.

Trócaire handed over the coordination of the CIDSE programme in Vietnam to one of their Belgian counterpart agencies in 1994, having been responsible for the coordin - ating role for ten years. But Trócaire remained part of the consortium. Life was becoming more normal in Vietnam by this time. The political issues began to recede in importance, and the programme began to focus on the more regular type of activities: sustainable development, primary healthcare and those more normal areas with which most programmes were concerned.

The major challenge was to enable the programme to be fully handed over and carried out by local NGO initiative. This process took a number of years and was mainly preoccupied with building the confidence of the Vietnamese government so that this would be allowed to happen. It took up to ten years to achieve but it can be said that it has, for the most part, been achieved at this stage.

Justin Kilcullen said that he recently met, at a gathering of NGOs from all over the world in Ghana, the head of the Vietnamese NGO platform, of which there are now 600 members. The government there still does not recognise NGOs, so the organisation is known as the Committee for Science and Technology. This Vietnamese man told Mr Kilcullen that the former CIDSE programme is the model in terms of professional work for NGOs in Vietnam. Mr Kilcullen considered this a fitting tribute – however late in the day – for the work that Trócaire had done.

CHAPTER 6:
The Killing Fields: The Khmer Rouge in Cambodia

Aftermath of the Khmer Rouge genocide

In 1974, Trócaire made its first contribution to Cambodia, with a small grant towards a health and development programme. The following year, the Vietnam War ended, as did the Cambodian civil war, which saw Pol Pot come to power, leading to the Khmer Rouge's genocide of two to three million Cambodians over the next four years.

Cambodia was more or less sealed off and little news of the terrible events that were happening there leaked out of the country. Nevertheless, Trócaire became increasingly concerned about the rumours of mass murder by the Pol Pot regime. Growing numbers of desperate Cambodians had been escaping across the border to Thailand and Vietnam. In late 1978, the Vietnamese invaded Cambodia, overthrew the Khmer Rouge early the following year and installed a puppet government.

That year, Trócaire became the first Irish presence in Cambodia since 1975 by flying in on the first relief plane to land in the capital, Phnom Penh, since the Khmer Rouge had emptied the city. (One of the first acts of the Pol Pot regime, after coming to power, was to move most of the urban population to the countryside.) Some of the other aid agencies were operating from the Thai border, but did not have any presence within the country itself. Trócaire's experience of working with the Vietnamese authorities facilitated its entrance and ability to operate within Cambodia, Brian McKeown said.

The scale of the tragedy that had taken place was unprecedented. A traumatised and bewildered population was facing starvation as rice stocks diminished. Many were looking for lost members of their displaced or massacred families. Trócaire committed itself to a major relief programme. This later evolved into a long-term development programme and began a long struggle for justice for the Cambodian people.

Of £20,000 that Trócaire allocated to help Indo-Chinese refugees in 1979, £5,000 was devoted to fund an international airlift of food and medicine to Cambodia. It was part of an international effort, organised by a group of voluntary agencies, to bring food and medical supplies to a country where, as Brian McKeown put it at the time, experts estimated that millions faced death from starvation and disease. This was the first time such an airlift had been permitted to enter the country since the fall of the Khmer Rouge.

In November 1979, collections at Masses in the Dublin archdiocese raised £150,000 for relief of distress in Cambodia and Archbishop Dermot Ryan handed over a cheque for this amount to Brian McKeown in mid-November.

While thousands were dying in the famine in Cambodia, strong allegations were made that outside aid was not reaching the starving. All the reports in the West claimed that the Vietnamese were diverting the aid while they practised atrocities against the Cambodian people and that the country was enduring mass starvation. In December 1979, Mary Cole went to Cambodia on behalf of Trócaire to investigate these allegations.

She spent ten days travelling the country and when she returned she gave an interview to the *Irish Press* (16 January 1980) about what she saw. She said it was hard to blame people for getting carried away with the sensational aspects of the famine but that there was not enough awareness of why the famine was caused. 'It's injustice – injustice all the time – the Third World is poor because our world is rich.'

She described Cambodia as a country that had been sealed off for four years but said that some parts were only mildly disrupted. The worst districts were in the south west and the south east, where the Khmer Rouge drove people from their homes, towns and villages, and killed many. The survivors fled to the mountains, without food or medical supplies, and when the Vietnamese began their offensive, people started the massive trek back to their homes while in the last stages of malnutrition. Pol Pot's dream of the most advanced and purest form of communism had cost millions of lives.

When Ms Cole arrived in Phnom Penh, she had difficulty getting a two-week visa. However, when she told the authorities that the Irish government had abstained on the UN vote on whether to recognise the Pol Pot regime, that the Irish people were worried the supplies they had paid for were not getting through, and that there had been a lot of negative publicity, the authorities' attitude softened and she was allowed to travel to areas of her own choosing. She was free to speak to the people, many of whom spoke French, and interpreters were available for those who did not.

In a recent interview for this book, Ms Cole recalled that she was treated very kindly. She had a room in the Phnom Penh Hotel, a massive and grandiose building that had almost returned to jungle due to years of neglect. She remembered that there was a python wound around the cistern of the toilet in her bathroom. Everybody was too busy to deal with the sleeping python so the toilet had to be flushed very gingerly!

Most of the people she saw were still dressed in the black pyjama-style outfit that was the 'uniform' imposed by the Khmer Rouge regime on the populace. She recalled that nobody smiled, not even children who were playing – so traumatised were they by the horror they had been through.

When she returned to Ireland, as well as arranging for food aid and other essential equipment, she also arranged for toys to be sent, especially to the orphanages, of which there were many.

In her *Irish Press* interview in 1980, Mary Cole said that at first Phnom Penh seemed to her like a ghost town, 'gutted, levelled, rat-infested'. Nonetheless, she discovered that there were plenty of people, but also that there was widespread hunger and terrible anaemia. The noise of trucks and the trundle of ox carts were constant as supplies were being moved to the stricken areas. Although there were only 1,500 lorries to service a country as big as England and Wales combined, she believed the administration had made remarkable strides towards getting some sort of normality back and she was certainly able to establish that the aid was getting through.

Ms Cole found Cambodia an overwhelmingly depressing place but what was most depressing for her was the position of women. The Khmer Rouge had killed so many husbands, brothers and sons that the women left behind were very vulnerable. They had been left with young children or were going from orphanage to orphanage trying to recover their lost children. Many wished to flee the country. The skilled, who were necessary for the reconstruction of Cambodia, were leaving the country and who could blame them after so much devastation, she asked. She was worried that some of the women who were left behind would turn to less desirable means of support, such as prostitution.

She stayed in the refugee camps on the Thai border for four days. In one, which accommodated 30,000 people, she found that food was plentiful and there was a good ratio of doctors and medical personnel. She said it was now vital for the Irish government to call for the de-recognition of the Khmer Rouge at the UN (where the Pol Pot regime was still recognised as the government of Cambodia).

She was astonished at the strength and resilience of the human spirit that she witnessed in Cambodia – the people there had been through sheer hell but somehow still had the will to go on. Despite the horror of the eradication of 2.5 million people, if the concern of the world 'could be translated to political will, to solve the situation and to ensure that these things do not occur again, then we might have learned something from the Kampuchean disaster,' she told the *Irish Press*.

In an article she wrote for the *Irish Times* shortly after her return (17 January 1980), Ms Cole described the reports of aid not getting through in Cambodia as dangerous. 'They affect the physical and political future of the estimated 4.5 million within the country who are in the process of reconstructing a fragile new Cambodia, while still suffering the effects of prolonged malnutrition, trauma and the complete destruction of the infrastructure through which aid could be effectively channelled.'

She also wrote about the determination she witnessed among the people to survive. 'Bamboo huts sprout around ruined buildings, people wade waist deep in canals and ponds, with nets, baskets, basins, anything that will catch fish. Intensive bartering of cabbages, palm sugar, fish and timber goes on in towns and villages to supplement the rice ration.'

The only virtue of the Khmer Rouge regime she could discern was its thoroughness. The detailed records kept by the various notorious prisons, listing all the information on the thousands slaughtered in them, with the stacks of photos taken before, during and after torture and execution, plus the mass graves seen in various provinces, she described as 'evidence of thoroughness gone mad'.

The Cambodian people, she wrote, were horrified at the mention of a Khmer Rouge return to power. (The Khmer were still strong on the Thai border.) Among Cambodians, that fear was even more intense than the fear of the Vietnamese, the ancient enemy. The officials in the new administration were working flat out, twelve hours a day and seven days a week, trying to get the country back on its feet, Ms Cole said. They expressed bewilderment and receding confidence to her at 'the negative Western publicity of their considerable efforts towards normalising the situation within the country'. The future welfare of Cambodia, she added, depended on how quickly the threat of a Khmer Rouge return to power was removed.

Following Ms Cole's report on her fact-finding mission to Cambodia, Trócaire and its sister agencies in Europe met and arranged for a major shipment of aid into the country. They liaised with warehouses and retail outlets in Singapore and Hong Kong. The aid agencies, headed by Oxfam, brought a huge barge of supplies from Singapore up the Mekong river.

Ms Cole said the barge, the size of a football pitch and piled high with food and equipment of various sorts, was 'an amazing sight' as it came up the Mekong and docked at Phnom Penh. Before that, any ships bringing in supplies had to stop at the coastal port of Kampong Som. The subsequent transport of supplies inland was slow because of the destruction of the road network during the Pol Pot years, and this new way of bringing in supplies opened up a whole new means of doing this vital job.

Within six months of the emergency in Cambodia coming to light in August 1979, Trócaire had donated half a million pounds in aid. As well as food and medical supplies, the money was used to buy rice seed, hoes, fish nets, irrigation pumps, assorted vegetable seeds, raw cotton for textile factories, drawing books and sets of crayons for schools, and diesel fuel for trucks.

In October 1980, Brian McKeown wrote to the Irish Minister for Foreign Affairs, Brian Lenihan, urging him to vote against the continuing recognition of the Khmer Rouge representation at the UN. In the letter, he said that there was a genuine fear among ordinary Cambodian people that the Khmer Rouge might return under another ideological label. He said the representatives of Trócaire and of the other European Catholic development organisations in Cambodia had testified to this fear and to the brutality that gave it a foundation.

In her recent interview, Mary Cole recalled graphic evidence of that brutality. One of the places she was taken to see on her first visit to Cambodia was the notorious Tuol Sleng prison in Phnom Penh. In this former school, 20,000 people had been tortured and slaughtered. She was one of the first Westerners to see this hellish place and she said it was akin to what it must have been like for those who were first on the scene at Auschwitz. The prison had not been cleaned or touched in any way: human tissue, hair and blood could still be seen on the walls and floors of the torture chambers. In the basement, the floor was strewn with photos of those who had suffered and died there – photos taken before, during and after their torture. It was as if the written account was not enough; there had to be a visual record as well.

On her second visit to Cambodia, Ms Cole was one of a CIDSE delegation taken to see a mass grave near Phnom Penh. It was a vast field, part of which was in the process of being dug up and bodies taken out. She was astonished at the number of bodies of children that were being disinterred. The skulls of a lot of them were exposed and the CIDSE delegates could see that the fontanelle in many of them had not closed, meaning that these infants could not have been much more than two years old – if even that – when they were killed; clubbed brutally and buried in mass graves, some perhaps not yet dead when they were dumped into these pits.

Ms Cole remembered that going out in the minibus to that mass burial site in the morning, the delegates were talking about various things and there was much chatter. During the day, they made themselves useful by helping to count and categorise bodies – they simply had to be occupied in some way to keep their minds from thinking too much about the horrific tragedy before them. Going back to the city in the evening, there was silence in the minibus. No one was able to speak after what they had been through.

Also in October 1980, Trócaire announced a further £250,000 allocation for development purposes in Cambodia.

Making the announcement, Brian McKeown said the situation there had moved steadily from one of dealing with an emergency to rebuilding the shattered economy. The allocation brought the amount Trócaire had by that time given to Cambodia to more than £1 million – a record in the seven years' existence of the agency.

Some of the money was spent in ways that might be considered surprising. Mary Cole recalled the Cambodian Minister for Agriculture impressing on her that they were able to get food from elsewhere but what they really needed from Trócaire was rat poison, so that the food would not be consumed or spoiled by rats before the administration could get it to the people. She also remembered that this same minister was wearing a big, heavy coat although the temperature was thirty degrees Celsius. He was shaking uncontrollably with malaria but was still at this desk doing his job for twelve hours a day.

Funding development and campaigning for de-recognition of the Khmer Rouge

The extent of Trócaire's (really the Irish people's) donation to Cambodia meant that significant support could be given to longer-term projects, which was what really was required. The aid was given gradually, according as the infrastructure could absorb it, and little, if anything, was wasted, Mary Cole explained in her recent interview. Her own role, when she returned from her second visit to Cambodia, was to disseminate information about the real situation that existed in the country. There was a great need for this to be done because of all the misinformation that had been and was still being put out by the Western media. In addition, people in Ireland had become so interested in what was happening in Cambodia that there was a huge appetite for information that needed to be satisfied.

Italian-born Onesta Carpene took on the running of the CIDSE programme in Cambodia and lived in Phnom Penh from 1980 onwards. Trócaire and its sister agencies in CIDSE pooled the considerable amounts of money they had raised into one large fund, which was administered by Ms Carpene. This was the basis on which the programme started, Justin Kilcullen said, and as the fund dwindled, Trócaire increased its own contributions to it.

He said there were about fourteen different NGOs operating in Cambodia at the time, all of them based in the same hotel in Phnom Penh. It was called the Monorom Hotel – 'monorom' translates into English as 'luxury' but he remarked that there was nothing luxurious about it in those early years after the genocide. Mr Kilcullen also said that there was even less of a presence of international people in Cambodia than there was in Vietnam at the time.

As well as its support for development work within Cambodia itself, Trócaire continued to devote much time and effort to the campaign for de-recognition of the Khmer Rouge at the UN. This was a slow, painstaking process and involved a consortium of thirty-six NGOs from all over the world working together.

Emergency aid had staved off disaster in 1979–1980, but what Cambodia really needed was technical equipment and assistance to rebuild its economy. Then it fell victim to the US, Western and Association of South-East Asian Nations' (ASEAN) hostility to Vietnam. The result was that agencies such as UNICEF were barred from giving development, as opposed to purely relief, aid to Cambodia. This meant, for example, that UNICEF could not even maintain a fleet of lorries it had supplied in 1979. The US and the EEC refused all development aid to Cambodia. Ireland and France had taken a less hard line at the UN and had abstained on the vote to seat the Pol Pot delegation, but neither country had challenged the overall EEC line.

In July 1984, the Irish Minister for Foreign Affairs at the time, Peter Barry, took a harder than usual line on Cambodia at a conference in Indonesia, while Justin Kilcullen of Trócaire, who had just returned from the country, appealed to the Irish government to urge the EEC to take a more conciliatory line towards the government in Phnom Penh. Speaking on behalf of the EEC at a conference of the pro-US ASEAN bloc, Mr Barry indicated that the EEC regarded the government of Cambodia as unrepresentative and demanded an end to the Vietnamese 'occupation' of the country.

In late August 1985, it was announced that the EEC was to give 1,000 tons of rice, worth more than £300,000, to Trócaire for distribution in Cambodia, where there were serious food shortages. This was only the second time since 1979 that the EEC had given emergency aid to the country (on the previous occasion, Trócaire was also the aid agency involved). The rice was to be sent to five provinces where heavy floods along the Mekong had completely destroyed the food crops and left the local population destitute.

Brian McKeown welcomed the EEC decision and said he hoped it represented a 'softening of attitudes' on the part of the community, which had consistently blocked all development aid to Cambodia. 'Trócaire and other European voluntary agencies will continue to press for the lifting of the EEC embargo on humanitarian aid to Vietnam and Cambodia. The people of both countries desperately need our help if they are to fight off famine and rebuild their lives after so many years of war. It is not right that, for purely political reasons, they should be denied that help,' he said. He added that the voluntary agencies had always stressed that aid to those in need should never be denied on political grounds.

In early July 1987, the Irish Department of Foreign Affairs refused to meet a delegation from Cambodia that came to Ireland to thank the Irish people for contributing so much aid to their country through Trócaire. Trócaire had invited the delegation to Ireland and had announced in advance that it would be visiting the department, so the agency expressed disappointment at the refusal to receive the Cambodian delegates. Representatives of all political parties met the delegation and these representatives expressed surprise at the department's attitude.

In January 1988, Trócaire sent £800,000 in food assistance to Cambodia, which was suffering serious drought at the time. By that time, the agency had channelled £2.5 million in EEC-funded food assistance to Indo-China. The shortfall in Cambodian food production was estimated by the UN at the time to be in the region of 200,000 tons.

In October 1989, Trócaire, Oxfam and Christian Aid arranged a fact-finding trip to Cambodia for Mary Banotti MEP and two British MEPs. On her return, Ms Banotti warned that peace was on a knife-edge there following the withdrawal of the last remaining Vietnamese soldiers. She said there was a danger that the murderous Khmer Rouge could bring the killing fields back. (Roland Joffé's film, based on the genocide between 1975 and 1979 and called *The Killing Fields*, had been released in 1984.) But if China stopped supplying arms to the Khmer Rouge and all outside military intervention ceased, she believed the Cambodian government could stave off the threat.

Ms Banotti said she was convinced the Cambodian government had popular support and that the former Cambodian leader, Prince Sihanouk (merely a figurehead presence during the Pol Pot years), was a spent force. He had allied himself with the Khmer Rouge in a so-called coalition, which was still recognised by the UN as the government of Cambodia, but it was time, she said, for that scandalous recognition to end. She praised the Irish government for not recognising it but said Ireland should go further and recognise the government in Phnom Penh so that the West could give financial assistance to the country.

In November 1989, the UN General Assembly adopted a resolution that called for a Prince Sihanouk-led interim administration, which included the Khmer Rouge, to replace the Vietnam-installed government that had ruled since early 1979. Brian McKeown condemned the resolution as an 'immoral and reprehensible' act. He also condemned the Irish government's support for the resolution. He said everyone knew that the superpowers, the US and China, the UN and

Britain were supporting the Khmer Rouge, and that the Special Air Services (SAS) and British Intelligence advisers were working with anti-government forces in Cambodia.

He suggested that the Cambodian seat at the UN, at that time occupied by a member of the Khmer Rouge, should be left vacant for a year. In addition, the Khmer Rouge and other members of the anti-government coalition should receive no recognition and the UN could confirm – what was already known – that Vietnam had withdrawn from Cambodia. He said that there should then be a UN-supervised referendum among the Cambodian people to ask if they wanted the Khmer Rouge to be part of any new government formed. He had no doubt that their response would be an unequivocal no.

In June 1990, Trócaire welcomed the decision of the Irish government to review previous government policy towards Cambodia. The agency also welcomed the government's allocation of £100,000 towards the UN trust for the Cambodian peace process. The Minister for Foreign Affairs, Gerard Collins, had promised that the Irish government would consider pressing for the withdrawal of the then current Cambodian delegation to the UN (which included a member of the Khmer Rouge), if progress towards free and fair elections was not achieved by the following September. Brian McKeown expressed the hope that this new departure in Ireland's foreign policy would stimulate the government towards playing a more active role in encouraging substantial international economic assistance for Cambodia.

The difficult transition to democracy
Near the end of October 1991, while many welcomed the signing in Paris of the Cambodian peace agreement, Trócaire warned of the possibility of a return to power of the Khmer Rouge. Pol Pot's group was one of the signatories to the agreement, but Bishop Casey argued that rather than returning to Cambodia with the legitimacy of the world community, as seemed to be happening, the Khmer Rouge leadership should be put on trial for crimes against humanity.

He said the prospect of them being again in a position of power in Cambodia was horrifying, and he asked how could the world possibly forget what they did during the Pol Pot years – causing the deaths of millions of people and the total destruction of the country's economic and social infra-structures. Referring to Trócaire being the only Irish development agency to have operated in Cambodia since the ousting of the Khmer Rouge, Bishop Casey said that the people who had survived the Pol Pot holocaust were living in fear of the Khmer Rouge going back into Cambodia and once again gaining control.

At the same Trócaire press conference, Brian McKeown said that Cambodia was one of the least developed countries in the world and had been denied any development assist-ance from the West, for political reasons, since the fall of Pol Pot. It had been left largely to NGOs, such as Trócaire, to help those who survived the genocidal regime of the Khmer Rouge to rebuild their devastated country. He explained that since the early 1980s, £18 million had been granted in development aid through the programme coordinated by Trócaire in Cambodia.

The Trócaire warning regarding the Paris peace agreement turned out to be justified. Although the Khmer Rouge had signed the agreement, they resumed fighting in 1992. They boycotted the 1993 elections, the first held since the 1960s, and rejected their results. They were now fighting the new Cambodian coalition government, which included the former Vietnam-backed communists as well as the Khmer Rouge's former non-communist and monarchical allies.

In April 1992, Trócaire announced it had channelled £1.35 million to a range of development programmes in Cambodia over the previous year. The projects included agricultural and rural development programmes, adult education courses, healthcare and skills training as well as emergency aid for people displaced by the ongoing conflict. Brian McKeown said there were still more than 300,000 refugees living in camps in Thailand, another 200,000 had been displaced within

Cambodia by the fighting and hundreds of thousands of lethal landmines were causing enormous problems for people in rural areas. Farmers who wanted to cultivate their land risked being blown up by mines dislodged by the rains and so this was causing severe food shortages.

At the beginning of December 1992, Justin Kilcullen, who had just returned to Dublin after four years living in south-east Asia, warned that the Khmer Rouge again controlled large areas of Cambodia and that there was a very real danger that Pol Pot would once again seize power. He blamed China for arming and Thailand for facilitating the Khmer Rouge. As a result, they had created a virtual separate state within Cambodia which they controlled. Mr Kilcullen also blamed the EEC and US for the 'political brinkmanship' they had indulged in for the previous ten years by keeping the Khmer Rouge alive through supporting a coalition of resistance forces (based in Thailand) opposed to the Cambodian government. He asked was there now the political will among the Western powers to do what should have been done fifteen years before, i.e. face down the Khmer Rouge. It was up to the UN and the US. He also thought it most important that the UN committed itself to a long-term peace in Cambodia after the elections the following May to ensure the Khmer Rouge could not take power from the newly elected government.

In February 1993, Trócaire warned that Cambodia was sliding towards full-scale war involving the Khmer Rouge, as it attempted to frustrate UN efforts to establish a democratic political system in the country. The statement, issued jointly with other international agencies working in Cambodia (including Oxfam and Christian Aid) was an urgent plea to the international community to take effective steps to prevent the return to power of the Khmer Rouge.

The statement said the Paris peace accords had been unsuccessful due to the failure to create a neutral political environment, and it pointed to widespread ceasefire violations, forced conscriptions and the failure to disarm the various armed factions. It also pointed out that Cambodia had received only around 10 per cent of the promised aid package of $880 million, which had been pledged by the international community.

The statement urged that the UN forces in Cambodia (UNTAC) be empowered to deal effectively with all perpetrators of human rights violations, that UNTAC take all necessary steps to protect all Cambodians against human rights abuses, and that the Khmer Rouge leadership be held responsible for crimes against humanity. The international community, it said, had to adopt a clear plan of action before the elections, detailing how it would help the newly elected government to deal with threats to peace and stability caused by the now legitimised Khmer Rouge.

Democracy, the continuing scourge of landmines and punishing the perpetrators of the genocide
The UN did play a central role after the May 1993 elections in helping the new government to establish its mandate. The threat from the Khmer Rouge persisted but lessened as the 1990s wore on, the movement being weakened by outside pressure and internal disputes. Foreign aid for development began to flow into Cambodia in greater quantity after the May 1993 elections, which also helped the new government to strengthen its position. Trócaire continued its active role in the country.

In February 1995, Bishop Kirby called on the Irish government to push for the banning of the manufacture and use of landmines, which, he said, were claiming more than 300 victims monthly in Cambodia alone. To mark International Mine Awareness Day, Trócaire, Pax Christi Ireland and the Cambodian Solidarity Group held a 2-hour picket outside the Dáil. Speaking in support of the picket, Bishop Kirby said that wars that had ended decades before were still claiming lives, especially in Cambodia where there had been more than 30,000 casualties in the previous fifteen years.

The three organisations demonstrating outside the Dáil called for a total ban on landmines, which cost as little as fifty pence to purchase but up to £700 to decommission. Bishop Kirby estimated that around ten million mines were produced each year, most of which were being used in Third World countries. He pointed out that Ireland's European Union (EU) partners, Britain and Italy, were exporters of large quantities of mines, mainly to developing countries, and he called on the Irish government to work to influence fellow EU members along the lines of the Belgian government, which had made a recent policy change.

'The main victims are civilians who get blown up collecting firewood, fetching water or tending sheep and goats. Only when you meet people whose limbs have been blown off by these appalling weapons do you fully realise the horrific consequences of their use,' Bishop Kirby said.

In April 1995, Mary Sutton, head of Trócaire's overseas department at the time, wrote to the papers on behalf of the NGO Forum on Cambodia to say that on the first anniversary of the genocide in Rwanda, the world was rightly calling for its authors to be brought to trial to pave the way for a future of renewed peace. The genocide in Cambodia, the twentieth anniversary of which also fell in 1995, should not be forgotten, she said, but its perpetrators still walked free and unjudged.

In the name of ethnic purity, her letter continued, the Khmer Rouge transformed Cambodia into an extermination camp and those responsible had never been brought to trial. She expressed the belief that in allowing the genocide in Cambodia to disappear from public attention and the Khmer Rouge to escape trial, the international community sent a message of impunity to the world. For the fragile peace then existing in Cambodia to be strengthened, it was vital, she said, that the international community be seen to uphold the basic tenets of human rights and justice.

She strongly urged, on behalf of the NGOs working in Cambodia, the international community to set a long overdue example by supporting the establishment of a Permanent International Tribunal where the Cambodian genocide and similar human atrocities could be tried and prosecuted in a fast and efficient manner, and by backing such initiatives as the US Office of Cambodian Genocide Investigations.

In June 1996, there were news reports of the death of Pol Pot (in fact they were premature by almost two years), which prompted Justin Kilcullen to write to the papers to say that if the reports were true, they would be greeted with great relief by the people of Cambodia, by the international donor community and by NGOs such as Trócaire. He said the former dictator's name was synonymous with 'one of the most brutal and heartless political regimes' of the twentieth century.

His letter said that it was estimated that Pol Pot's attempts at social engineering caused the deaths by starvation and disease of up to three million, in addition to the total destruction of Cambodia's social, economic and physical infrastructures. Having worked since the early 1980s on Trócaire's programmes aimed at helping survivors, and having lived in the region for four years, Mr Kilcullen said he himself witnessed at first hand the acute suffering caused by Pol Pot and the Khmer Rouge.

But for all the condemnations of the dictator, in the end he escaped any retribution for his crimes against humanity, Justin Kilcullen lamented. Although he was overthrown by the Vietnamese in early 1979, the realpolitik of the region required that the West play down the fact that he had been the ideologue of some of the worst crimes of the twentieth century. He survived, living in Khmer Rouge-controlled areas on the Thai border, his forces funded by lucrative logging deals with the Thai military. Even at the time that Mr Kilcullen was writing, the Khmer Rouge continued to wage a guerrilla campaign aimed at destabilising the fledgling Cambodian democracy struggling to rebuild its shattered economy.

Had the world anything to learn from the fact that Pol Pot died in his bed from the effects of malaria, Mr Kilcullen asked. War-crimes tribunals had been set up to bring to justice those responsible for atrocities in Bosnia and Rwanda, but apart from a tiny number of relatively minor participants, those who planned and incited massacres go free, he lamented. 'For anyone who stands in the killing fields of Cambodia, or who walks the corridors of the Tuol Sleng high school where the Khmer Rouge systematically tortured their victims, the name Pol Pot will continue to send shivers up the spine.'

But the dictator and his associates were saved from having to answer for their crimes by 'the cynical demands of international realpolitik'. Was one to assume that those who meticulously planned the 1994 massacres in Rwanda would also die peacefully in their beds in years to come, Justin Kilcullen wondered.

It was not until 2007–2008 that the trial began of some of those who may have been involved in the genocide in Cambodia thirty years before.

CHAPTER 7:
The Good Shepherd: Dark Days in El Salvador

The Catholic Church's fight for human rights in El Salvador
In July 1977, Fr Higinio Alas, who had to flee from El Salvador, visited Trócaire. He reported that the Catholic Church there was being persecuted because it supported the peasants' claim for land distribution. Both he and his brother José, also a priest, had to leave El Salvador after being threatened with death by a right-wing death squad. The same death squad threatened to kill all Jesuits who would not leave the country by a certain date, but all forty-seven Jesuits in El Salvador chose to stay.

Fr Alas explained that serious repression began in 1972 when Colonel Arturo Molina gained control of the government by electoral fraud. The university in the capital, San Salvador, was closed down in the hope that student agitation would be weakened but the opposite happened. Impoverished peasants who agitated for land division were ruthlessly resisted during 1973, 1974 and 1975 and forty of them were killed. Even greater force was used against students who campaigned for social justice and human rights; some forty were shot or disappeared after arrest. Only one body was recovered.

In El Salvador, Fr Alas said, 8 per cent of the people owned 90 per cent of the land, including almost all the good land;

fourteen families owned most of the country's wealth. Of a population of nearly five million, 61 percent were peasants. Some of the big landowners preferred to let their land deteriorate through lack of cultivation or irrigation rather than rent it to the peasants because they believed that if they did so, it would be hard to remove them afterwards. Sometimes, groups of peasants occupied some land but were ejected by the military or police.

Fr Alas believed the agrarian problem was central to the persecution of the church then taking place because the government considered the church too concerned with the peasants' plight. In 1968, the bishops of Latin America, at a major conference in Medellin, Colombia, drew up a programme for the implementation of the policies and declarations of Vatican Council II. Every attempt by the church in El Salvador to promote social justice and human rights brought accusations that churchmen were subversive or sympathetic to subversives.

The Catholic Church took a strong stand against injustice and repression. Fr Alas himself had been kidnapped by a right-wing group and beaten, almost to death. He denounced the greed and oppression of Salvadoran landlords. A Jesuit priest, Fr Rutilio Grande, had been murdered in March 1977. Afterwards, a force of 2,000 police and soldiers surrounded a town of 7,000 people in the area where Fr Grande lived and killed 350, depositing their bodies in the town church. Two months later, Fr Alfonso Navarro was murdered on the outskirts of San Salvador.

Trócaire supports the Salvadoran church
In 1978, Trócaire gave a total of £10,000 to two projects of the Catholic Church in El Salvador. These projects provided infor-mation on major instances of social injustice, and Trócaire's funds enabled the church to disseminate information both within the country and for the international community to counteract false media reports and the lack of information about dead and missing persons in El Salvador.

The following year, Trócaire began its support of the El Salvador Human Rights Commission, which had been set up by Archbishop Oscar Romero (Archbishop of San Salvador) and others in response to the unlawful killings of 8,000 people. Alongside this, Trócaire's development-education and campaigning teams focused on raising awareness in Ireland of worrying aspects of US foreign policy in relation to El Salvador. (The US supported the right-wing Salvadoran government, despite its abysmal human rights record.)

In a recent interview for this book, Bishop Casey said that Trócaire provided Archbishop Romero with the equipment for the radio station that he used every Sunday. In 1979, the bishop, accompanied by Sally O'Neill (head of projects), met the archbishop in San Salvador. Ms O'Neill said they had gone out to El Salvador because the Irish Franciscans based in San Francisco Gotera, a city in the eastern part of the country, had asked Trócaire for help. Their parish house had been badly damaged when the army drove a tank into their front door.

Archbishop Romero invited Bishop Casey and Ms O'Neill to lunch while they were visiting his country. At 5 a.m. on the day they were to go to that lunch, Human Rights Commission activists picked them up at their hotel in San Salvador and took them on the back of motorbikes out to a public dump on the edge of the city, where some bodies of people killed during the night had been thrown.

The dump was in a ravine. Ms O'Neill said that the bishop scrambled down the side of the ravine to find that there were three bodies lying there. Their hands were bound behind their backs and their blood was still wet. One of victims, a woman, was still alive and the bishop knelt beside her and gave her the last rites.

The young motorcyclists had cameras and they took pictures of the dead and dying. This was what they did every morning: taking pictures of such dreadful scenes to put them on display on large billboards outside the Human Rights Commission's office. Ms O'Neill said that every day there could be as many as seventy or eighty such pictures on display on these billboards. She recalls being in the commission's office and hearing the anguished screams of people outside as they recognised their loved ones' photos.

Bishop Casey and Ms O'Neill fulfilled their luncheon appointment with Archbishop Romero. They asked him what was the best thing they could do about such appalling savagery. He said that they had to speak out and let the world know what was happening, that it was important that there be voices from outside El Salvador telling of what was going on within the country.

In his recent interview, Bishop Casey said what they saw on that trip was frightening. He did not know how they witnessed such things and remained sane. The following day he and Ms O'Neill themselves had a close brush with death. They were returning from Gotera when they were stopped at a roadblock. Ms O'Neill recalled that those manning the roadblock seemed a motley crew; some of them were in military uniform but the majority were dressed like peasants and were armed with machetes.

The bishop was ordered out of the vehicle. His diary was taken and looked through. The lunch appointment with Archbishop Romero had been pencilled in, and when the guard saw this he poked a gun into Bishop Casey's chest. Those that were carrying machetes then surrounded the bishop. Suddenly, round the corner came an Italian journalist on a motorbike. He started taking pictures of the scene and said to Ms O'Neill that that might be the only chance they had of not being killed. Slowly, the group around Bishop Casey broke up and they were allowed to continue on their way.

On 24 March 1980, Archbishop Romero was murdered while celebrating Mass in the chapel of the Divine Providence Hospital in San Salvador. His murder was a reprisal for his unflinching defence of human rights and of the rights of the poor in El Salvador to social justice. Trócaire had been funding projects for him since 1977. These included radio school education and skills training for the poor. On the very day that he was murdered, Trócaire had received a letter from him thanking the agency for the support he had received from the Irish Catholic Church.

Bishop Casey attended his funeral and narrowly escaped injury when members of a death squad (possibly army men disguised as civilians) threw bombs into and opened fire on the huge crowds that had gathered outside the cathedral in San Salvador where the funeral Mass was taking place. In an emotional press conference at Dublin Airport on his arrival back from the archbishop's funeral, Bishop Casey dismissed any suggestion that he had behaved heroically during the panic that ensued when the crowd attending the funeral had been attacked. He described that attack as 'the greatest act of savagery ever performed'. He said there had been no provocation and the people who were at the funeral were there because they admired Archbishop Romero and wished only to pray for his eternal rest.

Grief showed on the bishop's face as he spoke of seeing the bodies of twelve victims being brought into the cathedral where the panic-stricken crowd had gathered. He said that people grabbed him as they ran into the cathedral and pleaded for a blessing. It took about an hour to calm the people. He was in no doubt that the government army, and not any left-wing group, was behind the shooting.

Under a headline that read 'The Good Shepherd', the *Irish News* (8 April 1980) reported eyewitnesses at the funeral as saying that Bishop Casey distinguished himself by the calm courage he displayed. 'He stood at the door of the cathedral while bullets were flying and guided people inside, trying to calm them and bring them to safety. Later he spent nearly two hours among the injured and terrified, administering the Sacrament of the Sick and trying to restore calm among the victims,' the paper reported.

Julian Filochowski of CAFOD, who was at the funeral, after-wards told Justin Kilcullen that the dead and dying were brought into the cathedral and that the visiting bishops were taken away for their own safety. He said that Bishop Casey, however, stayed and that when the dead and dying were laid out on the floor of the cathedral, he went round on his hands and knees among them, giving the last rites to each one. Mr Filochowski said that Bishop Casey was the only bishop to remain in the cathedral.

Archbishop Romero's murder and the bloody civil war that followed, which claimed at least 75,000 lives (some estimates are as high as 120,000) and led to more than a million and a half people being displaced or going into exile, drew Trócaire into one of the longest and most dangerous emergency-relief programmes in the organisation's history. Before the Salvadoran Peace Accords were signed in 1992, more than 180 of Trócaire's close partners had been murdered or had lost their lives in El Salvador.

Central America was also the venue for the first Trócaire-sponsored 'fact-finding mission' by parliamentarians. These were later successfully extended to other countries, including South Africa, Burundi and North Korea.

Campaigning to change US policy

On 6 December 1980, under a strapline that ran, 'The catalogue of horror that grows and grows' and under a headline that read, 'Slaughtered', the Irish Independent reported on the murder of three nuns and a lay missionary woman in El Salvador. Bishop Casey was quoted as describing the military rulers there as 'depraved' and as saying that he had recieved a letter from one of the victims just a few days before, in which she gave a detailed account of the daily atrocities being committed in the country's civil war.

The bodies were found in an unmarked grave about twenty-five miles from San Salvador. Two of the victims had been raped. When exhumed, two of the bodies were semi-naked and the clothing of the other two was in disarray. The victims were two American Maryknoll Sisters, Maura Clarke and Ita Ford, an American Ursaline Sister, Dorothy Kazel, and an American lay missionary, Jean Donovan. They had been Trócaire's partners for some time. Jean Donovan had just returned to El Salvador a few weeks before from her university studies in Cork.

Because of the outcry in the US, the government there suspended all economic and military aid to the right-wing junta in El Salvador until the killers – suspected to be members of the security forces – were caught, but in early 1981, Washington renewed aid to a reshuffled regime.

When the new Reagan administration announced increased military aid for the government in El Salvador, Bishop Casey called on the Irish government to break off diplomatic relations with the US unless this policy was reversed. He urged the Irish government to use every possible influence it had with the American government to get this disastrous move reversed.

On the first anniversary of Archbishop Romero's murder, Bishop Casey again called for renewed pressure on the US government to bring about a negotiated peace in El Salvador. He described Archbishop Romero as a man of peace who stood for human rights and championed the cause of the poor and oppressed – a man of outstanding courage. Bishop Casey re-echoed the call Archbishop Romero had made just before his death when he appealed to the US to withdraw support from the junta, a regime responsible for so much suffering among innocent people and which could not continue in existence without the support of the US government.

A few days later, Brian McKeown attacked the Irish government for not supporting Trócaire's programme for the relief of refugees in El Salvador. He said the Department of Foreign Affairs had refused a request, made the previous month, for £40,000 to match a similar amount given by Trócaire towards easing the problems of an estimated quarter of a million refugees. The government had responded that it had given £30,000 to an EEC humanitarian-aid package for El Salvador, but Mr McKeown said the package was being held up, possibly because of US pressure.

A Trócaire delegation, comprising Bishop Casey, Brian McKeown and Sally O'Neill, went on a fact-finding mission to El Salvador in August 1981. What they saw and heard there affected them deeply. In a recent interview, Sally O'Neill said that Bishop Casey was strongly of the view that while there were certain things Trócaire could do, there were also obligations the politicians had to take up. So, on their return from their 1981 visit, they called on the Irish government to support the Franco-Mexican declaration on El Salvador, which recognised the Farabundo Marti National Liberation Front (FMLN) and the non-combatant Democratic Revolutionary Front as representative political forces. The declaration also called for a new internal order, free elections and the restructuring of the armed forces.

Bishop Casey welcomed the declaration as the most helpful sign that had so far emerged on El Salvador; it showed the people there that for the first time they had major international backing for a solution to their terrible situation. He said the delegation saw a trail of murder, brutality and ill-treatment and that there was an urgent need for the US to end its military support for the junta. Bishop Casey petitioned the Irish government to use its influence to try to get the US government to discontinue its backing for the El Salvador military regime.

The bishop said that the oppression carried out by the regime had increased unbelievably in the previous year, with 10,000 murdered between January and July; the bodies of fifteen to twenty murder victims were found daily, usually on refuse heaps in San Salvador – the delegation had seen these bodies and the *Irish Times* carried photos of some of them on 3 September 1981.

He said that six members of the security forces, arrested after the rape and murder of the three US nuns and the lay missionary, had been released. He estimated that there were 200,000 displaced persons in the country and a further 200,000 refugees in neighbouring countries. The conditions in the refugee camps he described as 'sub-human'. So far that year, Trócaire had given £65,000 in aid to El Salvador and had decided to give a further £50,000.

A month later, Trócaire expressed disappointment and dismay at the Irish government's failure to support the Franco-Mexican declaration at the UN. Brian McKeown said that the Irish view of the situation in El Salvador was more or less akin to the US position. In a recent interview for this book, Mr McKeown said that he and Bishop Casey took the report they had written of their visit to El Salvador to the US and Canada, where they had a number of high-profile meetings to talk about their findings. One of the people they met with was Archbishop James Hickey of Washington DC (ordained a cardinal in 1988), who had also attended Archbishop Romero's funeral. He was very satisfied with the report the Trócaire duo had compiled, according to Mr McKeown, giving him support and encouragement for the stance he was taking in the US, where he spoke out against his government giving military aid to the regime in El Salvador.

Mr McKeown said that Professor James Dooge (who had become Irish Minister for Foreign Affairs in late October 1981) was on a visit to the UN at the same time that he and Bishop Casey were in the US. Because of the publicity they were getting in America, he said that Professor Dooge asked to meet them.

Sally O'Neill recently said that Professor Dooge took a great interest in the situation in El Salvador and held a number of briefing meetings with Bishop Casey and Brian McKeown. The outcome was that Ireland changed its position and supported the Franco-Mexican declaration on El Salvador at the UN.

In an end-of-year review of the situation in El Salvador for the *Irish Times* (30 December 1981), Bishop Casey said he was happy to put on record that both the Irish government at that time and the previous government had taken good positions on the question of US arms being sent to the junta, and on the human rights issues at stake. He added that the government of the day had now allocated £100,000 for the relief of distress in El Salvador, following the report submitted to them by the Trócaire delegation that had visited the country. Half of the £100,000 allocation had been channelled through Trócaire.

An all-party Oireachtas delegation, consisting of Niall Andrews, Michael D. Higgins and Patsy Lawlor, visited El Salvador in January 1982. Trócaire organised the visit, and the agency's Sally O'Neill and Tony Meade accompanied the delegation. The delegates said on their return that the elections in El Salvador planned for March 1982 would not return a government representing the true wishes of the electorate, and that the junta's decision to hold an election was a piece of 'window dressing'. Only the right-wing parties were interested in the election, they said, and the Christian Democrats led by President Duarte did not represent a real alternative for the country.

They described the voting system existing in El Salvador at the time as 'an invitation to murder' because voters would have to produce identity cards at polling stations and have them stamped, which meant people who did and who did not vote could be identified.

The junta claimed the majority of the deaths, at least 35,000 between 1979 and 1982, had been caused by in-fighting among guerrilla groups but the delegation believed the evidence suggested otherwise. They found the city of San Salvador tense. As well as government ministers, they also met Democratic Revolutionary Front members in Mexico and members of the Human Rights Commission in El Salvador. They said that there was on-going evidence of deplorable oppression of ordinary people and that this was being carried out with the backing of the US government. They visited camps for Salvadoran refugees in Nicaragua and found evidence from some of the people there of horrific torture and murders in El Salvador.

On 16 March 1983, the body of Marianella Garcia, the president of the Human Rights Commission of El Salvador, was found. She had been abducted by the national army in Las Bermudas refugee camp in Suchitoto. Trócaire expressed revulsion at the mutilation and murder of the thirty-four-year-old lawyer who had devoted herself totally to the defence of victims of oppression in El Salvador. She had visited Ireland the year before at the invitation of Trócaire and had addressed a number of meetings, including one with representatives of the Oireachtas. Trócaire called on the Irish government to protest in the strongest possible way to the El Salvador and US governments and to demand a full inquiry into her murder.

Archbishop Rivera y Damas, in his first sermon as Archbishop of San Salvador, strongly criticised the Salvadoran army for recent mass killings and called on the authorities to uncover the truth about the killing of Marianella Garcia. The British Council of Churches expressed 'grief and horror at the murder of this courageous woman and her companions'. (By that time, the press coordinator and the administrator of the Human Rights Commission had also been murdered by police or army men posing as civilians. Their deaths are documented in Amnesty International's report for Central America and Mexico, published in December 1996.)

On 22 April 1984, the *Sunday Independent* had an article on Trócaire under the headline 'Little Red Box Power' (referring to the cardboard boxes used in Trócaire's Lenten collections). The article said that in El Salvador the organisation had found it could not get development programmes off the ground any more because the people it wanted to help had all been evacuated to the mountains or to refugee camps. As a result, stated the article, Trócaire had come out strongly against the American foreign policy that it saw as creating this situation.

The article went on to say that Brian McKeown had no doubts about the propriety of the Catholic Church getting involved politically in the Third World. 'I don't think the church can avoid getting involved in politics. We follow the encyclical of Pope Paul VI on the development of peoples. And in doing that, we have to treat the problem, not the symptoms.'

President Reagan's visit to Ireland

President Ronald Reagan spent from 1–4 June 1984 visiting Ireland. Responding to critics of US policy in Central America, he said they were misinformed. He called them sincere but considered them victims of 'the Cuban-Soviet Union disinformation machine'. In reply, Bishop Casey said that the president made a number of serious errors of fact such as, for example, when he identified the regime in El Salvador in 1979 as an elected government. Equally, he must know that every election there since 1981 had been seriously flawed, the bishop continued. He pointed out that not only was there no electoral register in El Salvador but that those going to the polls had a stamp affixed to their identity cards, and people without such polling stamps were suspected of disloyalty to the state.

Only far-right candidates could campaign with any hope of safety and the murder of six leaders of the political opposition in 1980 had ensured that the elections would be one-sided, the bishop argued. However, the most serious defect he saw in the interview with President Reagan, which had been broadcast on RTÉ's *Today Tonight* programme, was the complete absence of any mention of the large-scale human rights violations that had occurred in El Salvador and were continuing daily. Amnesty International and the Human Rights Commission of El Salvador had consistently identified government forces as having most responsibility for the more than 40,000 murders that had happened between 1979 and 1984, the bishop said.

He went on to point out that, faced with this overwhelming evidence, Congress had insisted on certification of an improvement in the human rights situation every six months before further aid would be given to El Salvador. However, President Reagan had vetoed the requirement, so it did not matter how many murders the government of El Salvador committed because the US administration would continue to support it, Bishop Casey said.

The Galway West Fianna Fáil TD, Bobby Molloy, clashed with Bishop Casey about what sort of welcome President

Reagan should be given in Galway city, which was making him an honorary citizen. Mr Molloy said the city should give the president a warm and generous welcome. But Bishop Casey would be boycotting the reception for President Reagan and he said he supported those who would be protesting against the president's foreign policy.

In his recent interview, Brian McKeown said that one reason he vividly remembered the Reagan visit was that Trócaire's phones and his own home phone were tapped. He said Trócaire had done a lot to inform the Irish public about the issues in Central America and he praised Bishop Casey for refusing to meet with President Reagan, which drew a lot of publicity to the situation in El Salvador. He also pointed out that none of the Irish bishops met the president, with Cardinal Ó Fiaich 'diplomatically' going on a pilgrimage to the island of Iona during the period of the visit.

Mr McKeown also expressed the belief that the work Trócaire had done in getting publicity for El Salvador also contributed to the Taoiseach of the day, Dr Garret FitzGerald, publicly dissociating Ireland from US policy on the country at the State banquet for President Reagan at the time.

Trócaire had managed to get a copy of the president's address to the Houses of the Oireachtas, the night before he was due to deliver it, from an American journalist, Mr McKeown revealed. They spent most of the night checking it for factual errors and came up with a list of twelve or thirteen. As soon as President Reagan had finished delivering his address, Trócaire had arranged for an interview for Bishop Casey on the *Good Morning America* programme, which went out coast to coast in the US. To this day, said Mr McKeown, Americans have not been able to figure out how the bishop could have had knowledge of so many of the issues so soon after the president had finished delivering his address.

In December 1985, Bishop Casey, Brian McKeown and Sally O'Neill again visited El Salvador and they produced a report on their visit in early February the following year. The report covered the six-month period from January to June 1985. It found that during this period, 1,655 civilians had died at the hands of the security forces and right-wing death squads. This was a considerable reduction from the figure of 9,250 for a similar period in 1981, the previous time that the Trócaire team had visited the country. However, they said that despite this reduction, they got the impression that it was more a matter of tactics than policy.

They spoke of the number of civilians who had been forced to abandon their homes because of bombing raids by the airforce on civilian targets within guerrilla-controlled areas. They also got the impression that President Duarte had little real control and that he was largely tolerated rather than obeyed by the armed forces. It was the latter, with the financial backing of the US, who prolonged the war in the face of widespread human misery, with one million refugees outside the country, 600,000 displaced within and 56,000 civilians murdered up to that time in the struggle.

Archbishop Rivera y Damas had received death threats from right-wing elements shortly before that. He had condemned in the strongest terms the indiscriminate bombing of civilians and the destruction of homes and farms by the armed forces, Bishop Casey said. These actions directly contradicted the repeated denials by the government of El Salvador, by the armed forces and by the US embassy that villages in contested areas were not being bombed.

The tragic civil war dragged on in El Salvador, with human rights abuses and atrocities continuing. In November 1989, six Jesuit priests, one of whom had studied in Dublin, were murdered in the Central American University in San Salvador where they worked. Murdered with them were their housekeeper and her fifteen-year-old daughter, with some of the bodies being horribly mutilated.

Bishop Casey expressed his utter revulsion at the outrage as hundreds began a 24-hour fast outside the US embassy in Dublin, protesting at the US government's continuing support for the regime in El Salvador. The bishop expressed concern for the safety of Irish religious orders working there but asked: 'When does the church ever run away from their people because it is dangerous?' He said he had personally known some of those killed and that members of religious orders working in El Salvador had claimed that military death squads had been responsible for the murders. He urged the Irish government to highlight the situation in the country internationally and insisted that organisations such as the UN should respond to what was happening there.

In 1991, Mary Sutton accompanied Bishop Casey on what was his last visit to El Salvador as chairman of Trócaire. In a recent interview for this book, she said that what she recalled most about the visit was going to see the memorial to the murdered Jesuits and their housekeeper and her daughter. The man who was the husband of the murdered housekeeper and father of their slain daughter was gardener to the Jesuit house where the atrocity had taken place. Ms Sutton found it very moving to see him tending the plot of ground where he had six red rose bushes growing to commemorate the six priests and two yellow rose bushes in memory of his wife and daughter.

In October 1991, Bishop Casey welcomed the news that for the first time ever in El Salvador, a high-ranking military officer had been convicted of a human rights-related crime – the murder of the six Jesuits and their housekeeper and her young daughter. 'There was a time when such a crime would have gone unpunished, but the campaigning of human rights organisations within El Salvador, in the United States and in other countries has ensured that justice will be done. It emphasises for us, once again, that there can be no real human development unless the right of every individual is guaranteed.' (The officer and his deputy both received the maximum thirty-year sentence for murder but they were amnestied and released in 1993.)

Peace, rebuilding and rehabilitation

At the beginning of 1992, Trócaire welcomed the UN-sponsored peace accord between the El Salvador government and the

FMLN and said it hoped the accord would bring an end to the eleven-year-old war in the country. However, Bishop Casey warned that the peace agreement was but a vital first step towards a just and lasting peace, not a final settlement of the problems faced by the Salvadoran people, 80,000 of whom had been killed since 1980.

He recalled that Trócaire had been working in El Salvador since the early 1970s, during which time it had allocated some £2 million towards a wide range of human rights organisations, towards relief for displaced persons and towards development projects. Warning that the troubles of the people of El Salvador were far from over, he said the military, those who controlled them and the death squads were still in power.

Bishop Casey said that any successful peace settlement had to include measures that would rid the armed forces of those who had violated human rights and had to guarantee the security and economic reintegration of former combatants into civilian life. Just as the US had played a central role in the maintenance and training of the army through the war of the previous eleven years, so now it had an important role to play in effecting a just and lasting peace in the war-ravaged country, he maintained.

He said the Archbishop of San Salvador and the families of victims of the violence were expressing legitimate concern that the ceasefire would be followed by an amnesty for those in the military and others who had been guilty of human-rights abuses. He pointed out that such an amnesty had recently been proposed by the armed forces but he said that elements in the army who had carried out crimes and atrocities during the eleven-year war could not be given an amnesty and had to be brought to justice.

This latter plea from the bishop went unheeded. There was indeed an amnesty following the peace agreement and it seemed that the perpetrators of some terrible deeds done during the war in El Salvador would go unpunished. However, as Sally O'Neill explained, such people have not been allowed to get off totally scot-free.

Maria Julia Hernandez, a famous Salvadoran lawyer, is the founding director of Tutela Legal, the legal assistance office of the Archdiocese of San Salvador, established in March 1982. She had worked very closely with Archbishop Romero. Under Ms Hernandez's leadership, Tutela Legal has been a leading force for human rights in El Salvador. Trócaire supports its work.

Ms O'Neill said that, because it was futile to take cases to the Salvadoran courts, Tutela Legal took cases to the Inter-American Commission on Human Rights of the Organisation of American States. In 2003, she said, they succeeded in overturning the amnesty for people accused of major human rights abuses and that there are now a number of cases going through the courts.

She referred to Bishop Casey having visited Mozote in El Salvador where the Irish Franciscans worked. A massacre occurred there in December 1981 in which 1,281 civilians were murdered by an army battalion that had been trained in the US. Ms O'Neill said that a few years ago permission was given to exhume the mass graves there, and now a well-known American anthropologist, Dr Clive Snow, is giving his services to the Human Rights Commission to help with identification of those buried there. More than ninty of the children, brutally murdered by having their heads bashed against poles, have now been identified, according to Ms O'Neill. She said a court case in relation to this particular atrocity is now being taken.

The end of the war in El Salvador also meant the end of major media coverage of the country but for Trócaire it meant the start of a whole new phase of commitment in terms of rebuilding and rehabilitation. Trócaire's work in El Salvador gradually moved away from a human rights focus based exclusively on investigation and denunciation more and more towards prevention: what could the agency do to ensure that such terrible things would not happen again? The approach here has been to implement education prog - rammes in human rights.

On the occasion of Trócaire's twenty-fifth anniversary in 1998, Fr Jon Sobrino SJ of the Archbishop Romero Pastoral Centre sent this message to the agency:

> We remember how Trócaire stood by us in the terrible times of repression, terrorism and war. You shared with us other moments of hope, commitment and martyrdom. I do not know what would have been the fate of our people and our church had we not received your help. But also I ask myself what would have become of Trócaire had you not opened your hearts to the inspiration that comes from the poor and repressed of Latin America.

Trócaire continues its ongoing commitment to the people of El Salvador.

CHAPTER 8:
The Somoza Dictatorship: Nicaragua's Tragic Decade

The Somoza dictatorship

By 1978, Nicaragua was in the throes of the ruthless Somoza dictatorship. Trade unions were banned. Members of peasant movements were being massacred. All opposition was suppressed. Fr Ernesto Cardenal, a famous Nicaraguan poet from a family that has featured prominently in his country's history, was one of the fiercest critics of the Somoza regime. In mid-1978, he was running a community-development programme in Nicaragua and he approached Trócaire for funds to support the growing numbers of Nicaraguans fleeing south to Costa Rica.

Fr Ernesto and his brother Fernando, a Jesuit priest, came to Ireland and met with Bishop Casey and Sally O'Neill to tell them about the situation in their country and to discuss what kind of support Trócaire might give them. This heralded the beginning of a major intervention by Trócaire in Nicaragua.

Trócaire gave a grant of £5,000 to help those affected by the civil war in Nicaragua – civilians who got caught up in the conflict between the Sandinista Front and the Somoza regime and who had to abandon their homes, taking only what they could carry with them. Thousands of refugees were fleeing the country for neighbouring states, especially Costa Rica and Honduras, where they ended up in camps. An inter-church committee in Costa Rica assisted several thousand refugees there with tents, blankets and food.

Part of the Trócaire grant was given to the Nicaraguan Permanent Commission for Human Rights. The commission, comprising church leaders, trade unionists and businessmen, had been monitoring and documenting violations of human rights and promoting development programmes at community level. It was also helping people involved in the conflict by means of a relief programme.

Civil war: US support for the anti-Sandinista forces

When the Sandinistas gained power in July 1979, one of the most promising and provocative experiments in reform and community development in Latin America began. The new government tried to break the mould of traditional Latin American cycles of political violence and repression. Trócaire worked hard to support the new programmes to eradicate poverty and empower local communities. The agency also worked vigorously in Ireland, Europe and the US against the involvement of the US government who supported right-wing anti-Sandinista forces in a tragic civil war that was to divide the Nicaraguan people and bring the whole of Central America into an international conflict.

Trócaire published an information pack on Central America covering the history, political situation, human rights violations and US policy in the region. In 1981, a delegation from Nicaragua visited Trócaire to express their people's gratitude for the development aid they had received from the Irish people through the agency. The delegation represented the Sandinista Government for Reconstruction. Among the delegates was Fr Edgar Parales, the Minister for Social Welfare in that government and one of a number of Catholic priests in the administration. (Fr Ernesto Cardenal, who had approached Trócaire in 1978, was Minister for Culture.)

At a news conference at Trócaire headquarters in Dublin, Fr Parales explained that one of the first projects undertaken by his government was a literacy campaign. The project had mobilised the whole population, he said, and had brought townspeople into contact with deprived rural dwellers, which was key to unity and solidarity in Nicaragua. He said the campaign had reduced illiteracy from 53 per cent to 12 per cent of the total population. More than 400,000 men and women had learned how to read and write and 75,000 mainly university and high-school students, housewives and young workers had given their services as instructors and organisers.

Fr Parales said the dedication of these literacy workers was amply rewarded by the dramatic results and that the United Nations Educational, Scientific and Cultural Organisation (UNESCO) had recognised their achievement by awarding its 1980 prize for literacy to the Nicaraguan Ministry of Education. He also said that the Nicaraguan government was carrying out a major programme of agrarian reform designed to give land for the first time to hundreds of thousands of landless people who had previously faced starvation and virtual slavery. 'In a largely agricultural country, dependent on cotton and coffee, land reform is the only key to a socially just society.'

Fr Parales warned that the US was seeking a pretext for an open invasion of El Salvador by suspending a $15 million aid package to Nicaragua and claiming that that country may have been helping left-wing forces in El Salvador.

The Reagan administration authorised the CIA to finance, arm and train the Contras (the label given to various rebel groups opposing Sandinista rule), who operated out of camps in Honduras and Costa Rica. After the US Congress prohibited the funding of the Contras in 1983, the Reagan administration continued covert support, even after the 1984 elections, although impartial observers from the EEC, Canada and Ireland concluded that the elections in Nicaragua were free and fair. The US government also imposed a trade embargo on Nicaragua, which exacerbated an already bad situation.

In a recent interview, Sally O'Neill recalled how bad things were inside Nicaragua itself at the time. She said there were food shortages, practically empty supermarkets, lack of electricity – a daily nightmare for the ordinary people who were already among the poorest in the world. The Contra war also damaged Honduras, according to Ms O'Neill, as the Contra rebels were based in camps in Honduras where they were trained by American forces.

One of the tragic consequences of the Contra war, Ms O'Neill said, was seeing the programmes that the Sandinistas had tried to put in place to improve the quality of life for ordinary Nicaraguans being eroded. These programmes were concerned with such vital aspects of life as education and healthcare and really could have led to great improvements very quickly, especially for those who had so little. Instead, government resources had to be diverted to deal with the Contra threat.

Just after President Reagan's visit to Ireland in 1984, Bishop Casey said he was surprised by the reference in one of the president's speeches to the Catholic Church being persecuted in Nicaragua. The bishop said there was no reference to the persecution of the church in the most recent report on human rights published by Amnesty International (1983). Nor in the bishop's own three visits to Nicaragua had he either seen any evidence of such persecution or heard any reference to such persecution from any member of the Nicaraguan hierarchy. However, he said, there was definite evidence of persecution of the church in other Central American countries whose governments were supported by the US.

In October 1985, Trócaire and Oxfam held a public meeting in Belfast at which they said that the American government was causing misery in Nicaragua, and reported that they were finding it increasingly difficult to continue their long-term development projects there. Money assigned to these projects had to be diverted to help 170,000 smallholders who had been forced to leave their homes as a result of attacks by US-backed Contra forces. Trócaire and Oxfam invited delegates from the US consulate to the meeting to present their views but they declined.

In March 1986, Comhlamh, the association for returned development workers, hosted a coffee evening with a difference in the organisation's offices at Grand Parade, Cork. The beverage on offer was 'N-Café', Nicaraguan instant coffee from high in the mountains of that strife-torn country. Comhlamh launched the coffee on a non-profit-making basis as part of its ongoing solidarity marking Central America Week. The week's events were sponsored by Trócaire, Christian Aid, Oxfam and other groups to highlight the need for an end to US intervention in the region.

The emphasis on coffee was to stress that the crop accounted for a massive one-third of Nicaragua's foreign-exchange earnings. The country was in an economic crisis, with 40 per cent of its national budget being spent on defence. Despite this, the US had just banned Nicaraguan imports to try to further undermine the country's economy.

In August 1986, Trócaire called on the Irish government to dissociate itself from US policy on Nicaragua. Bishop Casey and Brian McKeown issued a statement condemning the recent decision of the US Senate to agree to the granting of $100 million to Contra rebels. They said the decision 'blatantly disregarded the principle of non-intervention in the affairs of another nation' and was a serious blow to hopes for a negotiated settlement.

The statement denounced the refusal of the Reagan administration to recognise a ruling by the International Court of Justice, a ruling which affirmed that US support for the anti-Sandinista rebels constituted illegal intervention in the affairs of another nation. 'Those who have a genuine admiration for the American commitment to the rule of law and democracy could not but feel betrayed and shocked that the most powerful democratic government in the world should so blatantly violate international law and ignore the ruling of the World Court.'

Trócaire called on the Irish government to use every opportunity to reject US policy and to support instead a renewal of the search for a negotiated settlement, which had been sponsored by a group of countries in the region. (This was the Contadora Group, which originally consisted of Colombia, Mexico, Panama and Venezuela. The UN Security Council and General Assembly had supported their initiative, as had a number of regional and international bodies. Argentina, Brazil, Peru and Uruguay had added their support in 1985.)

The end of the civil war and transition to normality

In 1988, the Nicaraguan civil war finally ended. In October that year, Hurricane Joan devastated the country. Trócaire allocated £50,000 to the relief of victims of the hurricane in Nicaragua and El Salvador. Brian McKeown said that some 300,000 people in Nicaragua had been made homeless, with the country's main port on the Caribbean totally destroyed. In a country with an economy already under such severe strain, he said the consequences of such devastation for ordinary people would be unimaginable.

In May 1989, Nicaragua's president, Daniel Ortega, and Foreign Minister Fr Miguel D'Escoto visited Galway on the final stop of their European trip seeking support and financial assistance for rebuilding their country. Their Irish host was Michael D. Higgins TD and they were greeted at Galway City Hall by Bishop Casey among others. President Ortega expressed his appreciation for the work Trócaire had done for Nicaragua.

When talking of the economic situation there, he referred to the extreme poverty that still existed. The previous year, he said, 300,000 people had been left homeless by the hurricane and the American-backed Contras were still waging war against the revolution. He said that the Contras would not defeat the revolution and expressed the hope of continuing Irish support for his country.

In a recent interview, Sally O'Neill told of a little known side to President Ortega's 1989 visit. He had had a serious eye injury since his time as a guerrilla leader, which the Soviets had offered to treat, but he was nervous of Russian tech -

nology. He knew an eye surgeon in the Royal College of Surgeons in Dublin, who was from Grenada and whose brother was a minister in the government of that country, and so decided to go there to get treatment. He wanted to do this anonymously and quietly and return to Nicaragua as quickly as possible.

However, at this same time a US invasion of Panama appeared imminent. (It actually happened a few months later.) There was rumour and speculation that Nicaragua would also be invaded. As rumour mounted that Nicaragua would be invaded, it would be the case that its president and foreign minister and some other cabinet members were in Ireland. President Ortega needed to be kept quiet and tranquil for a few days until his eye recovered from the surgery. Bishop Casey decided to invite him and his entourage to Galway to stay with him.

The bishop said he would have him brought to Connemara, where nobody would bother him, and gave him a present of an Aran sweater to keep him warm. So, while his country seemed in danger and its Cuban allies were frantically trying to make contact with him, Daniel Ortega was enjoying some healthy walks in the relative obscurity and beauty of the Connemara landscape. He got safely back to Nicaragua after a few days and the feared invasion of his country did not materialise.

In the elections of 1990, President Ortega lost power to a fourteen-party coalition led by Violeta Chamorro. After a decade of civil war and economic sanctions, the Nicaraguan people were exhausted and wished for an end to the conflict and the economic blocade.

In June that year, Fr César Jerez SJ, Professor of Political Science at the Central American University in Managua, and a recognised authority on Central American politics, visited Dublin. At a press conference at Trócaire's headquarters in Booterstown, he said that the participation of the Sandinistas in the Chamorro government (for example, Daniel Ortega's brother, Umberto, was retained as military leader) was a positive step, given that the government was representative of many political elements in the country, ranging from the far left to the far right.

Referring to the continuing violence in El Salvador, where over 3,000 had died in the previous year, he said that although he was hopeful of an end to armed conflict, he was not too optimistic about an end to what he called the 'structural violence' in the country. He also said that the Contra guerrillas were still a force to be reckoned with in Nicaragua and that the 3,000 hard-line Contras that continued to exist out of a force of 14,000 posed a serious threat to peace.

At the same press conference, Brian McKeown said that Trócaire would continue to support those who were working for human rights and a decent way of life for the poorest of the poor in countries such as El Salvador, Honduras, Guatemala and Nicaragua. Many of those involved in this work were risking their lives, he said, to bring about changes for the better in those countries. He concluded by saying that it was Trócaire's intention to continue its support at that crucial time more than ever before.

Not only did Trócaire continue its work in Nicaragua but in 1994 it strengthened its presence there by opening a new field office in Managua, which is still very active.

Carlos Garcia Agurto, deputy Minister of the Environment in Nicaragua, sent Trócaire the following message on the twenty-fifth anniversary of the agency's founding: 'Trócaire's willingness to provide support at the most difficult moment for the social re-insertion of ex-combatants was a key decision that brought social and economic comfort to thousands of families, sick of war and seeking a better life. Your trust in us helped achieve a lasting peace and genuine reconciliation among divided Nicaraguan communities.'

CHAPTER 9:
The Ethiopian Famine and its Aftermath

The 'great' famine

Trócaire had been involved in relief and development work in Ethiopia for ten years before the defining event that was the famine of 1984/85.

Kate O'Brien recalled, in a recent interview for this book, a visit she made to Ethiopia in the early 1980s on behalf of Trócaire. She said that the agency's relief efforts in the country were coordinated at the time mainly by Brother Gus O'Keefe of the Holy Ghost order. He founded the Christian Relief and Development Association (CRDA) of Ethiopia. She described Ethiopia as 'a stunningly beautiful' country and also as a totally different place from the rest of Africa, with a very different 'feel'. The people there are of a different origin and they had never been colonised (apart from brief incursions by the Italians). However, wars and climactic conditions had led to a series of famines there, she lamented.

The famine of 1984/85 in the Horn of Africa – especially in Ethiopia – was to prove the watershed event of the 1980s. It was the first major famine to be televised, almost as it happened, day by day, and had a major impact on the Irish public. It led to huge fund-raising activities, including Live Aid. The Trócaire African Appeal at that time remained the largest response by the Irish public to any single Trócaire appeal until the Rwanda (1994) and Tsunami (2005) appeals, but in terms of currency value, it probably surpassed either of those appeals. The generosity of the Irish public (at a time of economic recession) enabled the agency to set up a major relief and rehabilitation programme that provided assistance to the seven famine-affected countries in the region.

The Ethiopian famine of the mid-1980s opened up a vital debate about the nature of aid and the role of relief agencies and the media in times of emergencies. Trócaire, as an agency primarily interested in strengthening local capacity, felt that media coverage of African famines tended to stress the role of Irish volunteers while often negatively portraying Africans as inept, passive or unwilling to help themselves. Exploitative and sensational images were used – by the media and aid agencies – which offended human dignity and reinforced the traditional prejudice about Africa. With NGOs in the developing world increasingly voicing their opposition to these types of representation, this debate was to continue through the next decade and beyond.

The emergency in Ethiopia opened up an important debate within Trócaire itself about its own role in emergencies. This debate centred on the extent to which the agency should become involved in emergency humanitarian relief as opposed to devoting itself primarily to development activities. Sally O'Neill contended that the extent of Trócaire involvement in humanitarian relief in Ethiopia was the beginning of a trend for the agency, which has seen its emergency-response work grow to become almost as important as the development side of its activities.

Ms O'Neill also made the point that Trócaire's involvement in Ethiopia at this time led to a greater focus within the agency on Africa generally. Before the mid-1980s African crisis, she said that much of the ethos of the agency had been heavily driven by its experience of development in Latin America and to some extent also in Asia, where there were strong linkages with countries such as India, Sri Lanka and the Philippines. Trócaire's interventions in Africa in the middle of the 1980s changed that focus somewhat. The different situations in Africa, the weaker capacity and the various issues that needed to be tackled (famine, certainly, but also war and the conflict between Eritrea and Ethiopia where the regime used food as a weapon of war) – all of these problems provided a focus for change, she said.

Joe Feeney joined Trócaire in 1985 during the Ethiopian famine and his first year's work for the agency was devoted to dealing with that disaster. In a recent interview for this book, he pointed out that the civil society and church structures that existed in a country such as the Philippines, for example, did not exist in many parts of Africa. As a Catholic agency, Trócaire had been able to work through church structures and organisations in Latin America and the Philippines but in Africa, he said, the church was not as widespread and did not have the same roots.

He said that in Ethiopia, for example, less than 1 per cent of the population was Catholic. It was not that Trócaire worked only with Catholic organisations; it worked with other Christian and secular groups generally, but such groups, he said, hardly existed in Africa. He also pointed out that in Ethiopia there were high levels of illiteracy associated with incredible levels of poverty; there was widespread disempowerment and no history of voluntary involvement in addressing problems.

Such organisations as did exist in Ethiopia had very heavy foreign involvement, Mr Feeney said. One that Trócaire worked with, as already mentioned, was the CRDA. A core Trócaire founding principle was to support and work through indigenous structures but if those structures did not exist, and if some other structures were already in existence, it was better to work through them, even if they were non-indigenous, rather than set up parallel structures in an emergency situation, Mr Feeney observed.

He referred to the justice, health and education structures, outside of the main cities such as Addis Ababa, being weak and he said that they got weaker the further one moved away from the cities. With 85 per cent of the people of Ethiopia living in rural areas, this meant dealing with a massive population. This situation provided a huge challenge for Trócaire, Mr Feeney said, which it faced by working through existing organisations and structures – mainly foreign – while at the same time gradually trying to set up, nurture and facilitate indigenous counterparts.

He believes that the agency's decision to involve itself in the provinces of Tigray and Eritrea showed both its commitment to doing things differently and the influence of its experiences in Latin America on its approach in Ethiopia. Many of the other big agencies, he said, would not have been working in Tigray and Eritrea at the time. They tended to be more conservative and to work with governments, which he acknowledges was understandable when trying to deal with such massive levels of starvation as existed in the mid-1980s. However, this approach also demanded compromises and could lead to reinforcing, supporting and giving legitimacy to a government which was quite brutal, he observed.

Mr Feeney said that many people now accept that the terrible Ethiopian famine of 1984/85 was man made. It is true that there was a drought, he said, but the government was spending vast amounts on fighting an internal war rather than trying to deal with the problems the drought brought. Most of the people who were affected by the drought were in the north of the country, where the rebel movement that was fighting the government was based, and the government was content to let the consequence of the drought take its toll rather than ensuring that aid got through.

Trócaire's decision to support aid going into the areas controlled by the rebels from Sudan, Mr Feeney saw as very important. Travelling in with the aid, often at night, there was a sense of achievement and a feeling that one was making a big difference for people on the ground, he said, because there was no other way of getting food aid into those people in Tigray and Eritrea. Trócaire, he said, was also involved at a very early stage, before many of the other big international agencies made a contribution.

A record church collection for Trócaire
In 1984, Trócaire raised a massive £11.8 million throughout Ireland, and on one day alone brought in £5.7 million when it organised a nationwide church collection for famine relief. An independent report in the August 1985 issue of *Business and Finance* magazine, which studied the workings of ten major Irish charities, found that in terms of channelling money from donor to intended recipient during 1984, Trócaire was by far the most efficient, with 97 pence out of every pound being put directly to work in the Third World.

Trócaire pointed out that alongside the immediate food crisis at the time, there was a general trend of under-nourishment and hunger, with its associated diseases and its overall negative impact on development prospects for the years ahead. Twenty-two of the countries most seriously and immediately affected were in sub-Saharan Africa. Airlifts of food, medical supplies, blankets and other necessities – while absolutely vital to save lives – were only a drop in the ocean, designed to alleviate the crisis in a desperate stop-gap fashion. However, such resources would not prevent further horror, the agency warned.

Brian McKeown argued that voluntary agencies could not substitute for national and international efforts to deal with the crisis on a long-term basis. He warned that unless the relief efforts of the rich countries were accompanied by a commitment to increase development assistance sub-stantially, there would be more Ethiopias but on a worse scale. There was no point in dealing with the symptoms unless the cause was tackled as well, he said.

He appealed to the Irish government to increase its aid to the Third World, and said the unprecedented response of the Irish public to the voluntary agencies, in response to the famine in Ethiopia, clearly told the government its perfor-mance had not kept pace with public concern. The public response also showed that a restoration of the UN aid target (0.7% of GNP) would have the broad support of the people of Ireland, he said.

At the launch of Trócaire's 1985 annual Lenten Campaign, Bishop Casey said the situation in Africa at that time was as bad as when television brought the first awful reality of the famine home to the Irish people. Shortly afterwards, Cardinal Ó Fiaich and Brian McKeown departed on a ten-day visit to Ethiopia and Sudan.

At a press conference when they returned, the cardinal said that famine-stricken Africa would need relief and development aid on a massive scale for years to come. Although the situation there was tragic, there were signs of hope, he said. He acknowledged that nothing could prepare one for the reality of the starvation and human misery on the scale that they had witnessed. However, he said that the hope was that along with dealing with the famine situation, there was also a great deal being done to rehabilitate the affected people and to develop the resources necessary to prevent a recurrence of famine.

By that time, Trócaire had allocated £1.2 million to the crisis in Ethiopia and had spent £3 million by the end of the year. The agency also planned to spend £4.3 million on rehabilitation and development programmes over the subsequent three years.

Cardinal Ó Fiaich explained that Trócaire was involved in an integrated development programme with health, education and soil-conservation elements to it. He saw for himself that those programmes were working and were an excellent investment in the people of Ethiopia. It was vital that the Irish people maintained their interest in and ongoing commitment to Africa and its suffering people if their assistance was to have real and lasting value, he said.

Emergency and development aid 1986–1992
In 1985, one Trócaire experiment involved sending 500 tons of seed potatoes to Ethiopia. The venture proved so successful

that in April the following year, the agency sent 1,000 tons of seed potatoes to the country. The potatoes were purchased from small farmers in Donegal, at a cost of some £200,000, by Trócaire. The Third World organisation, Self Help, paid for the transport of the potatoes to Dublin where they and a quantity of fertiliser were loaded on board the *Band Aid Star* ship and taken to Ethiopia.

The shipping of seed potatoes to Ethiopia was repeated in April 1987 when 300 tons of Donegal seed potatoes were shipped from the port of Larne in Northern Ireland. The potatoes were sent to the northern Ethiopian provinces of Eritrea, Tigray and Wollo. Once again, Self-Help organised the project and it was assisted by Trócaire, Gorta, Oxfam, the Irish Farmers Association and the Department of Foreign Affairs. The Ethiopian Ministry of Agriculture also cooperated in the project. It was found that the Donegal seed potato, especially the Cara variety, yielded many times more potatoes in Ethiopian soil than native Ethiopian varieties.

In late July 1987, a plague of locusts sweeping across parts of Ethiopia, Sudan and neighbouring countries threatened to bring famine in its wake on a scale worse than that brought by the 1984/85 drought. Trócaire donated £20,000 in an attempt to halt the destruction of the growing crops. The donation went to Tigray, one of the worst affected areas of war-torn Ethiopia.

Late in 1989, evidence suggested up to four million were on the brink of starvation in Ethiopia and Sudan. Reports reaching Trócaire indicated a famine on the scale of that of 1984/85 threatened unless food aid was sent in the subsequent months. The combination of almost total crop failure and the Ethiopian government's refusal to allow relief supplies into the stricken regions meant there was every likelihood of severe famine by March of 1990.

In January 1990, Brian McKeown called for an immediate and radical response by the EEC and its member governments to the developing famine in Ethiopia. He was speaking at a press conference to announce the largest single emergency allocation (£500,000) made by Trócaire since its foundation. He said that the EEC had placed itself in a poor position to respond adequately to Ethiopia's needs. The 1989 food-aid allocation was completely used up and there were no EEC food surpluses; the heavy aid allocations to Poland and Hungary threatened the provision of adequate food aid to four million people facing famine in Ethiopia, he said.

While he was not questioning the need for assistance to Hungary and Poland, he said that there was something seriously wrong if food was diverted from people on the brink of starvation to eastern Europe, where the need was demonstrably not so great. He pointed out that the Irish government itself had allocated more than twice its share of the EEC's aid programme to Poland and Hungary than to Ethiopia.

Joe Feeney, Trócaire's emergency officer, who had returned from a five-week tour of the affected area, said at the same press conference that 1.9 million people in Eritrea and an estimated 2.2 million people in Tigray were in need of food aid. Tigray was far from the main supply centre and it was taking two or three weeks to deliver each truckload to each distribution point, with around 10,000 tons getting into Tigray each month. He said that the best available evidence indicated that roughly 30,000 tons were required each month. The solution would be the opening up of supply routes to Tigray through government-held territories. If the government did not allow this, the prospects for more than two million people were very grim indeed, he said.

In June 1990, Trócaire announced it had received £880,000 from the EEC as a contribution towards its famine-relief programme in Eritrea and Tigray. The agency said the money would be used to buy 1,500 tons of lentils, sugar and rapeseed oil as well as providing vital mobile truck-repair shops for Trócaire's partners in the famine-stricken region. Trócaire added £315,000 from its own funds to the EEC allocation to bring the total contribution to almost £1.2 million.

Announcing the allocation, Brian McKeown emphasised the need to ship large quantities of food through Massawa, the port nearest the famine-stricken areas. There was growing pressure to have Massawa operated under UN control to effect a safe and speedy supply of food aid. He pointed out that while famine on the scale of that which ravaged Ethiopia five years before had been avoided, there was still a serious shortage of supplementary foods, such as milk powder and oil. Therefore, all possible avenues for the movement of food supplies had to be continued if mass suffering was to be avoided, he said.

At the beginning of 1991, Trócaire expressed the fear that famine in Africa was now off the Irish political agenda, with the focus having switched first to eastern Europe and then to the crisis in the Gulf. In the meantime, Africa found itself caught up in a 'silent famine' and was badly affected by drought, wars and food shortages.

The Irish government's allocation of £1 million for emergency relief for the Third World in that year's budget estimates contrasted sharply with the £7 million that had been found to assist with the Gulf crisis. Trócaire had allocated £3 million in the previous year to those countries affected by the crisis. The agency continued to issue appeals and to send aid throughout 1991. In May, it welcomed news of a possible ceasefire in Ethiopia, as it allocated a further £350,000 worth of food aid.

In late September 1991, Trócaire began a special appeal for funds for the silent famine in Africa. It warned that up to 30 million people faced starvation, more than half of them in Ethiopia and Sudan. Stories of people trying to survive by eating weeds and roots in countries devastated by drought and the effects of long-term war should be contrasted with the superabundance of food which had been created by the EEC's Common Agricultural Policy (CAP), it said. The agency pointed out that in Kerry, for example, farmers were spraying milk into the ground because EEC regulations did not allow it to be sent to the Third World.

Tragically, it was no longer fashionable for comparatively affluent nations, such as Ireland, to make dramatic contributions to Africa, Trócaire argued. That year, the Irish government had again reduced its level of ODA. Trócaire had no doubt that the Irish people would once again respond generously to the agency's appeal but surely, it maintained, what was needed was the political will in Europe to translate the massive overproduction there into desperately needed supplies in Africa. If it were possible to help the people of the former Soviet Union without upsetting world trade, then some continuous system of aid could be devised, not only to send food to stricken African nations, but also to help them to produce their own life-saving products, Trócaire reasoned.

Joe Feeney, who visited the stricken areas, was quoted in some Irish newspapers (on 25 October 1991) as follows: 'Millions of mothers are having to make a decision no mother should have to take: to decide, where there is any food, which members of the family should get priority. You pass through deserted villages, where you will often find elderly people who stayed behind because they would slow the rest of the family down.' He said that 'deserting the village is the end of a cycle of desperation'. Once people moved, they were a totally dependent population and extremely vulnerable.

He stressed the urgency of Trócaire's appeal, the target of which was £500,000, which the agency hoped the EEC would match pound for pound. To bring home the reality of the situation, he explained that it cost Trócaire £100,000 to send 1,000 tons of food where it was most needed in Africa; 1.2 million tons were needed to avoid famine.

One of the most tragic sights from his trip to Ethiopia was that of more than half a million ex-soldiers trying to make their way southwards and home. 'They are trailing the roads, often with horrific injuries. They are totally humiliated; hated by the people and the government because they supported the old regime, even though most were conscripts with no choice. It is estimated that 50 per cent have AIDS. None of them has boots or shoes. Their feet are swollen. They are dying at the side of the road.'

Trócaire wanted primarily to support the development of local structures to enable local people to become self-sufficient and independent of outside aid, Mr Feeney said, but the situation was so grave that the agency had to respond to the emergency. He questioned what the international community was doing spending so much on the war in the Gulf, with thirty million facing starvation in Africa.

Throughout 1992, Trócaire continued to issue appeals on behalf of and to send aid to Ethiopia and to sub-Saharan Africa in general, which faced the worst drought in over half a century, with up to forty million people in danger of starvation.

Brian McKeown said that the effects of years of conflict, acute underdevelopment, soil erosion and drought had left millions on the verge of famine; eight million in Ethiopia were in need of immediate aid. In Eritrea alone, he said, more than 80 per cent of the population were at that time dependent on food aid; there was an acute shortage of essential medicines, agricultural seeds and tools, and shelter material to re-house over 50,000 people returning from refugee camps in Sudan. He said that with very few resources, the Eritrean authorities were struggling to rebuild the country's shattered infrastructure.

Rebuilding in Eritrea, Tigray and in Ethiopia generally
The year 1993 saw independence for Eritrea from Ethiopia after a UN-supervised referendum. Trócaire had been supporting the Eritrean Relief Association during the years of the struggle. In February 1993, Ato Teklewoini Assefa, director of the Relief Society of Tigray (REST), briefed Trócaire staff. Some 60 per cent of the £3.8 million channelled to Ethiopia by Trócaire in the previous six years had been sent to Tigray and the agency had worked in cooperation with REST since 1983.

Mr Assefa said that now that the war was over, less attention was being paid to vital medium- and long-term intervention. Tigray was particularly underdeveloped, he said, having been deliberately neglected by both previous regimes in Ethiopia. During the war with the Mengistu government (1975–91), roads, schools and hospitals were badly damaged. More than 90 per cent of the population was engaged in agriculture but the legacy of war, coupled with several successive years of drought, had left Tigray facing acute food shortages.

He also said that the overuse of poor farming land, overgrazing, deforestation, outdated farming methods and declining rainfall had contributed to a pattern of falling agricultural production and environmental degradation. Trócaire had identified soil erosion as the biggest single factor limiting food production and there was an urgent need for a major soil- and water-conservation programme in the region.

REST was an African success story in development terms. Established in 1978, it was the only organisation channelling vital relief aid to rural Tigray during the sixteen-year war. Mr Assefa said it was trying to change the attitudes of people to fight the root causes of war and drought. He said the time was then right for the international community to recognise and support the sound political base then existing in Ethiopia (based on the local-government system established in the June 1992 elections) by assisting with resources and skills. The country needed time to overcome the effects of war and drought, and at that particular time Tigrayans were on the threshold of needing emergency relief, but they wanted to link it to recovery and rehabilitation, he concluded.

In April 1993, Dr Nerayo Teklemichael, director of the Eritrean Relief and Rehabilitation Agency (ERRA), met Trócaire representatives in Dublin. Trócaire had spent almost £2 million in Eritrea up to that time. Dr Nerayo said it would take $2 billion to reconstruct Eritrea but that it was already too late for the 60,000 who had died as a direct result of war. There were also 60,000 orphans, as well as more than one million refugees, half of them in Sudan, who needed immediate rehabilitation. He added that up to 85 per cent of the population depended on emergency food aid.

In 1995, on the 150th anniversary of the start of Ireland's Great Famine, Trócaire made 'Hunger in a world of plenty' the theme of its Lenten Campaign. One of its advertisements stated: 'In Ethiopia, £5 will get enough drinking water for a week. In our box, £5 will help sink a well.'

The advertisement referred to how some years had passed since the stories of hunger and famine in Ethiopia had first appeared in the news, and how Ethiopia had been replaced in people's awareness by the tragedies in Somalia, Rwanda and elsewhere. But, the advertisement warned, despite the great progress made by the Ethiopians themselves in the intervening years, the problems of hunger and poverty still remained. For this reason, Trócaire also remained, working in cooperation with local people to make their communities less vulnerable to famine, providing clean water, training farmers, providing seed banks, cultivating hardier crops and vegetables and developing livestock.

In Addis Ababa, Trócaire was helping impoverished slum dwellers by providing leadership training, community health-care, sanitation, employment schemes and support for AIDS victims and their families. As the advertisement said, Trócaire was committed to the long-term struggle for lasting solutions to hunger and poverty throughout the developing world.

Kevin Carroll, Trócaire's representative in east and the Horn of Africa, noted in March 1995 that Ethiopia had a 600,000-ton food deficit the previous year. He said that war and deforestation, which led to soil erosion, were largely to blame. One of Trócaire's programmes involved promoting the construction of stone terraces to prevent topsoil being washed away.

He noted that Ethiopia suffered from the additional burden of a rapidly increasing population. Most people dep - ended on subsistence farming, and food production had been unable to match the rise in population, he said. Trócaire was involved in schemes to train people to use better farming techniques to achieve higher crop yields. Because of cyclical droughts, most farmers were in a very vulnerable position.

They had enough to feed themselves and grew a cash crop, usually coffee, as well; they were totally dependent on just a few commodities and if there was a drought, they had to sell everything, including all their possessions, to survive.

Trócaire supported food-aid programmes, he explained, that bought from the more fortunate farmers in different parts of the same country who would have a surplus. He also explained that if nothing was available locally, food aid was brought in by international bodies, with the goal being to give people the kind of food they ate as part of their staple diet, for example, sorghum.

Kevin Carroll was optimistic about the progress he saw in Tigray, where there was a tremendous effort to get agriculture going again after the twenty-year war that ended in 1991. It was one of the poorest regions in the world, very dependent on food aid, but the people were determined to become self-sufficient within the subsequent ten years, he said.

Trócaire continued to work in Ethiopia and Eritrea throughout the second half of the 1990s. In early 2000, Irish aid agencies had again to warn that serious famine would hit Ethiopia within the following month. Justin Kilcullen said that the emergency had not come as a bolt out of the blue, that the international community had been given ample warning and simply had not responded fast enough. He added that Trócaire had been implementing an emergency food-security operation in Ethiopia since March 1999, and had invested some £120,000 in emergency initiatives. This was in addition to £180,000 the agency had spent the previous year on promoting long-term food security.

Between 1999 and 2000, Ethiopia and Eritrea fought a border war – two of the poorest countries of the world squandering a huge amount of money on a war that had little significant outcome. Writing in the *Irish Times* in late May 2000, Justin Kilcullen referred to the populations of both countries facing severe food shortages as their governments engaged in a brutal border war. An estimated 40,000 displaced Eritreans had fled the fighting throughout May.

Twenty years after Live Aid had focused world attention on Ethiopia, Trócaire made the country the central aspect of its 2005 Lenten campaign. It was part of the agency's 'Make Poverty History' campaign because Ethiopia reflected the issues the Millennium Development Goals (MDGs) were trying to address, such as maternal health and child mortality, the right to primary education, the right to clean safe water, and freedom from HIV/AIDS and other killer diseases.

Trócaire continues its vital work in Ethiopia.

CHAPTER 10:
Brazil: 'A Social and Economic System of Injustice'

The Brazilian Catholic Church, social justice and early Trócaire involvement

From 1964–1985, Brazil was ruled by a military dictatorship. The three years following that was a transition period, and since 1988, the country has been a democracy.

In a recent interview for this book, Sally O'Neill said that from its foundation, Trócaire had been involved in working in Brazil. There were two main reasons for this. One was the extensive presence of Irish missionaries over a long period in the country. She said that the Columban, Redemptorist, Kiltegan and Holy Ghost orders all had presences in Brazil. Many of the Irish missionaries there were working in areas of urban poverty or of rural deprivation. A second reason for early Trócaire involvement was that the Brazilian Bishops' Conference was one of the most progressive of the Bishops' Conferences in Latin America.

Ms O'Neill said that Brazil was the centre of a lot of the innovative work that was taking place in the Catholic Church. She referred in particular to the two major meetings of Latin American bishops that occurred in Medellin in Colombia in 1968 and in Puebla in Mexico in 1979, at which Brazilian churchmen played a leading role. She said that a lot of the church thinking and challenging about social justice came from those two meetings. Cardinal Paulo Arns, Archbishop of São Paulo, and Dom Helder Camara, Archbishop of Olinda and Recife, were the two leading proponents of what was called 'liberation theology' in the Brazilian church.

A Trócaire advertisement, at the launch of the agency's Lenten Campaign on 7 February 1975, referred to Brazil's booming economy but said that the so-called 'economic miracle' had bypassed the masses. The advertisement gave the statistic that in 1970, a certain 1 per cent of Brazilians earned more than half the entire population. The poorest and most neglected region of the country was the north east, with a population of thirty million. There, life expectancy was just thirty years and illiteracy and unemployment were wide-spread.

Many from the region, the advertisement said, went to Recife, the capital, seeking a better life but ended up in shantytowns such as Dos Coelhos. Trócaire was helping a job-training centre there, set up by locals, by financing equipment and assisting it in expanding to provide community leadership training and healthcare.

In March 1975, Trócaire approved the allocation of £66,500 towards twenty-six projects. Two of these were in Brazil. A grant of £8,500 went to an education and community-development programme in the southern city of Porto Allegre, which had expanded rapidly in the previous twenty years to become the third largest industrial centre in Brazil. There was heavy migration from the surrounding country-side during that time.

The population was then 1.5 million in an area of 2,500 square miles, one-thirteenth the size of Ireland. Most of the people there were very poor, and there was high unemploy-ment and inadequate health and education services. Trócaire's grant went to the Federation of Organisations for Social and Educational Advancement, which was engaged in an extensive education and community-development prog-ramme in the area, including adult-education courses for women and for factory workers.

Trócaire also gave a grant towards the operational costs of a leadership training centre in Goias, in the centre of Brazil, where the majority lived and worked in very poor conditions; 70 per cent of adults in the area were illiterate and consequently without the right to vote. The aim of the training centre was to enable smallholders and labourers to be the agents of their own social and economic advancement. Besides running literacy and training courses, the centre helped small rural communities to organise on a cooperative basis with the objective of buying land.

Among the grants Trócaire announced for 1976 was one of £8,000 towards a programme initiated by the National Bishops' Conference of Brazil. The programme was designed to generate a greater awareness in the country and throughout the world of the growing abuses and violations of fundamental human rights and to study the causes. The project culminated in a series of international study days in October 1977, which examined the possibilities of educating people to understand, overcome and transform the structures and mechanisms that resulted in violations of human rights.

In March 1979, Trócaire gave a grant of £6,000 towards a land-reform programme in Brazil. Half the population of the country depended on land for survival at the time, yet owned no land themselves, and many of the people were unaware of their rights. The grant went towards the work of the Pastoral Land Commission, which had been set up by the Brazilian Bishops' Conference to assist and advise people of their rights to land and to provide legal assistance.

At the launch of Trócaire's 1979 Lenten Campaign, the agency described Brazil as one of the largest countries of the Third World, and argued that with its population of almost 100 million and vast natural resources, it could be one of the wealthiest countries in the world. Trócaire went on to point out that over the previous fifteen years, the country's military government had embarked on a massive programme of economic and industrial expansion. Within ten years, GNP had doubled, foreign investment had flowed in and exports had rocketed. It was hailed as an 'economic miracle'. However, the so-called miracle aimed only at profit.

The wealth that had been generated did not reach the majority. In fact, while the rich minority became even richer, the poor majority actually became poorer, and the ruling regime made sure their voices would not be heard. Thousands had been jailed and torture had become a standard practice.

For example, two priests in the diocese of Conceicao do Araguaia in Pará in northern Brazil, whose bishop was the Irish-born Redemptorist, Patrick Joseph Hanrahan, were shot dead, murdered by an armed gang employed by big land - owners.

An extract from a pastoral letter of the Brazilian bishops summed up the situation: 'Only the great and the powerful have rights. The humble ... have only what is strictly necessary in order to stay alive and continue serving those in power.'

Cardinal Paulo Arns

Representatives of the Catholic Church in Brazil continued to speak out about the social injustices in the country over the subsequent years, just as they had spoken out during the 1970s. Cardinal Paulo Arns, Archbishop of São Paulo, one of the church's leading promoters of social justice, was a keynote speaker at Trócaire's tenth-anniversary seminar at University College Galway in June 1983. He spoke of the church as an instrument for the promotion of development and justice.

By that time, he had been Archbishop of São Paulo for thirteen years, Brazil's sprawling industrial metropolis with a population of twelve million. He had long been a critic of Brazil's headlong rush to industrial growth at the expense of the poor majority. He was also a constant critic of the military regime's repressive policies and did not spare his energies in defending human rights. This earned him the abiding hatred of the military establishment and the respect of the overwhelming majority of the people, who placed their hope in him.

He had presided over a number of major studies and publications on the causes of poverty in Brazil and had also been involved in the development of the trade union movement in São Paulo. In 1979, he was named president of the Latin American Human Rights Commission and he acted on behalf of the committee of the Mothers of the Disappeared from Argentina (during the military dictatorship in that country from 1976–1983, some 30,000 disappeared), raising their case at the Organisation of American States and within the UN Commission for Human Rights. He published numerous works on social issues and on the new international economic order.

Cardinal Arns had made contact with Trócaire at an early stage. He was greatly interested in Irish history and especially in the land issue, which formed such a part of that history, from the plantations of the sixteenth and seventeenth centuries to the struggle of the Irish tenants to gain ownership of land in the latter part of the nineteenth century. He asked Trócaire to support the work of the Pastoral Land Commission in Brazil, which he had been instrumental in setting up. Trócaire worked with the commission in some ten different dioceses around the country.

In the course of his address to Trócaire's tenth-anniversary seminar, he said: 'Eighty-five per cent of our population is oppressed and its oppression clearly shows us that we live in a social and economic system of injustice. The poor are exploited in all aspects of the system, from the little fisherman who sells his shrimp for two cents a pound to the factory worker in the transnational industry.'

During Brazil's worst years of oppression, when the Catholic Church's voice was the only one left to be heard, he denounced human rights violations and set up the Justice and Peace Commission to investigate the widespread abuses.

Kate O'Brien, who worked on the issue of land in Brazil for Trócaire, met Cardinal Arns on a few occasions. In a recent interview for this book, she recalled feeling that there was something serene and 'saintly' about his presence. Yet, at the same time, she said, there was a steeliness in him. She got the sense that here was a person with a very long-term vision who had the strength to follow through on it but who knew that to realise it would not be easy.

He came from a relatively humble background, being one of thirteen children of German immigrants, which perhaps explains his feelings of solidarity with the poor. Ms O'Brien recalled seeing him in a favela in São Paulo on one occasion and noticing how at ease he was with the people who lived there. She said that they were mobbing him and that it was clear how much they adored him. His leadership, she remarked, was hugely important both for the laity and in the Bishops' Conference.

Little change from the transition to democracy
The military regime fell from power in 1985 and democracy was re-established in 1988 but, for the vast majority, change at the top brought little actual difference to their day-to-day lives, which continued to be an unrelenting struggle. Trócaire made 'shelter' the central theme of its 1987 Lenten Campaign because of the plight of the urban poor. The agency said the gap between rich and poor was widening daily in the Third World and nowhere was this more acute than in the cities. It was possible to pay a visit to a city like Rio de Janeiro and see slums and shantytowns alongside modern skyscrapers and luxury hotels.

'Life in the slums is tough and the inhabitants have a hard time surviving. Many of them are rejected by the more estab - lished citizens because of the shortage of work. They are exploited by ruthless landlords and their access to essential services is minimal. The dream of greener pastures turns barren and many social problems set in' (from a Trócaire article which appeared in a number of local papers, e.g. the *City Tribune*, Galway, 3 April 1987). The 1987 Lenten Campaign attempted to focus attention on the appalling poverty in cities in Brazil as well as in other urban centres in the world.

The following year, Trócaire representatives visited Brazil as part of an international CIDSE delegation to investigate the perennial issue of land conflicts in that country. Sally O'Neill was part of the delegation and, in a recent interview, told how they managed to get access to very valuable information about workers' conditions in a rather unusual way.

They were aware that bonded labour was being used on some of the massive Brazilian estates but they found it very difficult to get access to any of these estates. One of the delegates was a member of the Dutch ministry of social welfare. She was aware of an Italian company that was growing thousands of acres of tomatoes for canning and export. She phoned the landowner and said that they were representatives of an Italian company that were looking for business and that they would like to view his enterprise. The owner sent his private plane to collect them and bring them to his estate. Ms O'Neill said the delegates had to go and kit themselves out in suits and such like so that they would look like genuine Italian buyers.

When they met the owner, the Dutch delegate asked pertinent questions, such as could the company guarantee constant supply, what was the situation of the workers, and could they see their conditions. The owner assured them that they had nothing to worry about on that score, that he did not allow any trade union to represent the workers, that, in fact, the workers were not allowed to leave the estate. At a lunch he organised for the visiting 'Italian business people', the delegates were able to talk directly to the workers and learn of their poor pay and conditions. Ms O'Neill said that the CIDSE group left the estate with the most valuable, first-hand information they could have hoped to gather.

The delegation's report was dedicated to Chico Mendes, president of the Rubber Tappers Union, a distinguished ecologist and human rights activist who had been murdered in 1988 while trying to prevent further devastation of the Brazilian rainforest.

That year also marked the fortieth anniversary of the UN Declaration of Human Rights. Trócaire dedicated its Lenten Campaign that year to marking this significant anniversary and to publicising the declaration itself. Deputy director Tony Meade wrote an article on the role of Trócaire in relation to human rights. One of the points he made was that the organi- sation had found itself, over the years, having to defend its partners in the Third World when their human rights were infringed.

He gave the example in Brazil of the peasant farmers who found their land taken over by speculators because they had neglected to register legally their holdings. In cases such as this, Trócaire undertook the defence of the farmers' rights through the court process, as well as engaging in education work among them to show them how to set about registering their claim.

As well as working with the Bishops' Conference Pastoral Land Commission, Trócaire also worked in Brazil with the Movement for Landless Workers, a secular organisation that would have been considered more radical than the church body. However, although they may have had their differences, the two groups frequently worked together. Their work covered a wide range of issues because land was of such key importance in Brazil.

Kate O'Brien, who visited Brazil many times on behalf of Trócaire, said that it was important to keep in mind just how enormous the country is, especially coming from a country so small by comparison. Brazil is 121 times bigger than Ireland. In addition, she pointed out that Brazil is also a huge melting pot of people of all kinds, being the recipient of many waves of immigration, both voluntary and forced. In the south, immigrants came primarily from Europe, many from Germany especially. Some 37 per cent of all African slaves traded were taken to Brazil. Today about 7 per cent of Brazilians classify themselves as black and nearly 43 per cent as 'pardo', a mixture of Amerindian, black and white. The Portuguese colonisation in the sixteenth century proved disastrous for the indigenous population; and although many indigenous peoples continue to exist, they are disappearing quite fast, according to Ms O'Brien. She said that although all smallholders have suffered in terms of land ownership, those who have suffered most are the indigenous peoples. Land for them is their life-blood because they do not have any other way of life. If their land is taken away, they lose their core identity as a result.

There is more than enough land for everybody in Brazil, Ms O'Brien pointed out. The totally unjust distribution of this precious resource is related to greed, as well as to the demands of the marketplace in North America and in Europe for soya products and for those other products that take up huge areas of land, such as palm oil and sugar cane. Over the years, the rural smallholders that Ms O'Brien has talked to have told her that they are not looking for vast amounts of land; they seek just enough for a decent life. She found it quite shocking that they have been denied even that little in a country that has so much in terms of natural resources.

In September 1989, Trócaire organised a study-visit to Brazil. The participants spent three weeks in the country, visiting Trócaire-funded projects in Rio de Janeiro, São Paulo, Salvador and Tefe Amazonas. The visit was part of a range of development education programmes involving clergy, Macra na Feirme and trade unionists. During their stay in Brazil, the group worked alongside Trócaire's partner agencies, gaining a fuller understanding of the extremes of poverty and inequality in the country. They focused on the major issues facing Brazil at the time: the land question, urbanisation and poverty, the exploitation of the Amazon Basin and the role of the churches.

One member of the study group was Gerry O'Hare, head of Trócaire's Belfast office, which had been opened in December 1986. He described Brazil as a place of 'stunning contrasts between the lives of the haves and the have-nots'.

The delegation spent the first few days in Rio, visiting the favelas there. These shantytowns had sprung up around Brazil's major cities and were a harrowing manifestation of the country's appalling economic and social problems.

'These places have come about as a result of peasants leaving the land to look for a better life in the big city. Almost invariably they end up living in the cardboard shacks of the favelas,' Mr O'Hare said. The group met with priests and local activists who were trying to deal with all the problems that arose in the terrible living conditions of the favelas.

The group then split up into smaller groups to visit other parts of the country. Gerry O'Hare's group went to the remote rural area of Conceicao in the north east to examine the problems of land distribution besetting the peasants who were coming under growing pressure from big landowners, greedy for their land. The peasants were trying to protect their lands; the Catholic Church was setting up groups to help them and Trócaire was involved in that work. Conceicao da Araguaia was the diocese of Bishop Hanrahan who was a strong supporter of the work of the Pastoral Land Commission.

The following year, in cooperation with Mary Immaculate College (MIC), Limerick (a primary teachers' training college), Trócaire organised a teachers' study visit to Brazil.

When the Trócaire Teachers' Network held its second annual conference during the schools' autumn mid-term break in 1990, the focus was on the problems of Brazil. Delegates attended from the primary and post-primary sectors in the Republic and Northern Ireland. At the confer -ence, Graffiti Theatre Company created the atmosphere of a shantytown in São Paolo where the people grappled with great poverty, greed and lack of interest from the authorities. The presentation showed the teachers a method of effectively communicating serious and contentious issues in the Third World to students of any age.

After the presentation, Fermio Fecchio, a Brazilian human rights lawyer and a member of the municipality recently appointed in São Paulo, addressed the conference. He out -

lined the patterns of migrations in Brazil. The population in urban areas had increased six-fold since 1940 and by 1990 constituted 75 per cent of the population as a whole, he said. He explained that the reasons for such a growth in urbanisation ranged from the corrupt politics of land ownership to violence in rural areas. In addition, he said, Brazil was crippled by a foreign debt of $150 billion in 1990, the burden of which was borne by the impoverished masses. The title of the conference was 'Solidarity has no frontiers' and it outlined the role of education, both in Brazil and Ireland, to create an awareness of Third World poverty; it also showed that a long-term solution strategy was necessary. The Trócaire Information and Resource Centre, in Cathedral St, Dublin, made invaluable new resources available for teachers, and the topic of development education had become part of the Junior and Leaving Cert syllabi in a number of subjects.

The rights of indigenous peoples and the continuing battle for land rights

In November 1993, Dr Aldo Mongiano, bishop of one of Latin America's largest and most remote dioceses, Roraima in north-western Brazil, visited Ireland at the invitation of Trócaire. He appealed to the Irish people to support the rights of 35,000 Amerindians struggling for survival against powerful mining and ranching interests in his diocese. He said that between 1987 and 1991, at least 2,000 Yanomani Amerindians had been exterminated as a direct result of the invasion of their territory, by up to 40,000 gold miners, in the far north of the vast Amazonian region. Two years before, the Brazilian government had demarcated a special area for the Yanomani, who started to have real contact with Europeans only in the 1970s. The demarcation made it illegal for anyone else to live and work there but the gold miners ignored this.

Dr Mongiano had received a death threat earlier in 1993 because of his defence of indigenous rights. Local politicians, business interests and the military had consistently opposed the demarcation of Amerindian territory, and the bishop feared proposed amendments to a revised Brazilian constitution might weaken existing guarantees for indigenous land rights.

The Yanomani population had been reduced to 8,000 but was still the second largest group in his 230,000 square kilometre diocese. The largest group – 80 per cent of whom, unlike the Yanomani, had been converted to Christianity – was the 15,000-strong Makuxi people. In Brazil, there were around 220,000 Amerindians in a population of 150 million.

Bishop Mongiano said that the world should know that this was a racial issue, which was exploited by very powerful and greedy people. He said that the Irish could do a great deal to help stop the attacks on the indigenous peoples because the Brazilian government did not like bad publicity. The more attention that was focused on the bad treatment, the greater the likelihood was that the Brazilian government would take action to uphold indigenous rights, he said.

The bishop had organised a scheme, mainly with money raised in Italy (his home country), to provide cattle for the Yanomani and the scheme had proved very successful. In 1991, 7,000 cattle had been bought; in 1992, this grew to 12,000 and he hoped the numbers would rise to 20,000 in 1994. Trócaire was supporting the work of Dr Mongiano.

In 1993, a Trócaire delegation had visited Brazil and its report, 'Brazil Now', was launched in March the following year by a Brazilian priest, Fr Alfeo Prandel. Fr Prandel, one of the coordinators of the Brazilian bishops' Pastoral Land Com - mission and a leading human rights worker, came to Dublin for the occasion. At the launch, he referred to the following October's Brazilian presidential election and said the country's political right would view a victory for Luis Ignacio Silva, the former leader of the metalworkers, as 'the end of Brazil'. Fr Prandel said he himself would view such a victory as a new beginning.

He explained that 80 per cent of Brazilian land was owned by 5 per cent of the people. The extreme concentration of land in a few hands was increasing, he said, with large multi -

national companies such as Fiat, Mercedes Benz and Volkswagen among the landowners responsible for thousands of smallholders being forced off their lands. In the previous ten years, he said, 1,600 rural community leaders had been killed all over the country. Because the judiciary defended the interests of the oligarchy, only eighteen people had been brought to trial for these killings; only nine had been convicted and as few as four were in jail at that time.

The bishops' Pastoral Land Commission was struggling against powerful agri-business interests who were spreading the belief that small landowners did not produce and that only large landowners were productive and efficient, Fr Prandel said. The policy of extreme land concentration was leading to untold misery for millions of Brazilians, who had been forced from their lands and had flocked to favelas, where conditions were often intolerable. Fr Prandel said that in 1992 his commission documented eighteen different cases of slavery in Brazil, involving neary 16,500 workers, with more than 50 per cent of those affected living in the southern state of Mato Grosso.

The authors of 'Brazil Now' were Kate O'Brien, Mary Sutton and Sr Isabelle Smith. Ms Sutton pointed to the tragic paradox of the world's tenth largest economy officially acknowledging that thirty-two million of its citizens were hungry. Brazil had the sixth highest rate of hunger and malnutrition in the world, she said. The size of Brazil's foreign debt was also crippling, even by Third World standards. Brazil had been one of the largest recipients of Trócaire funding since the agency was founded and Ms Sutton said it would continue to support Brazilian organisations working for comprehensive and just land reform, without which there would be little lasting improvement in the lives of the people. She said that Trócaire also gave priority to requests for assistance from the seven most marginalised groups in Brazilian society: Afro-Brazilians (the world's second-largest African population after Nigeria), migrants, the homeless, street children, prostitutes, prisoners and the handicapped.

In her recent interview, Kate O'Brien told of taking Fr Prandel, when he came to Ireland in 1994, to visit some schools in the diocese of Ferns in Wexford. She recalled that in one of the schools, the children asked him what fields were like in Brazil. On his drive from Dublin with Ms O'Brien, he had been fascinated with the patchwork effect of the fields in rural Ireland because nothing similar existed in Brazil. He struggled to convey in a comprehensible way to the Irish schoolchildren just how big a field might be in his own country and they, in turn, struggled to understand that a field could be so enormous.

In May 1995, Trócaire invited the Brazilian human rights activist, Fr Ricardo Rezende Figueira, to Ireland for the publication of his book, *Rio Maria: The Song of the Earth*. The book traced human rights abuses in the Amazonian state of Pará. Fr Rezende was parish priest of Rio Maria, where 550 people had been murdered in land-related conflicts since 1986 – community leaders, smallholders and indigenous peoples cut down mercilessly because they got in the way of ranching and mining interests.

In her recent interview, Kate O'Brien elaborated on the readiness of the ranchers to resort to violent methods to get their way. Around Conceicao in the state of Pará, she said, the approach of these landlords might be described as to 'shoot first and ask questions afterwards'. They simply did not brook any opposition, and hired gunmen were easy to come by amidst such poverty and high unemployment. She said that a few dollars here and there could get as many gunmen as a rancher might want.

Despite the vastness of the country, where one could travel for a whole day and not see anything but cattle, if one tried to move in on a piece of land, the owners would soon know one was there, she remarked. The policy of the Movement for Landless Workers was to occupy a piece of land after they had identified that it was unused. They would set up their camp, always made of black plastic tents, and display their flags and banners. They would organise a school and a basic health clinic, and people would begin to till the land. Ms O'Brien said that on a number of occasions she had been driven for hours to one of these remote camps and what was remarkable about them was the normality of the life there for the people, although they were living under black plastic in the heat of the day and the cold of the night.

The effort people expended, the energy they put into it and the suffering they endured to get such a piece of land, she described as quite extraordinary. The piece of land would be no bigger than a decent-sized Irish field, and would constitute only a tiny fraction of the whole of a ranch, and yet the people occupying it would be persecuted by the rancher and his employees, she said. The ranchers' attitude was, if they gave an inch, the landless would take over. It was a rigid, unyielding and inflexible attitude, Ms O'Brien observed.

Campaigning for the rights of street children and slum-dwellers

In December 1995, Trócaire ran a newspaper advertisement with a photo of a bullet and beside it the message: 'In Brazil this Christmas, street children will receive a little present from some local shopkeepers.' The advertisement gave the example of a little girl, Teresa Alves. She lived in a shanty-town in Rio, in a house made of wood and cardboard. She and her brothers had to beg on the streets for money. Circumstances forced her to stay away from home and live with other street children, probably involved in petty crime. At the age of nine, on 22 May 1989, she was tortured and killed by a vigilante death squad employed to 'clean up' the streets. Her killers were almost certainly members of the military police.

The advertisement said that that Christmas the best present such children could get would be a better future. There were up to 100 million street children all over the world, the advertisement said. By removing serious threats to their health and well-being by offering them a structure for development, Trócaire could give children like Teresa a real chance. This could mean physically protecting children from execution or exploitation, trying to reunite parents and children separated for whatever reason, providing them with a fair source of income so that they did not have to beg or steal, or simply continuing to campaign for justice.

Among the many groups worldwide to benefit from Trócaire's Lenten Campaign in 1996 were the slum-dwellers who faced eviction and squalor in São Paulo. Most of the city's eighteen million inhabitants lived in tiny shacks made from whatever materials were available. With rubbish piled up in the street and little or no running water, at least three million in the city got their water supply from sewage-polluted wells.

By 1996, the Dublin priest, Fr Pat Clarke, had been working in São Paulo for twenty years. He was one of the founder members of the Movement for the Defence of Slum-dwellers (MDS). By that time, Trócaire had given more than £100,000 to the MDS to help the poor hold on to their homes and to try to convince the city authorities to provide clean water and a proper waste-disposal service. Over the years, the MDS had battled the authorities who were trying to move people from their homes, and had helped residents to organise to stop evictions.

Fr Clarke said that the MDS did not give handouts. 'We help people in their efforts to analyse their situation and find the solutions to the great problems they face. This involves us in providing legal aid and advice, and in organising adult-literacy, childcare and basic healthcare facilities.' They were determined to make a difference in people's lives, he said.

In May 1996, concern over the massive increase in suicide among some of Brazil's indigenous peoples, due to problems such as land ownership, prompted Trócaire to host a dele - gation from Brazil to discuss the issue. Rosalino Ortiz, a member of the Guarani indigenous nation, and Mauricio Pauletti, a lawyer working with the Council for Indigenous Affairs of the Brazilian Bishops' Conference, came to Dublin to highlight the problems facing Brazil.

The Guarani were Brazil's second-largest indigenous group and had been pushed aside by ranchers and sugar-cane plantation owners, and at that time occupied less than 1 per cent of their original land. The incidence of suicide among them had grown alarmingly during the previous ten years. Trócaire said that suicide was a new phenomenon linked to the destruction of the traditional Guarani way of life. The previous year, fifty-four Guarani had committed suicide, many of them young people.

A decree signed into law on 8 January 1996 by Brazil's President Cardoso had modified considerably the previous legislation governing the demarcation of indigenous land. This made it easier for ranchers, gold prospectors and lumber companies to invade what was left of indigenous land. The Brazilian delegation invited by Trócaire also highlighted the considerable opposition, both inside Brazil and internationally, to the decree and expressed the hope that the pressure from all quarters would be maintained.

In October 1997, Trócaire held a two-week sponsored walk in Brazil to raise funds to help street children there. The huge numbers of such children in the country faced a bleak future. Parents who found they could not afford to raise all their children often sent them out on the streets, where the problems they faced involved prostitution, theft and drugs.

Seventy-three people from all over Ireland took part in the walk and each one raised £3,250 in sponsorship. The money raised went to financing centres to take the seven million street children in Brazil off the streets. The walkers witnessed first-hand in Brazil the grim reality for so much of the population there. The people who lived in slums had little chance of escaping from their daunting existence. The slums were governed by drug lords who offered more money than the people who lived there could ever hope to earn, and so a lot of them had no choice but to become involved in the drug scene themselves. The average wage was $110–$120 per month, but the drug barons offered slum children $30 per day to peddle drugs for them.

The government showed little interest in the people who lived in the slums – they were considered worthless and treated accordingly. Members of the walking group said that what they had raised, while it would be of some help to the street children, was a mere drop in the ocean, and that there was an urgent need for a change in the government's attitude and policies. Worldwide media coverage was the only way this could be achieved.

Members of the group met Fr Tony Sheridan, who had worked with the poor of the slums of Rio de Janeiro for the previous thirty years. He said that the situation had not improved in all that time. He told them that because of Pope John Paul II's visit to Brazil the previous week, buses had been sent around the city to pick up homeless people. The purpose was a major 'clean up' of the streets – people had been put on buses by force and deposited in the mountains. He also told them that forty children had been shot over the previous month; again, another 'clean up' of the streets.

A lot of Fr Sheridan's work was done through the use of drama. He used the techniques of drama when working with young people as a way of building self-esteem and confidence and also as a way of raising their social and political aware-ness. He used the methodology of Agusto Boal, the Brazilian theatre director, writer and politician, author of the influential *Theatre of the Oppressed* (1973) and founder of the Centre for the Theatre of the Oppressed in Rio de Janeiro.

However, some of the things they saw lifted the spirits of the members of the walking group, such as a project in Rio that was part-funded by Trócaire. The project was based on personal development, self-awareness and self-worth. The project team visited children in school one hour per week, where they were given time for arts and crafts self-expression. The official school-going age in Brazil was four but many parents could not afford to send their children before the age of seven.

Kate O'Brien's work in Brazil brought her frequently into the urban favelas and into touch with the people who lived there. She found them a warm people who welcomed her into their homes. Brazilians, she said, love to talk and to party and, when a visitor arrived, they were delighted to throw a little party to make that visitor feel welcome. She recalled being in favelas on days such as Mother's Day or International Women's Day and thinking to herself, 'What do these desperately poor people have to celebrate?' That would be the typical selfish mindset of the privileged European, she said, but she soon came to realise that they deserved to celebrate, more than most, because of what they were coping with and managing to survive.

She was also struck by their sense of sharing. Everyone brought some little thing and they pooled everything in a communal spirit and welcomed occasions to sing and dance and tell stories. It made their lives somehow more bearable, she believed. Ms O'Brien also recalled that no question was too big or too small to ask; the people were insatiably curious to find out about the visitor and also expected her to reciprocate by asking them questions about themselves. Westerners, she remarked, might consider their questions intrusive but they were completely open about themselves – they were not being intrusive but were genuinely interested in and wanted to know about the visitor's life.

Trócaire's twenty-fifth anniversary
On the occasion of the twenty-fifth anniversary of Trócaire's founding, Cardinal Arns sent the agency a message that is worth quoting at length.

'The generous giving of time and personal effort in the construction of citizenship and partnership and of a transform - ing humanism are living signs of God in our midst. Trócaire has been one of the sacramental instruments of hope to encourage us in our tasks. The work on behalf of justice and of human rights at this time of celebration was born after Vatican Council II as a sign of joy and hope in a Latin America that was so beaten down and wronged in international relations.

The partnership that brings to life a new vision of womanhood and manhood has gained the status of indis -

pensable citizenship in our countries. The nights and days of terror throughout the twenty-one years of military dictatorship (1964–1985) suffocated our best sons and daughters who offered their own blood and intelligence while dreaming and building the democratic resistance. Thanks to Trócaire's financial aid, we were able to constitute and maintain lawyers to guarantee justice in a time of fear and torture.

These new times of exclusion require greater dedication and an always new preferential option for the poor. Centuries of exploitation and suffering have not succeeded in drowning out from the Brazilian soul a priceless generosity.

I would like to finish by calling attention to our supporters in parishes and communities throughout Ireland. Theirs is like the work of ants, responsible today for a great microscopic revolution that can convert the world in a non-violent way. May you continue to be faithful to this grand cause, which is constructed with small gestures of sharing.'

The death of Dom Helder Camara

In late August 1999, Dom Helder Camara died at his home in Olinda in north-eastern Brazil. Bishop Kirby described him as a bishop who very much lived out the spirit of Vatican II as the founding president of the Brazilian Bishops' Conference established in the wake of the council. In his life, he expounded the social teachings of the church, which were detailed at the time by Pope Paul VI in *Populorum Progressio*, Bishop Kirby said, and as such he became known as a champion of the poor and a promoter of justice. Bishop Kirby said Trócaire was privileged to know him through its work in Brazil and that he was a great inspiration for the agency.

Justin Kilcullen described him as small in stature but a giant to his people – the poor, the landless and the oppressed. For decades, Dom Helder had been behind the struggle for human rights and social justice in Brazil, he said. His words and actions made him a hate figure for the military who had ruled Brazil between 1964 and 1985; they made him a 'non-person' for nine years and banned all references to him. They sent an assassination squad to kill him but the hitmen could not bring themselves to murder him and instead asked his forgiveness, Mr Kilcullen said.

He went on to say Dom Helder's crusade for justice in the face of such danger made him a hero to millions of Brazilians; they respected him because he lived and worked among them. World leaders had issued statements on the occasion of his death but Mr Kilcullen said that the words of the slum-dwellers, the street children and the landless labourers he cared so much for would have meant most to him.

He referred to a poster that hung in Trócaire's Dublin office that featured Bishop Camara's photo and one of his most memorable quotations: 'When I give food to the poor, they call me a saint. When I ask why the poor have no food, they call me a communist.'

Justin Kilcullen concluded by saying that because of Dom Helder's influence and the organisations he set up in Brazil, the demand for social justice did not end with his death; he would live on through the organisations he established and the people he inspired.

Brazil continues to be important to the work of Trócaire worldwide. Regrettably, the country is still one of the most unequal countries in the world in terms of wealth and resources' distribution. The agency's main focus now is in the north east of the country, in one of the poorest areas of Brazil.

CHAPTER 11:
Somalia's Humanitarian Crisis

Trócaire faces a new challenge

In 1991, the Somali dictator, Mohamed Siad Barre, who had ruled since 1969, fled the country, having been deposed by rebel coalition forces. International attention began to focus on hunger and disease as fighting within the coalition forces caused the blocking and diversion of NGO and international food aid to Somalia.

After the Ethiopian famine of 1984–1985, many observers said that it could never happen again. Somalia proved them wrong. This was one of the most difficult situations that Trócaire had ever faced. There was no government, no history of local NGOs, no infrastructure, and a total collapse of national institutions. A staggering 300,000 Somali children had lost their lives since the beginning of the war between the rival clans that had made up the coalition that had ousted Siad Barre; 1.5 million people – a quarter of the population – had left the country.

In a recent interview for this book, Mary Sutton said that Somalia really challenged Trócaire's existing modus operandi. Up until that time, the agency had been comfortable with a model of development based essentially on working through local partners rather than setting up parallel structures or systems or sending volunteers from Ireland. However, when

Somalia fell apart so dramatically, she said, that option was no longer there. This led to major debates within the management team in Trócaire concerning what approach the agency should take.

Ms Sutton recalled that there was even a suggestion that Trócaire should not get involved in Somalia because the situation there was so unsuited to the agency's model of working. They discovered very quickly, however, that that was simply not an option. Large numbers of people – ordinary members of the public who were Trócaire supporters – were daily ringing the agency wanting to know what it was going to do about the suffering in Somalia.

In this way, said Ms Sutton, Trócaire was posed with a real challenge to rethink the way it did things. The situation in Somalia meant getting involved on the ground, setting up a programme where nothing, or virtually nothing, existed and starting to deliver that programme from scratch. She added that it is easy to forget now how great a test this was for the agency's mindset, which had been content with the way it had been operating for almost twenty years. She believed the organisation rose to the challenge and came through this particular 'moment-of-truth' milestone very well.

Setting up a new operational programme

Sally O'Neill was Trócaire deputy director and head of programmes in 1992. She and Joe Feeney went to Somalia, she said, to assess the situation and see what could be done. Most aid agencies, including some Irish, were going into the capital, Mogadishu, or into Baidoa, Somalia's third-largest city located in the south-central part of the country, and one of the main centres of the famine at the time. Ms O'Neill spent her time in those two cities working on the legal side of any possible Trócaire involvement while Joe Feeney travelled around to observe for himself the situation in various parts of the country. He recommended basing the agency's activities in Gedo province, in the south west of Somalia, because there were no other relief agencies active there and the people living there had received no food aid from the outside world.

Trócaire set up its own operational programme, staffed by Irish people on the ground, because there was no choice but to do so in the existing circumstances. It was Joe Feeney who opened the agency's office in Gedo. Sally O'Neill said that for much of the first two years, a large part of Trócaire's activities involved providing food relief, because the famine conditions were so bad. At the same time, it was felt passionately that the agency should commit itself to a long-term programme of support that would link disaster support to rehabilitation and development activities. This involved training local people in Gedo to manage their own programmes so that they would not become dependent on aid. The programme was delivered in a highly insecure situation with the ongoing civil war.

Ms O'Neill said that Trócaire was one of the few agencies that made a decision from the beginning not to use armed guards despite the volatility of the security situation. Somalia was a heavily armed society, with AK-47s freely available. Ms O'Neill said that of all the countries she worked in, she felt most nervous working in Somalia.

Joe Feeney said that the challenges facing him as he set about establishing a Trócaire office in Gedo were enormous. He regarded it as an achievement for Trócaire that they were able to go into a region of Somalia and begin working there without making any 'protection' payments, and he felt that perhaps the other agencies were a bit too quick in agreeing to make them.

Trócaire chose to establish itself in Mandera, on the Kenyan-Somali border (Mandera is in an ethnically Somali area on the Kenyan side of the border). Mr Feeney said that he simply walked across the border (there were no border posts on the Somali side) and kept walking until he met someone who took him to one of the local warlords. He told this man that Trócaire wanted to help and to support structures in that area. The idea was to support any sort of local-government structures, however tenuous or attenuated, that existed in the region. Trócaire was optimistic that it could establish basic services such as a health centre and water supply and provide basic education, thus creating a semblance of normality so that the people there could see some tangible evidence that things were getting back to normal.

For that to be able to take place, Mr Feeney said, some sense of security was, of course, needed. One always knew that if one built a clinic, for example, that it could be destroyed very quickly. However, one had to go ahead and take that risk because if one did not, he argued, that would be to give a message to the local community of a lack of confidence in their ability to act to solve their own problems.

As it happened, Mr Feeney said, Trócaire set up a long-term rehabilitation programme in the area and established a lot of credibility with the local community, but not before enduring some hair-raising experiences along the way. For example, while the clinic was under construction, they arrived one morning to find someone with a machine gun at the entrance. He said he was not letting anyone in or out unless his brother was recruited as a guard on the enterprise. In such situations, it took a lot of patient and delicate negotiation, involving quite an amount of time, before a solution could be worked out to the satisfaction of all.

In spite of the obstacles, Trócaire rebuilt the clinic and school and restored the water supply in that area. Mr Feeney said that even if they were destroyed three or four years later, the process of rebuilding and restoring them had been worthwhile. That was Trócaire's mandate, after all: to support people in dire need, people who had endured the most appalling levels of savagery and deprivation. The issue for him, he said, was solidarity, letting the people know the world had not forgotten them.

Trócaire recruited Liz Higgins, who had previous experience of working in a number of African countries such as Sudan, Kenya and Lesotho, as a programme manager in Somalia in 1992. At first, she worked under Joe Feeney, and then took over management of the programme when he returned to Ireland. In a recent interview for this book, she described this programme as an integrated rehabilitation programme in Somalia for refugees who had returned from the camp in Mandera. A number of NGOs were working in that camp but Trócaire had decided, she said, to try to improve the situation across the border in Somalia itself to encourage and enable refugees to return home.

The medical area was one very important area that needed attention, according to Ms Higgins. Also, because there were no education facilities and there were so many children who were missing out on this vital aspect of their development, it was also decided to start an education programme, she said. This involved setting up primary schools in conjunction with a number of other agencies, and particularly UNESCO. This organisation was supporting teacher education in Somalia and Trócaire worked with the organisation to try to train teachers and, with the longer term in view, to try to redevelop a system of teacher training that could be used as the situation improved in Somalia.

Ms Higgins said Trócaire believed it was important to get a sense of community going again within the country and she believed the work devoted to the education programme contributed to that aim. Other important community-development activities undertaken by the Trócaire team involved agriculture and water supply. The involvement of local communities was considered vital from the outset, Ms Higgins remarked, so that they would claim ownership of what was being undertaken and sustainability could be ensured.

Given her experience in other parts of Africa, what Liz Higgins found different about Somalia was the extreme clan loyalty, the inter-clan relationships and the absence of any government structures. She said it was important, therefore, to seek to identify community leaders, the people who had some sort of legitimate role within their communities. It was a dangerous situation because of the widespread availability of guns and it was not unusual to be held up at gunpoint when going out to visit communities. To ensure that staff would not be in danger as they went about their work, she said, strong relationships had to be build with community leaders.

Building these relationships called for delicate diplomacy. Because of the inter-clan rivalry, it was important not to be seen to be favouring one clan over another. Therefore, jobs had to be distributed on as equal a basis as possible. Ms Higgins recalled one difficult situation where Trócaire had to dismiss a locally recruited staff member because he was misusing resources. Doing something like this in Somalia was risky because of the danger of retaliation against other staff members. She met the man's family to explain why he had been dismissed and found that a number of clan elders were among his family. She said that, fortunately, the good relationship Trócaire had built with the elders smoothed out this particular difficulty.

President Robinson's visit
In August 1992, the Irish Foreign Minister, David Andrews, went to Somalia to see for himself the conditions there. Brian McKeown warned, on the minister's return, that 'vague promises do not fill stomachs'. He welcomed the minister's initiative in going to Somalia to see at first hand how 'horrendous and desperate' the situation there had become. But, while also welcoming Minister Andrews's efforts to take the issue to the EEC and the UN, he reminded him that if the Irish government was not putting its hand in its own pocket, then it lost a lot of moral clout when preaching to its European partners.

Mr McKeown said the generosity of the Irish people towards famine relief and Third World development was cancelled out by the government's policy of cutbacks in overseas aid. Irish ODA had fallen since 1986, despite the government's stated commitment to increasing it. Ireland's ODA, as a proportion of GNP, was at the time the lowest of any country in the Organisation for Economic Cooperation and Development (OECD), Mr McKeown pointed out.

The following month, Trócaire launched a £1 million appeal for Somalia. The agency adopted a three-pronged approach to the disaster: (i) assisting Somali people inside the country; (ii) assisting Somali refugees in both Kenya and Ethiopia; and (iii) supporting an airlift of food to Mogadishu from Kenya. Trócaire's operations inside the country were concentrated in the province of Gedo, where more than 70,000 people were in desperate need and had not been reached by any outside aid. As well as immediate food aid, medical help and shelter were also vitally needed.

In mid-October 1992, Trócaire warmly praised President Mary Robinson's efforts on behalf of the people of Somalia. Describing her visit to the famine-stricken country as 'an act of great compassion', Brian McKeown said the visit might well be recalled in years to come as a turning point in the relationship between the rich and poor nations of the world community. He thought President Robinson's eloquent response to what she had witnessed in Somalia would do more than 'all the carefully worded platitudes of world leaders'.

Not only had she become 'a voice for the voiceless', he continued, but in her justifiable indignation she had become a voice for those in the rich countries of the world who were incensed at the international indifference and bureaucratic bungling that had caused the catastrophe in the Horn of Africa. Her indignation was an expression of the indignation felt by all of them in recent months at the largely man-made famine in Somalia and other African countries, he contended.

He said that she had given all of them the courage to continue to speak out against 'the shameful reality of forty million starving people in Africa'. This was at a time when governments were not meeting their responsibilities in terms of aid to the Third World, when the structure of trade ensured that the rich nations became richer at the expense of the poor nations, and when vast sums of money continued to be wasted on armaments, he went on.

Mr McKeown said that the crisis facing Somalia and other African countries warranted a completely new and original approach to disaster relief and a renewed commitment to the Third World. He had no doubt that having seen for herself the situation in Somalia and of the Somali refugees on the Kenyan border, President Robinson would impress on Dr Boutros Boutros-Ghali (Secretary-General of the UN) the need for rapid UN action to save hundreds of thousands of lives. She knew only too well that every day's delay meant thousands more dying of starvation and disease.

He believed her absolutely right in her view that the security question was central to the problems in Somalia and he thought UN forces should be sent immediately to the country in sufficient numbers to ensure that food was no longer an issue in the conflict between the factions there. Until definite moves were made to disarm the factions, there would be little hope that people could sow and harvest their crops in the following months, he argued.

He also supported President Robinson's view that the international community had not adjusted to the 'post-Cold War world', adding that the superpowers that had competed for decades for strategic advantage in the Horn of Africa had now washed their hands of any responsibility towards the people of the region. They had flooded Somalia with their weaponry and now they looked the other way when the consequences of their actions became so apparent.

Brian McKeown had just arrived back from Somalia and Mandera in northern Kenya, where Trócaire had established a £1 million emergency relief and rehabilitation programme for the 55,000 Somali refugees living in Mandera camp, and the population of 300,000 in Gedo province. President Robinson and Minister David Andrews had visited Mandera on the last day of their trip to Africa. Mr McKeown said that the camp would become a 'death camp' as soon as the rains came in the following weeks. The shelters would be demolished and because there was no sanitation, there was the serious risk of a cholera epidemic, which would decimate the population there.

He said that Trócaire's priority at that particular time was to provide urgent medical care and to resettle in Somalia, on a voluntary basis, as many refugees as possible. The Trócaire programme had already identified 1,000 families (approx - imately 10,000 people) who had agreed to return to their homes in Gedo. Trócaire was providing each family with a basic kit of kitchen utensils, clothing and seeds to help their resettlement. The water pumps that had been destroyed in the areas of resettlement would be repaired to assist the rehabilitation process. It was estimated that the cost of resettling one family was £20 and Brian McKeown appealed for funds towards the programme.

The US/UN force in Somalia

In December 1992, Trócaire gave a cautious welcome (in contrast to a more widely held view) to the decision by the UN Security Council to accept the US offer to send troops to Somalia to protect relief aid to the famine-stricken popu- lation. Trócaire's deputy director at the time, Sally O'Neill, said the agency's main concern was that such a move would 'let the UN off the hook'. Brian McKeown warned that the action could lead to further suffering for the people of Somalia if the intervention sparked off a hostile reaction among the warring clans. The danger with that kind of operation, he said, was that it could result in even greater loss of life for a people who had already suffered terribly from war and famine.

Trócaire feared that aid workers would also become targets for the clans and warned that any US/UN action had to take into account the safety of aid workers in the country. He noted that Trócaire's emergency personnel in Gedo had reported increased tension in the region in the face of the speculation about military intervention by the US. Mr McKeown remarked that the difficulty with that kind of operation was that it offered no long-term solution to the problems of Somalia because the solution could not be a military one. He argued that what the country needed was a political initiative.

Shortly afterwards, Trócaire was forced to abandon its feeding stations after gunmen launched attacks on aid workers. The expected landing of US troops caused a movement of heavily armed Somali gangs from Mogadishu to the south-western province of Gedo. Some of these gunmen made their way into the countryside round Mandera and the Kenyan army was unable to stop them. As a result, the Kenyan authorities closed the border, trapping many of Trócaire's Somali workers inside Gedo.

A Trócaire vehicle was hijacked and a Trócaire Somali agronomist fired on. Trócaire's emergency officer, Joe Feeney, said the agency thought it prudent to withdraw their personnel to Nairobi for some days to watch how the situation developed. A heavily armed band had invaded a town three hours south of Mandera, well inside Kenya itself, and had taken three aid vehicles from Médecins Sans Frontières.

The result was the temporary closing down of the Trócaire feeding stations in Gedo, which were feeding seriously malnourished children. If they had had to stay closed for a week, an estimated 10 per cent of the children being fed would have died. The fear was that the warlords would use Gedo province as a base for operations against the Americans, which would endanger the population of the province and the relief programme being operated by Trócaire and other agencies.

In late January 1993, Brian McKeown expressed concern at the deteriorating security situation in the Gedo region. He said the shooting dead of a Swiss aid worker in Bardera and the wounding of a Somali worker employed by the American CRS (a sister agency of Trócaire) were the culmination of a series of incidents which reflected the increased tension in the region in the previous weeks. Large numbers of armed gangs had moved into Gedo province since the arrival of the

US-led UN force in December, he said. These gangs had arrived in Gedo to dump arms and ammunition and to escape the attention of the US/UN forces. Their arrival had resulted in increased tension and harassment of aid workers, both foreign and local.

Trócaire's Somali aid workers were bearing the brunt of the increasingly difficult situation in Gedo, he pointed out, and it was they who were most at risk. He said it was absolutely essential that the US/UN force extended its operations to Gedo and other remote areas in Somalia to where many gunmen had fled. The UN-backed forces would achieve little in the long term, he contended, unless effective action was taken by them to disarm the gunmen and prepare the way for a peaceful transition to a democratically agreed civil authority.

In July 1993, Trócaire's newly appointed director, Justin Kilcullen, visited Somalia. On his return, he said that the UN was failing the people who had rebuilt the country. The root of the crisis then existing, he argued, was that the US/UN intervention was failing to tackle the underlying political and economic problems. While Trócaire had given an initial cautious welcome to the intervention, he said, it had warned about the dangers of a purely military operation and had stressed the need to consult the Somalis themselves about what they wanted for their country. The agency had stressed especially the need to support local elders, professionals, business people, women's groups and others in their efforts to establish some kind of democratic administrative structures.

The media concentration on the increasing violence in Mogadishu detracted from the very real progress being made elsewhere, especially in the north and the west, where there was minimal UN presence, Mr Kilcullen observed. In the western province of Gedo, where Trócaire was implementing its programme, it had developed a working relationship with local elders built on trust and mutual respect. This had been achieved slowly and painstakingly but bore fruit in that

Trócaire staff could go about their work with the full support of the elders, unhindered by the armed factions present in Gedo. The reason was the elders saw the Trócaire programme as their programme; Trócaire had four expatriate staff providing medical, engineering and agricultural advice, but Somali personnel ran the programme – doctors, nurses and highly skilled administrators. They were putting huge efforts into increasing crop yields, restoring water supplies, reopening schools and providing vital healthcare to their communities. These people – the ones who would rebuild Somalia – were the ones who should have been receiving UN support, Justin Kilcullen contended.

He urged the Irish government to call for action, at UN and EU levels, for a full reassessment of the US/UN operational methods in Somalia, and to support the Italian call for a suspension of the UN combative role. He also wanted Ireland to urge the UN to set a date for a reconvened peace conference to work towards the establishment of an interim government, which could begin the process of normalisation. The Irish government had to press for policies that would strengthen the elements in Somali society that would work to bring about the stability and peace that were needed above all else in the country, he argued.

In October 1993, Mr Kilcullen welcomed the announcement by the US government that it was to give priority to reaching a political settlement in Somalia. He said that the policy it had been pursuing of seeking a strictly military solution had been a costly error in terms of loss of human life, in postponing an eventual settlement and in undermining much of the work of the NGOs active in the country.

Trócaire's health programme 1994–1996
Mary Healy, with a background in nursing and midwifery, joined Trócaire in 1994 and took over responsibility for managing the health programme that the agency was running in Somalia at the time. She was based in Mandera,

SOMALIA'S HUMANITARIAN CRISIS

for security reasons, but travelled to and from Gedo every day. In a recent interview for this book, she said that it was a huge health programme involving a district hospital, a number of clinics and village outposts as well. There were 100 Somali staff employed to work on the programme, many having been trained by Trócaire since its arrival in the region.

Part of Ms Healy's work was with traditional midwives, training them to work within the health structure rather than outside of it. She trained them to provide a service in outlying areas because that part of the country was sparsely populated in places and there was a lot of travel involved. As well as this, people in this part of Somalia lived a nomadic, pastoralist way of life. So health staff were needed to go out to the people rather than expect them to come into hospitals, at least as far as preventive measures were concerned.

She said that she found the Somalis one of the proudest peoples that she has ever worked among. They treated expatriates as equals and expected to be treated as equals in return. Ms Healy speculated that this might be a legacy from their experience of (limited) Italian colonialism. Italians of all walks of life came to Somalia and integrated well with the Somalis – they worked among them as equals and inter-married with them.

One of the strongest memories she carries with her from her time in Somalia is how most of the other aid agencies left the country around 1995. During the time that she was there, she said, most other organisations were leaving rather than arriving and contracting rather than expanding. However, Trócaire remained and is there to this day.

She herself stayed there for about fifteen months, leaving only for security reasons. It became increasingly dangerous for expatriates to be working there so Trócaire's programmes came to be run almost exclusively by local Somali staff. She recalled that when Somalis negotiated with Trócaire they said that they found the agency not the most generous giver, i.e. it did not throw its money around as plentifully as some of the other international agencies. The Somalis used the analogy of the cow, as befitted a pastoralist society: Trócaire, they said, was not the most plentiful giver of milk but it never dried up.

Another memory she had of her time in Somalia was that whenever she introduced herself, even in the smallest, most remote or poorest Somali village, the people used to say to her: 'Oh, your name is Mary, like Mary Robinson. We remember when she came.'

Trócaire's programmes 1995–2001

Unfortunately, fighting continued and the UN withdrew its UNOSOM II mission to Somalia in early March 1995. Interviewed at the beginning of Trócaire's Lenten Campaign that year, Justin Kilcullen pointed out that two years before, when the crisis in Somalia was at its height, the Western world's attention was riveted by the horrors that unfolded. Two years later, the international relief agencies and the media camera-crews had packed up and left. However, Trócaire was committed to remaining for the subsequent three to five years, he said.

Severe flooding in southern Somalia in October–November 1997 focused world attention on the country once more and Trócaire launched an appeal for help for the people of the area. An estimated 800,000 people were affected. The immediate needs were for shelter, blankets, food, drinking water and medical supplies. The damage to infrastructure, to homes and shops, and to the agriculture and food-supply system was widespread. The only access to the affected areas was by air and the roads had been washed away in the floods.

Trócaire was one of the few agencies to have continued to work extensively in Somalia since 1992. In 1996, it had built a new district hospital and continued to run health, education and agriculture programmes. Now it also warned of a risk of cholera as tankers that normally distributed water were unable to get their regular supply and instead collected water from ponds. Trócaire also reported that many of the canals dug for irrigation systems had been destroyed and would need to be cleared out and repaired, and that many of the local primary schools had been seriously affected. Made of sticks, with iron roofs, the schools stood no chance against the rain and rising floodwater.

Many of the rural health posts that provided a service to the nomadic and farming communities were similarly affected. Throughout 1998, Trócaire worked with other international agencies, such as Cordaid (the Dutch Catholic development agency), the African Medical Research Foundation (an international African voluntary organisation with headquarters in Nairobi) and Médecins Sans Frontières, to mitigate the worst effects of the severe flooding in late 1997.

In March 1999, Trócaire warned that one million Somalis were again threatened by a devastating famine caused by war and drought. Continued fighting and the failure of five successive harvests had forced 30,000 Somalis to flee their homes. Trócaire said that it estimated that in the Gedo region alone, 52,000 would need food aid and that children were already suffering malnutrition. Because of the drought, farmers had been forced to sell their livestock despite falling cattle prices. With rivers drying up, farmers had little water to irrigate their land.

Once again, emergency work by a number of agencies, especially the UN bodies, the Food and Agricultural Organisation (FAO), the WFP and the World Health Organisation (WHO), averted a humanitarian disaster on a massive scale. Some thirty NGOs assisted in this vital, life-saving work, Trócaire being the chief Irish one among them.

Kathleen Fahy, who worked for Trócaire for a number of years, first visited Somalia in 1992 to help with the setting up of the agency's programme there. She returned in 1994 and was Trócaire programme manager in the country for the next seven years. In a recent interview for this book, she said that throughout the period of her association with Somalia, outside commentators described the country as anarchic and ungovernable, with the splintering of the clan system and the endless power struggle that followed the overthrow of Siad

Barre. In fact, she pointed out, the twenty-two years of the Barre dictatorship and the stripping of power from the clan elders (which was a deliberate exercise in control) had left the country with no natural leadership able to command authority and respect or to pick up the pieces when things fell apart.

Ms Fahy said that Gedo did experience a few years of uneasy peace, which allowed an opportunity for some rehabilitation and development to take place. But this peace was always fragile, she remarked.

Trócaire, she said, worked very closely with the local leadership in Bulla Xawa and Dolow districts in northern Gedo. She recalled that this involved interminable meetings and negotiations, where the smallest of details would be discussed before the agency was able to proceed with a prog-ramme. The elders' main agenda was always to maximise jobs and contracts for their area or their clan group. This was not necessarily avarice, Ms Fahy pointed out, political expediency demanding a balancing of employment oppor-tunity and the even distribution of contracts (for vehicle hire, supply of materials etc.) among clans.

She also pointed out that there was a tendency for a sub-clan to view a particular post within the organisation or a specific project as 'theirs', simply by virtue of the fact that a member of their group was the first appointee to that particular position. She recalled that this attitude led on one occasion to an absurd situation where the family of a nurse fought hard to have another clan member appointed to his position when he left – solely on the grounds that it was 'their' job.

Ms Fahy said that Trócaire made a decision from the outset that they would always try to hire local expertise and work through local contractors. She believed that this was a very wise decision. At the height of the programme, the agency had a payroll of 140 employees and their monthly income meant a regular injection of cash into the area. This was hugely advantageous to the entire community. After all, as Ms Fahy pointed out, a steady job is generally accepted as the best guarantee of moving out of poverty. She contended that it was also a contributor to the peace process because no one wanted to jeopardise these benefits and, so, when an incident occurred that risked the Trócaire programme's closure, the clans were willing to get together to resolve the issue.

From her attendance at general NGO meetings in Nairobi, it struck Kathleen Fahy that Trócaire had stronger support from the local community than did most other organisations and she believed this certainly had a positive impact on the agency's day-to-day interactions. In a country where foreign NGOs found it extremely difficult to operate, and where the opening argument was as likely to be the firing of a gun or the throwing of a hand grenade, she said that Trócaire's incessant meetings did serve a purpose.

Consensus was the aim and everyone had a right to express their opinion and be heard, she said. And heard they were and their clan's particular perspective clearly articulated. Leaders depended heavily on their powers of persuasion and negotiation; Ms Fahy said that in her experience and almost without exception, they were oratorical masters. If the devil really is in the detail, she remarked, then they all gave themselves ample opportunity to explore the minutiae of every intervention and anticipate reactions and pitfalls that might lie ahead. She believed this approach played a key part in whatever success Trócaire had.

She recalled that these meetings always ended with liberally sugared tea (six or seven spoonfuls to a cup), a habit which probably developed because of the very salty water which the local wells yielded. And despite the tough negotiations, she also recalled that there was lots of laughter and witty exchanges. The people there had a great sense of humour, she said, and conversation was lively. They also had a strong sense of identity and of pride in being Somali, she observed.

Trócaire was involved in many different initiatives in the region, according to Ms Fahy, involving health, education, agriculture and water, all with varying degrees of success. She pointed out that a credit programme targeting women involved in small enterprises proved particularly successful and seemed to have a positive and hopeful impact well beyond anything anticipated when the programme was started. Many women told Trócaire with pride how their involvement in the programme had enabled them to expand their small businesses, pay school fees or feed their families twice a day (instead of once) – something Ms Fahy described as small incremental steps in rebuilding their lives and as women gaining a new measure of confidence and independence.

She described Somalis as having a strong sense of fairness and equality and said that they demanded equal access and equal opportunity. She added that, unfortunately, when viewing a situation through the tribal lens, merit on the other side was usually overlooked and, as a result, charges of unfairness were brought against Trócaire if the job did not go a particular person's way. These charges were often accompanied by threats of violence, which were sometimes carried out, Ms Fahy explained. The only mechanism for dispute resolution was through the elders, who had the unenviable task of dealing with delinquent or criminal action without the back-up of a functioning legal or policing system.

Continuing involvement since 2002

Sadly, the new century brought no escape from war and no return to normality for the suffering people of Somalia. The climatic conditions continued to contribute to the people's misery from time to time as well. Early in 2006, the UN announced that six million people were on the brink of starvation in the Horn of Africa because of severe drought, crop failure and the depletion of livestock herds. Trócaire responded by saying it was at that time developing a targeted response by expanding its work in both Somalia and Kenya.

Emer Mullins, Trócaire communications coordinator, told the *Irish Catholic* newspaper that the agency was expanding its existing programmes in Gedo to cope with the current

SOMALIA'S HUMANITARIAN CRISIS

crisis, where two million were in need of food. Trócaire was operating a three-month emergency food-distribution programme, and a supplementary feeding programme for severely malnourished children and mothers was being developed. The UN's FAO had said that around two million people needed urgent humanitarian help in Somalia.

Trócaire launched an emergency response, committing €750,000 to combat the food crisis, called on the international community to help the millions at risk of starvation in east Africa, and warned that it could turn into a full-scale famine – the worst for more than a decade.

In February 2006, the Irish government announced that €5 million would be made available to Trócaire and other NGOs to combat the worsening food crisis in the Horn of Africa.

In the *Irish Medical Times* (10 March 2006), Orla Fagan, of Trócaire's communications office, wrote that the drought in the Horn of Africa at the time was causing up to eleven million people to go hungry, according to UN statistics just published. She said that nomadic farmers roamed the arid plains in Somalia, with their camels, in search of pasture and water for their livestock and that dead animal carcasses lined the roadsides. Compounding matters in Somalia was the widespread breakdown of law and order.

Trócaire continues its long-term commitment to Somalia, running its health, education and agriculture programmes in Gedo from Mandera. In a recent interview for this book, Eamonn Meehan said that the focus of the Trócaire programme in Somalia has changed slightly and has concentrated on its health and education aspects, as well as undertaking occasional emergency-response initiatives during times of key crises. A recent example of the latter would be providing clean water for some 20,000 people, many of them displaced from other parts of Somalia.

Mr Meehan said that the health programme currently operating in the Gedo region provides a health service to about 200,000 Somalis and that the education programme

TRÓCAIRE Veritas House Lower Abbey Street Dublin 1

WHERE'S
MY SHARE?

BISHOPS' NATIONAL APPEAL
FOR DEVELOPING COUNTRIES
THIS SUNDAY MARCH 11th

The poster for Trócaire's first Lenten campaign in 1973.

Namro Gul pictured with her daughter Meer (2) in a cave in Haripur outside Pakistan's capital Islamabad, where they were forced to live following the violence in 2009. This photo was awarded 'Picture of the Year 2009' by Caritas Internationalis, the international federation of Catholic aid agencies, of which Trócaire is a member. Photo by Kim Haughton.

L–R: Elizabeth Korio, Jemima Moonka and Grace Moti of a Maasai women's group in Kenya. The group is supported by Trócaire and educates girls and women about the dangers of female genital mutilation. Photo www.simonburch.com

LEFT: Brian McKeown 1939–2009. Brian was director of Trócaire from 1973 to 1993. RIGHT: Brother and sister Vanneth Kahn (5) and Vannuth Kahn (3) peeping out from their home, which looks onto Phnom Penh's largest rubbish dump. Families in this area scavenge on the dump to survive. Photo by Kim Haughton.

'Give them justice, they will reward you with peace.' Graffiti on a section of the wall built by Israel around Palestinian lands.

LEFT: Bishop Eamon Casey, chairman of Trócaire, speaking about the agency's campaign against apartheid in 1985.
Right: The Dunnes Stores strikers outside the Henry Street store in 1985.

Cardinal Paulo Evaristo Arns, Archbishop of São Paulo, Brazil, receives the freedom of Galway in 1983 from Lord Mayor Pat McNamara.

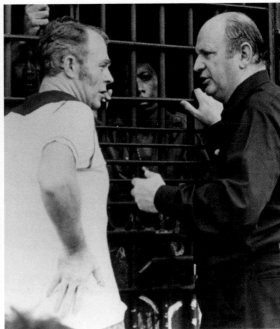

LEFT: Bishop Eamon Casey stopped at a checkpoint in Central America while travelling with Trócaire.
RIGHT: Bishop Eamon Casey visiting Fr Niall O'Brian and the 'Negros Nine' in Bacolod prison in the Philippines in 1984.

Ken Wiwa, son of Nigerian activist Ken Saro-Wiwa, pictured with Trócaire's head of campaigns, Annette Honan, and the late Niall Toibín, head of Trócaire's International Department.

LEFT: Archbishop Raphael Ndingi of Nairobi with Bishop Donal Lamont of Umtali. RIGHT: Cardinal Oscar Andres Rodriguez Maradiaga of Honduras pictured delivering the annual Maynooth College/Trócaire lecture in St Patrick's College, Maynooth, in 2006.

Bishop John Kirby, chairman of Trócaire, during a visit to Timor Leste in 1999, with Bishop Carlos Belo of Dili, pictured holding the Nobel Peace prize he was awarded three years earlier.

LEFT: President Mary Robinson pictured with Brian McKeown, Sally O'Neill and Joe Feeney visiting a Trócaire project during the president's visit to Somalia in 1993.
RIGHT: Ethiopia's Olympic champion Haile Gebreselassie pictured during his visit to Ireland in 2005 to support Trócaire's Lenten campaign. Photo by Conor Healy.

Throughout 2005 Trócaire gathered thousands of signatures and lobbied the government to commit 0.7% of Ireland's Gross National Income to development aid through the 'Keep Our Word' campaign.
LEFT: Justin Kilcullen presents Minister for Foreign Affairs, Dermot Ahern, Minister of State for Overseas Development, Conor Lenihan, and Taoiseach Bertie Ahern with the agency's petition at the UN Summit in New York in 2005.
RIGHT: Justin Kilcullen, Bono and Tom Kitt, Minister of State for Overseas Development, pictured during Trócaire's 2005 campaign.

Children pictured in North Korea during the famine. This photo, which was taken by Justin Kilcullen, was chosen by *Newsweek* as one of its pictures of the year, 1997.

LEFT: A Trócaire poster highlighting the North Korea famine in 1997.
RIGHT: Justin Kilcullen, current director of Trócaire.

provides a primary education for about 3,700 children. What he considers of major interest about these programmes is that they are owned by district health committees and community education committees, formed of local people in Gedo, who provide the link between the local communities, the programmes and Trócaire. He said that this is an interesting model and provides a contrast with other NGOs in Somalia who simply go in and run their own programmes without any real community engagement.

Recently, he participated in a meeting of the district health committees, which took place in Mandera. He found it inspiring to see the extent of their engagement with the programme. Even in what is a very difficult period in Somalia, they are working hard at their health programme and value it greatly, he said, and engage as genuine representatives of their communities. There are always issues to be considered in relation to the quality of service of the health and education programmes, he acknowledges, but he was glad to say that the structures underpinning them are solid.

The struggle of the people of Somalia for survival goes on. The country receives little media attention, yet it is the scene of probably the worst ongoing humanitarian crisis in the developing world.

CHAPTER 12:
The Response to Genocide in Rwanda

The genocide
The Rwandan civil war, which erupted in October 1990, reached its bloodiest point in April–July 1994, when at least 800,000 Tutsis and thousands of moderate Hutus were killed by Hutu extremists.

In April 1994, a Trócaire advertisement in the Irish newspapers drew attention to the human tragedy unfolding in Rwanda. It said that many thousands had died that week as a result of the four-year civil conflict and that many more were being forced to flee as rebel troops moved in on the capital, Kigali. Human rights abuses continued daily, carried out by the regular Rwandan army and by the militia known as the Interahamwe. Thousands were in need of food, medicines, water and shelter. Some 350,000 refugees from neighbouring Burundi, now living in camps in southern Rwanda, were also threatened. Medical facilities were stretched to breaking point. All foreign personnel had had to leave and support from international agencies had ended. However, Trócaire said that, working with Caritas Rwanda, its church partner, it could provide the basic essentials: food, medicine, water and shelter. It appealed to the Irish public for help.

The following day, Trócaire announced that the terror was increasing and that the killings continued. Innocent people were being terrorised and killed and Trócaire warned that the mass exodus of refugees would cause severe pressure on neighbouring countries, especially Burundi, to where up to 125,000 had fled.

Around the middle of April 1994, Justin Kilcullen strongly criticised media coverage of the crisis. He was speaking at a news conference in Trócaire headquarters where three Rwandans living in Ireland expressed frustration at the emphasis being placed on alleged tribal or ethnic rivalry between Hutus and Tutsis rather than the underlying economic and social injustices in Rwanda.

Mr Kilcullen said that the tragic events of that time illustrated yet again the unjust and exploitative nature of the relationship between Africa and the West. He reiterated what the three Rwandans had said and added that the focus on rescuing expatriates made it seem as if the people of Rwanda or Burundi did not count. The attitude seemed to be, he said, 'Let them get on with it; it's their fight'.

Putting the crisis in a wider context, he said that colonialist and exploitative attitudes towards Africa still dominated Western thinking. The West dumped its unwanted beef on Africa, destroying local livelihoods and economies in the process, and signed a General Agreement on Tariffs and Trade (GATT) deal that would cost African economies $2.6 billion a year, he said. And it delivered its toxic waste to Africa and salved its conscience by saying that Africans wanted this as a means to earn foreign currency, as if they had any choice, he added.

He went on to say that the West 'extracted' commodities from the continent and paid paltry sums for them; for example, Rwanda depended on exports of coffee and cocoa, the prices for which had fallen by 34 per cent and 46 per cent respectively in the previous decade. The resulting poverty fuelled conflict, he said. The West continued to demand enormous debt repayments, which crippled development; the debt repayments were four times more than Africa could spend on its health services. The International Monetary

THE RESPONSE TO GENOCIDE IN RWANDA

Fund, of which Ireland was a shareholder, was one of the players involved.

A few days later, Trócaire launched a massive appeal for funds during which it warned that Rwanda could become another Somalia unless the international community took immediate action. Justin Kilcullen said that the crisis should not be ignored by the EU and the UN despite their preoccupation at the time with events in the former Yugoslavia.

The crisis was raised that day with the Department of Foreign Affairs by Eamonn Meehan, Trócaire's acting head of projects at the time. Trócaire particularly wanted the government to ensure that Rwandan nationals working with international development agencies would be protected. Mr Meehan said that Trócaire was working with local church networks in both Rwanda and Burundi to try to channel humanitarian aid to the millions displaced by the fighting. Reports from Trócaire emergency officer Mary Sweeney in northern Burundi indicated that thousands of Rwandan refugees were pouring into Burundi, thus increasing the likelihood of the conflict spreading there.

Ms Sweeney was caught in crossfire in Burundi as she returned from a hospital on the Rwandan border, where she said the conditions were the worst she had ever seen. 'I saw recently arrived refugees, many of them children as young as four or five, with serious machete wounds. I spoke to women and children who had been very badly injured, many of them with limbs missing. Many were dazed and had lost members of their families.'

Trócaire advertisements kept the Irish public informed of the developing tragedy. In May 1994, one advertisement warned that at that particular time the biggest threat to those who survived the genocide was those who did not. Thousands of bodies were polluting the water supply, creating a huge risk of disease and epidemic, and Trócaire's immediate priority at that time was healthcare to avoid further disaster. But, the advertisement said, the agency could do more: with the help of the Irish people it could bring hope for the future.

When the killing was over and the refugees could return home, they would have nothing and would need the resources and assistance to rebuild their lives. That meant a long-term commitment, the advertisement concluded.

At the end of May 1994, a Trócaire-sponsored study of Third World debt was published under the title, 'Third World Debt – Towards an Equitable Solution', written by Tom and Mary McCarthy. Justin Kilcullen described Third World debt as economic genocide. Defending the publication of a report on debt while thousands died in Rwanda, he said that the debt situation in Africa fuelled many conflicts and that tackling that situation would, in effect, relieve many other problems.

The following month, Eamonn Meehan went into Rwanda by crossing the border from Burundi and heading for Butare. In a recent interview for this book, he told how he travelled with a Croatian priest, Fr Curic, who had been working for many years in the country. Fr Curic was closely involved in the work of Caritas and part of his responsibility was bringing food in through the Caritas structures. With them in their jeep was a two-person German TV crew. They spent five days in Rwanda, calling at various parishes and church houses.

Mr Meehan said that they encountered many roadblocks; every few kilometres from the border with Burundi there were makeshift roadblocks, essentially just trees that had been felled and pulled across the roads. At these obstacles were armed people, some with pistols and hand grenades but most had more primitive weapons, especially machetes. There was much evidence of drunkenness and some of drug abuse as well. Looking back on the event, Mr Meehan said they took a major risk trying to travel around Rwanda at such a time. They got through many roadblocks by giving cigarettes, chocolate and fruit to the people manning them. Fr Curic did all the negotiating and explaining and he managed to get them through safely.

Butare, Mr Meehan described as a garrison town at war, with tens of thousands of people milling around it. Paul Kagame's Rwandan Patriotic Army (RPA) had taken Kigali and was approaching Butare. On one occasion, just a few kilometres north of Butare, on the Kigali road, Mr Meehan witnessed tens of thousands of people moving like a human deluge. These were Hutus, fleeing in front of the RPA forces making their way towards Butare. He said that he met many frightened people in the days he spent in Rwanda during that tragic summer of 1994. When he and his travelling companions left Rwanda and returned to Bujumbura, they brought some Tutsis with them in a small convoy. These were people who had been in hiding and were now being brought out under the protection of the church. Eamonn Meehan gave the credit to Fr Curic who, through the force of his personality and his patient diplomatic and negotiating skills, got them through many obstacles and difficulties.

Trócaire expands its involvement

The worst excesses of the genocide came to an end in July 1994 and the long, slow, painstaking process of rebuilding within the country was stepped up. In September, Trócaire appointed an assistant programme manager, a medical doctor and an agro-economist to its existing team in Rwanda. Its programme manager in Kigali oversaw projects in agriculture, health, education, community development, women's development and human rights. At that time, Trócaire's medical programme was serving 200,000 people in the south west of Rwanda. It operated in four camps as well as running mobile health units for displaced people in the area. The agency was also running a variety of agricultural rehabilitation projects, mainly centred on seed and tool distribution for people returning to their homes. Trócaire was also working with local organisations, helping them to re-establish agricultural-support projects such as seed stations and extension services.

By September 1994, Trócaire had spent more than £700,000 on materials for its programmes in the huge camp of Cyanika, where there was a sixteen-person Irish team comprising a doctor, nurses, water and sanitation engineers and logistics personnel. The same month, Trócaire welcomed the decision by President Robinson to visit Rwanda as part of her two-week tour of central Africa. The president had been scheduled to visit only the refugee camps in Zaire and Tanzania, but after strong representations from Justin Kilcullen and Mary Sutton to the Irish Department of Foreign Affairs that she should also visit Rwanda, her schedule was changed accordingly.

In mid-October, Trócaire ran a newspaper advertisement with the title, 'Rwanda – out of sight but not out of mind'. The advertisement referred to how just a few short months previously, the tragic events in Rwanda had dominated newspaper, radio and TV coverage. Now other stories had pushed Rwanda into the background but the people there still needed Irish support, the advertisement said. It explained how up to two million were homeless and destitute, hundreds of thousands were orphaned and the country's institutions were in ruins. But, it continued, against all the odds, some Rwandans were endeavouring to pick up the pieces and were working to ensure that their children would live without violence and fear.

Trócaire was working with these energetic and resourceful people, in the same way that it worked with like-minded people in so many other countries, the advertisement said. Just as in Somalia, where, long after media attention had faded, Trócaire was working to provide the means whereby hundreds of thousands of Somalis were rebuilding their lives and communities, so Trócaire was in Rwanda for the long term, the advertisement declared.

The extensive diocesan collections that Trócaire held for Rwanda in the autumn of 1994 were the first time that such collections had been held since the Ethiopian famine of 1984–1985. The total raised all over Ireland was almost £6 million, the third highest amount for a single collection that the agency has achieved in its existence.

Mary Sutton had returned from South Africa to Ireland in late 1994 and, in a recent interview for this book, she said that her first trip abroad after that was to Rwanda, where Trócaire had set up a programme in Gikongoro in the south west of the country. She found the visit disturbing, particularly the sight of so many mass graves and the other sites where the victims' bodies had been kept and were on view in the buildings where they had been so brutally slain. To her it was horrific and frightening evidence that such genocide as had happened in Europe during World War II could indeed happen again.

On a more positive note, she was impressed by the Irish engagement in the country, particularly on the part of the Medical Missionaries of Mary sisters, with whom Trócaire had established a new partnership. This partnership, she said, became a very important part of Trócaire's programme in Gikongoro. In addition, and following on so quickly from the agency's new experience in Somalia, Trócaire established offices on the ground in Kigali and Gikongoro. Ms Sutton said that this brought the organisation into the whole area of management of volunteers, an area in which it had had no history before its involvement in Somalia and Rwanda. For the first time ever, she said, Trócaire had about thirty Irish volunteers working on the ground and managing such a number was a completely new experience for the agency.

It was a very difficult and tricky environment to be working in, Ms Sutton remarked, because 'you never knew who you were talking to'. The history of individuals and what side they had been on during 'those desperate 100 days' of the genocide gave rise to much self-questioning. 'Are we being duped here?' 'Are we on the right track?' 'Is this what we should be doing?' These were the questions that arose almost inevitably in a situation that involved huge responsibility and the spending of such vast sums of money that had been given so generously by the Irish people, Ms Sutton said.

Interviewed at the beginning of the 1995 Trócaire Lenten Campaign, Justin Kilcullen said that the agency had recently committed itself to a five-year development programme in Rwanda, which would support local NGOs and human rights groups. The problem in Rwanda, he said, was never one of starvation; it was a massive human rights issue. He acknowledged that feeding and medical programmes were initially necessary to see the people through the trauma, but he argued that if there was going to be any long-term hope for the country, the issues of justice and reconciliation had to be tackled.

Angeline Ludakubana did a Trócaire-funded degree in development studies in Dublin in 1993 and returned to her native Rwanda in 1995 to work as a development planner for the Rwandan government. She told Trócaire in March 1995 that life there was approaching some sort of normality – people could walk around freely and go to work – but almost all the physical infrastructure had been destroyed. Economic resources had crumbled, a lot of land had been left to grow wild and exports were virtually non-existent. Every aspect of the country needed rebuilding and Rwanda clearly needed international assistance. She said that the best thing the Irish people could do at that time was to continue to support Trócaire to carry out long-term development projects.

Her sister was Rwanda's Minister for Women's Affairs and among her tasks was to organise programmes to help the orphans, traumatised women, rape victims and widows of the recent fighting.

Andy Storey, assistant programme manager for Trócaire in Kigali, said in March 1995 that out of an original population of eight million, four million were by that time dead or displaced. Normally, he added, there would not be a problem with food shortage, because Rwanda was a very fertile country, but large swathes of the countryside had been left uncultivated. Much of the population was still living in refugee camps where they were given food by bodies such as the Red Cross and the WFP.

Trócaire was encouraging people to go back to their own communities by giving tools and seeds to those who had returned to their farms. But many were still afraid to leave the camps because they had been so traumatised by the war.

It was difficult but necessary to persuade them to leave the camps, said Mr Storey; otherwise, the camps would become semi-permanent with people dependent on handouts.

He added that land rights were also an issue; large numbers of men had been killed in the war and their widows were having problems in claiming their land. He explained that under traditional law in Rwanda, women had no right to property. There was a local organisation to promote the rights of women called Haguruka, which Trócaire was grant-aiding.

Mr Storey dismissed the popular misconception that Rwanda's most urgent need was short-term food, saying that flooding the country with cheap food was a disincentive to people to regain their independence. The most urgent need he saw was to rehabilitate local agriculture. At that time, Trócaire was paying an Irish agricultural adviser to work with the Rwandan Ministry of Agriculture.

In early May 1995, members of the RPA killed some 4,000 people in a Kibeho camp. Following this, the EU Commission decided to cut off development aid to Rwanda, a decision that Trócaire deplored. In a recent interview for this book, Justin Kilcullen said that the agency took that view based on consultations with their own staff on the ground as well as with missionaries (such as Fr Nicky Hennity, a Kiltegan Father, and Sr Therese Flynn, a Holy Rosary Sister) who were working in Rwanda.

The situation was naturally extremely volatile there and outbreaks of violence could occur at any time, although the government was doing its utmost to keep a lid on any such possible outbreaks. The considered opinion of the people in contact with Trócaire was that it was better to stay put and do what could be done in the circumstances, Mr Kilcullen said. At least by being present, they represented some sort of an international presence that could bear witness to such incidents and bring whatever pressure they could to try to ensure that such outbreaks did not occur again.

Mary Healy moved from Somalia to Rwanda around this time in 1995. She said that Trócaire had asked her to put together manuals and toolkits for the running of health programmes in the country and had expected that what she would be engaged in would be a fairly standard piece of work. This did not turn out to be the case, however, because her arrival in Rwanda coincided with the Kibeho massacre, and her two-week visit was spent working on night duty in a hospital.

Her time was devoted to treating those who had suffered in the massacre, and this experience was probably the one that had the most profound effect on her in her fourteen years working for Trócaire, she said. She felt deeply the trauma of those who had been through the horror and was shocked to witness such an example of 'man's inhumanity to man'. Machetes had been widely used during the massacre, and those who had survived lived with the horrendous wounds that that awful weapon can inflict. Other survivors were so traumatised that they had no idea where they were or what was happening.

At the hospital where the victims were being treated, anyone who could offer any sort of possible medical help or expertise was needed. Ms Healy recalled in particular the invaluable help given by the Holy Rosary Sisters, some of whom were veterans of running bush hospitals and whose experience really told on an occasion like that after Kibeho.

Just over a month after it had decided to cut off development aid to Rwanda following the Kibeho massacre, the EU Commission reversed its decision and Trócaire welcomed the announcement. Mary Sutton said at the time that Trócaire believed the Rwandan government, as then constituted, represented the best possibility for a peaceful long-term solution to the crisis in Rwanda. Any reduction in aid would have lessened the government's ability to rule the country and could ultimately have led to its collapse, she said.

As well as providing an agricultural adviser to the Rwandan government on a longer-term basis, Trócaire had also provided that government with some basic supplies such as photocopiers and stationery so that it could do its work in the early days of its existence. Brian McKeown, who had retired as Trócaire director in 1993, had gone to Rwanda and had established a good working relationship with some key ministries, especially health, agriculture, education, social affairs and women's affairs.

Persuading the refugees to return

In late August 1995, Irish aid agencies, including Trócaire, urged the UN to 'flood' Rwanda with peace monitors to prevent reprisals against returning refugees and so encourage a major voluntary repatriation of up to two million people. The call came as the same agencies welcomed the halting of Zaire's gun-point expulsion of thousands of refugees from camps along its border. The UNHCR, they said, had to ensure the safety of those who had already returned to Rwanda in order to engender the confidence in other refugees to return home.

At the same time, Justin Kilcullen expressed concern at the overcrowding in Rwandan prisons where prisoners suspected of genocide were being held. He said that more than 2,000 had already died and many more would die unless the conditions improved. The international tribunal to try these people was not yet up and running and even the Rwandan government admitted that more than one-third of the prisoners were probably innocent.

As the refugee situation continued to worsen in Rwanda, in September 1995 Mr Kilcullen strongly criticised the inter - national community for its continuing inaction in relation to the crisis. Speaking in response to reports from Trócaire staff in Rwanda about the recent arrival of more than 10,000 refugees, forcibly repatriated from Zaire, he said it was a crisis that had been waiting to happen. Zaire had more than 1.5 million Rwandan and Burundi refugees for over a year, and had made repeated calls on the UN and the international community to create the conditions inside Rwanda whereby the refugees could return safely, but this had not happened, Mr Kilcullen pointed out.

Sr Therese Flynn had been working with Trócaire in Rwanda for a year when the Gay Byrne Radio Show aired an unusual appeal from her in June 1995. It was for Irish households to donate old football boots and football gear to teams in the Rwandan Football League, which Sr Therese herself had set up. In September, the gear was flown to Rwanda, thanks to the sponsorship of the Anglo-Irish Bank corporation.

Sr Therese had known nothing about soccer, but by September 1995 she had nineteen teams up and running and hoped to have a national Rwandan team good enough to take part in the 2002 World Cup. (Rwanda did not make the 2002 competition but participated in 2006.) As the *Irish Catholic* remarked at the time (7 September 1995): 'It is a wonderful image for us all to have in our heads of these children running about enjoying themselves on a football pitch in colourful jerseys and football boots, and not just images of starving children like we see on our television screens.'

Limerick woman Pauline O'Callaghan set about raising funds to build a sports field in Rwanda. The cost was £120,000 and by February 1996 she had raised £32,000. Trócaire's annual 24-hour fast donated all the money raised in Limerick city to what was known as the 'Limerick/Rwanda Sports Facility'. CAFOD also supported the project, which was eventually realised.

Mary Sweeney, Trócaire emergency officer in Rwanda, returned to Ireland in mid-December 1995. She said seeing children smile like children, act like children and play like children at the classes Trócaire had established in Cyanika and Kiraro camps in south-west Rwanda 'does something for the soul'. Several thousand children attended classes in the open air and each class was known by the name of the tree they sat under, e.g. Eucalyptus Class, Avocado Class. Ms Sweeney said Trócaire's projects for children were 'giving back something of their childhood, the chance to be children again'.

In the aftermath of the war, many children had been orphaned, separated from their families or left wandering around on their own. Young as they were, many were traumatised by the horrific experiences they had suffered. One child, who had lived with her grandmother in Kigali because her parents had died when she was still a baby, told how men came and burned down the house and killed her grandmother. They then took her and buried her near a papaya tree – they threw her in a hole and put a lot of soil on top. Then they beat her on the head even though she was under the soil. She did not know how long she was there but she was eventually found and taken out of the soil.

Trócaire's projects were educating children to be independent and self-sufficient while at the same time providing emotional support. The children were taught technical and agricultural skills and healthcare also.

In the autumn of 1995, Trócaire recruited one of the few Rwandans living in Ireland at the time to work as a resource person advising the agency's team in Rwanda. Her name was Mukangiliye Nkunda but she was known as Colette Craven because she had married Offaly man Noel Craven in Rwanda in 1987; he was working there for the EEC at the time. They and their son were evacuated during the genocide and came to live in Ireland. Ms Craven lost her mother, her brother and eighteen other relatives during the tragedy and their bodies have never been recovered. In a recent interview for this book, she said that despite the major change in her life that moving to Ireland involved, and despite being traumatised by the losses she had suffered, her settling into Ireland was made easier by the welcoming attitude that she experienced from the Irish people that she met.

Her knowledge of Rwanda, its cultural differences and its many complexities was invaluable to Trócaire's work there. In her recent interview, she said that her first return to the country, since her hurried evacuation in the summer of 1994, was extremely traumatic. Her job was to aid in the drawing up of a strategic plan as to how the funds donated by the Irish people to Trócaire should be spent in Rwanda. She said that the agency's approach, as always, was based on partnership and they thus set about finding good partners who were firmly rooted in their local communities. She said that they also played to Trócaire's strengths and focused on areas such as justice and human rights. It took some time, Ms Craven said, to identify really good partners, ones that could make some impact on what she described as such a deprived society, but the time taken was time well spent, she believed, and for her the results were positive.

A major part of the programme was trauma counselling. There was a widespread need for it, especially among women and children. However, in their culture, Ms Craven explained, they did not have any kind of counselling. Suffering was meant to be endured and the attitude was, 'We have to be strong'. Thus, trauma counselling was something completely new and they even had to invent a new word to mean 'counselling', she said.

Ms Craven also drew attention to another aspect of the Trócaire programme in Rwanda – its dealings with the country's government. Parts of the programme worked with a number of ministries: Justice, Women and Gender and Agriculture. As an NGO, Trócaire had to exercise special care when working with government organs, she said. She referred in particular to the work the agency did in relation to the key area of justice and prisons. Trócaire had to be very careful to maintain a balanced approach at all times. She was always especially aware of the importance, for Trócaire's image, of not becoming labelled a pro-government NGO.

In February 1996, Alphonsine Mutabonwa Abia, a Trócaire project coordinator in Rwanda, came to Ireland. She spoke to church congregations and schoolchildren in Dublin and Belfast about Rwanda and Trócaire's work there and said that the international community had a vital role to play in helping the Kigali government to bring the perpetrators of the genocide to justice. Failure to punish those involved in previous genocidal outbursts was a factor in the recurrence of such outrages.

Some work had already been done by the new regime in building a judicial system and genocide trials would shortly begin. She expressed the belief that people would become reconciled when that work began, but warned that the process cost a lot of money and said that Trócaire wanted the international community to assist the Rwandan government in bringing people to justice. Some 60,000 were being held in Rwanda in relation to the genocide, she explained, and there were many other suspected perpetrators outside the country.

Ms Abia explained that following earlier massacres and the flight of large numbers of refugees, mostly Tutsis and Hutu moderates, governments then in power had worked against people returning, arguing that Rwanda did not have land to accommodate them. Her own father had been killed in 1963 and the rest of her family had fled to Uganda where the children grew up in a refugee camp. She herself, a psychiatric nurse, social worker and counsellor, had lived in a number of countries before returning to work for Trócaire in Rwanda, where the agency was training local people to work as trauma counsellors.

Most of the people they saw, she said, were widows. With genocide, because everyone suffers, people suppress their feelings. But Trócaire received a positive response to their counselling service, with people saying it was good to express feelings and the community reaction showed the need was there, Ms Abia said.

She would not discuss her own ethnic background and said that Tutsis and Hutus did not fulfil the criteria for being called tribes – they did not have the characteristics unique to one group. It was like clans in Ireland, e.g. O'Briens and Martins, she said. She denied a report that 100,000 Hutus died in 1994 in systematic killing 'tolerated if not organised' by the RPA. Trócaire representatives on the ground said that there had been arbitrary killing for revenge by RPA forces in 1994 but it had not been systematic or at the level claimed in the report.

Upheaval in Burundi and danger of regional war

In the summer of 1996, Trócaire made an urgent appeal for funds because a crisis in Burundi led to thousands of Burundian refugees fleeing to Butare in Rwanda. In addition, the forced repatriation of Rwandan refugees was ongoing. Rosemary Heenan in Butare said that an extra 8,000 had moved into Magara camp, which already had a population of over 50,000, including possible armed elements, so there was a lot of concern about the possible closure of that particular camp. Ms Heenan said that at the time the situation was very tense with the continuing escalation in the crisis a few miles away from them in Burundi, and the concern in Rwanda was that there would be problems in the communes when people returned.

With the coup in Burundi in late July 1996, there were a number of massacres in the camps and the Burundian army began to repatriate forcefully 85,000 refugees who had fled the genocide in Rwanda in 1994. There were more than 10,000 people at the Trócaire-run transit camp in Butare, just across the border from Burundi, and hundreds of refugees were arriving by the day because of the forced repatriation. Though most of these refugees were in good physical condition, Trócaire found several suffocated to death in the container trucks being used to transport them.

The agency sent emergency supplies of plastic sheeting and blankets. Refugees who left the transit camps to return to the homes they had fled from three years before were given two months' supply of maize, beans, oil and other necessities.

As the violence continued in Burundi, Trócaire denounced as totally inadequate the EU presidency statement (held by Ireland) on the situation there. Justin Kilcullen said that Burundian society was disintegrating and all the EU could offer was platitudes, a reaction that was 'morally and legally bankrupt'. He said the Irish government had to take effective action immediately to stop what was in effect genocide in Burundi.

By October 1996, a dangerous situation had developed on the Rwandan/Zaire border, in Kivu Province in south-eastern Zaire where about 250,000 people of Rwandan Tutsi origin had been living for 200 years. These people, known as the Banyamulenge, were coming under increasing pressure to move to Rwanda. The Zairean authorities called their legal status into question although they had lived in that area for generations.

Eamonn Meehan, who had returned from Rwanda shortly before that, said the Banyamulenge were coming under increased pressure from both the Zairean government and Hutu militias who remained very much intact in the refugee camps. Local militias were trying to take their land from the Banyamulenge and force them into Rwanda although they had never lived there, he said.

Trócaire had a representative working in a Rwandan refugee camp for around 15,000 Tutsis who had been forced out of their homes in Masisi in Zaire. Mr Meehan said that it was a very volatile and dangerous situation and part of the larger problem in Rwanda, Burundi and eastern Zaire. The UN was working on a plan to reduce the numbers in the refugee camps by encouraging those willing to return to Rwanda, he said, adding that the situation was getting worse every day.

The 'Banyamulenge uprising' followed and the Tutsi-dominated Rwandan and Burundi governments supported them, while the old Rwandan army supported the Zairean forces. The danger existed of full-scale war erupting involving Rwanda, Zaire and Burundi but also Uganda and Angola.

In the same month, Mayo priest and writer Fr Colm Kilcoyne visited Rwanda on a Trócaire-sponsored trip. Buildings full of dead and rotten corpses and the numerous mass graves he saw were, he said, the stuff of nightmares. However, he had good memories of the Trócaire workers he met in Rwanda to counterbalance the memories of the horrors. Among these workers were a young engineer helping survivors to rebuild bridges and schools; a health educator working with Rwandans to put the medical service back on its feet; another training Rwandans in trauma counselling; and a religious sister who was into 'honey production, fish ponds, women's groups ... These are all part of the Trócaire team in just one area, Gikongoro. They'd say they are just doing a job. I'd say they are heroes,' he wrote.

As fighting intensified along the Rwanda/Zaire border, large numbers of refugees fled into Rwanda. Trócaire was asked by the UN to provide water and sanitation facilities in a camp in the Gisenyi Prefecture of Rwanda, some twenty kilometres from Goma, to deal with the anticipated influx of refugees. Trócaire rushed £130,000 worth of aid to the area to cope with the new crisis. The aid was sent via Caritas Rwanda and was used to buy food, medicines and shelter for the displaced.

Eamonn Meehan said that the crisis was more difficult to cope with than the original tragedy in 1994, when all the refugees congregated in a specific area. Now the camps were being emptied, people were moving deeper into Zaire and a war was raging, so from a security point of view it was not possible for NGOs and the UN to provide a humanitarian response. He warned of the danger of Zaire disintegrating as the many factions within the country would take the opportunity to rebel against Kinshasa. There was also the danger that more than a million Rwandan refugees still in camps would seek arms to return to Rwanda to fight.

The intensified fighting caused the aid agencies to pull back their workers, and the refugees became increasingly difficult to reach in early November 1996, but the prospects for an intervention to save some 1.2 million stranded refugees in eastern Zaire improved after President Mobutu gave permission. The Rwandan government also changed its position and asked UN agencies and the NGOs to launch a major operation across its border. But Hutu militias and Tutsi rebels made the agencies' task a difficult and dangerous one as they tried to get aid through to the Zairean town of Goma and to the nearby Mugunga camp.

In mid-November, the estimated 800,000 refugees in Mugunga camp (until that time among the largest refugee camps in the world) were forced to leave the camp and return to Rwanda. Trócaire's emergency team warned that the situation on the Rwandan border had reached a critical point. The agency's coordinator, Niall Tóibín, said that Trócaire had a team preparing for the arrival of the refugees on the Rwandan side of the border, with trucks laden with beans, high-energy biscuits, plastic sheeting and medical supplies being unloaded. It was a massive logistical undertaking for the relief agencies to look after so many refugees. Trócaire launched a successful appeal in Ireland, which raised £1.1 million.

Some Trócaire workers on the ground gave an idea of what was involved in coping with the flood of returning refugees. The small Trócaire team in Gisenyi was quickly augmented by staff from other parts of Rwanda and from Ireland, including a doctor, a nurse, sanitation and water engineers and logistics personnel. Once news of the huge exodus from Magunga came, they sprang into action. By the time the first refugees reached the Rwandan border, they were provided with water and other needs by the Trócaire team.

Then, emergency officer Mary Sweeney led a team across the border to Goma, where tens of thousands were queuing patiently to gain entry into Rwanda. Working with missionary priests and sisters and the local Caritas organisation, Trócaire provided vital quantities of oral rehydration salts and other medicines to the refugees.

On the Rwandan side of the border, Trócaire staff did everything possible to help the mass of refugees flooding across from Zaire. Some of the staff worked in the large reception camp on the border while others served in the way stations that stretched along the road leading from Gisenyi to the town of Ruhengeri, twenty miles inside Rwanda.

Mary Sweeney said that she had never seen so many refugees on the move at any one time despite her long experience of African emergencies. She said that Trócaire did everything possible to help as many as they could but that the numbers needing assistance were of biblical proportions. She found it infuriating and heartbreaking to see small babies and children on the verge of death because their families had been unable to get water for days due to the fighting.

Bishop John Kirby, who visited the area, described the tide of human suffering flowing into Rwanda as 'awesome', the likes of which he had never imagined. He was particularly disturbed by the sight of tens of thousands – men, women, children and the elderly – sleeping out on the sides of roads in the pouring rain, all of them exhausted after days without adequate food or water.

Nevertheless, there was hope that the massive return to Rwanda would bring some kind of resolution to the crisis in central Africa. It was felt that a real possibility of peace now seemed to exist with the return of the refugees.

However, there were still many and huge problems to overcome. In early December 1996, Trócaire reported that Zaire, Burundi and Rwanda were on the verge of a catastrophe. Hundreds of thousands had been displaced as a result of the fighting and were threatened with sickness and death from hunger and disease. The agency made an urgent appeal for funds to help it continue with its work in central Africa.

Slowly returning to normal

A report in the *Irish Times* in early January 1997 showed how life in Rwanda was very slowly beginning to return to normal and it also showed Trócaire's involvement in that snail-like but vital process. The report was headlined 'Women's co-op could be best hope for Rwanda', referring to Promotion Feminine, described in the article as 'a women's cooperative designed to keep what little money there is in Gikongoro in the local economy'.

At lunchtime, the co-op served fish harvested in ponds in Kavili. A group of twenty women managed two ponds, harvesting around fifty kilograms of perch twice a year. The fish were sold in the market in Gikongoro and the resulting profits were reinvested in the farm or distributed among the women for their own use. The common link in these projects was outside involvement because in a country as damaged as Rwanda, where the cash economy was virtually non-existent outside the towns, the wherewithal to improve the lot of the rural poor was limited.

The *Irish Times'* report said that development projects such as those coordinated by Trócaire in Gikongoro were crucial to the future of Rwanda. Now that peace, however uneasy, reigned, and most of the refugees had returned, the hard task of rebuilding the rural infrastructure was beginning. The bloody genocide in 1994 was completed in just six weeks but the reconstruction of society would take decades. The report remarked that whatever hope there was for Rwanda might lie in applying the cooperative and self-help principles that were so successfully used to develop Irish agriculture in the past. The positioning of women as the linchpin of rural development also paralleled the Irish experience, the report said.

Trócaire's £1 million development programme in Gikongoro included a number of schemes in which local farmers and women's groups were given low-interest loans to buy new stock or open a business. The schemes were integrated into the local economy and were run by locals. Some of the agricultural schemes provided seeds, tools and technical help to plant new crops (Irish potatoes proved very popular and successful). These new crops partly went to feed goats and chickens bought with a loan from Trócaire.

In early March 1997, President Robinson visited Rwanda to address a women's conference at which she was critical of the incompetence and slowness of the UN tribunal set up to try perpetrators of the genocide. She also visited the Trócaire-run project in Kigali.

At that time, Zairean rebel advances into eastern Rwanda raised the prospect of a new refugee crisis after up to 170,000 refugees had to flee makeshift camps at Tingi Tingi to avoid the fierce fighting. Mrs Robinson called for a comprehensive international conference involving the UN and the Organisation of African Union states to look for a stability pact for the region and to settle peace, security and development issues.

In mid-April 1997, the Irish soldiers stationed at Collins Barracks, Cork held a fund-raising walk to build a drop-in centre for street children in Gikongoro. Mike Williams, Trócaire director of operations in Rwanda, praised the military personnel's effort and predicted their project would greatly benefit the street children. He described the latter as the 'forgotten' ones and explained that as well as lacking basic necessities such as food and shelter, many of them suffered from malaria, TB and scabies and were subject to all kinds of harassment. All of this was on top of the trauma they were experiencing having witnessed the awful atrocities of the 1994 genocide.

The new centre would be somewhere the children could come to be fed, educated and in general cared for; it would offer them some kind of security in an existence that had up to that time offered them none. He hoped that in a few years the scheme would be self-funding, when the agriculture and carpentry projects the organising committee were hoping to put in place would provide the centre with a small income. The project had also received the assurance of support from the Ministry of Youth in Rwanda.

At the end of July 1997, Justin Kilcullen wrote to the papers referring to a letter of a fortnight before in which a group of agencies and individuals had rightly highlighted the need for the Irish government to support moves to arrest war-crimes suspects by the International Criminal Tribunal at The Hague. He said that the failure by the international community to administer justice and to end impunity was what caused further violence. He expressed the belief that the vast majority of those responsible for the millions of grave human rights violations, which had occurred since World War II, had escaped justice, and he remarked that the domino effect of impunity was evident in conflicts throughout the world.

Concerning Rwanda, he said that up to the previous month, only twenty-three people had been issued with indictments by the Arusha International Tribunal (the International Criminal Tribunal for Rwanda set up by the United Nations in Arusha, Tanzania in 1995). The trials of three of those were going on but none had been completed. These delays, he argued, were leading to an increasing lack of confidence in the tribunal and had to be urgently addressed.

At the same time, the international community had a crucial role to play in rebuilding the justice system within Rwanda and providing adequate resources to this end. At a regional level, African governments bore a key responsibility for arresting suspects in the genocide whom they knew to be sheltering in their jurisdiction. History told us that old conflicts had a habit of repeating, unless a just peace was achieved, he concluded.

(The Arusha International Tribunal is continuing and its mandate is to have completed proceedings by 2010. So far, twenty-nine individuals have been convicted. A number of trials are in progress and a number of suspects still await trial. Some suspects are still at large and some may be dead.)

The sheer numbers arrested and imprisoned for suspected involvement in the genocide threatened to overwhelm the Rwandan court system (the Arusha Tribunal limited itself to high-level accused only). In response, the Rwandan government in 2001 set up the 'gacaca' system: community-based courts that traditionally settled village or familial disputes. Under this system, people are elected and trained locally and serve as village juries to try genocide suspects. The system is not without its flaws but it is serving to administer some sort of punishment and, at the same time, provide some sort of satisfaction for victims of the atrocities.

Mary Healy, who has attended some sittings of the gacaca, said in her recent interview for this book that there have been some very profound moments where people confessed and the relatives of their victims became reconciled – or not – to them. She said that such proceedings may seem very small-scale if one compares them to Arusha but, for people living in the villages, they are of great importance. The process is ongoing and has worked very well in some places and less well in others, she said; overall, she believes it has done much more good than harm.

In the context of what happened in Rwanda overall, Ms Healy sees the role the church played in particular, whether the Irish missionaries or the local Rwandan church, as being very important. She singled out for mention Fr Nicky Hennity, who arrived in Rwanda when the genocide was happening. She believes he has played an extraordinarily important role in reconciliation at a community level, and also in the exhumation of mass graves and the reburial ceremonies for the people found there.

On the negative side for the church was the involvement of some of its members in the genocide and a failure to be as supportive of its members as it could perhaps have been. Ms Healy said that there are questions about whether the church in some areas was quick enough to open its doors to people who were in danger or did enough to defend them when they took sanctuary in churches. It is probably fair to say that the church, as a moral authority, did not do enough to try to prevent the tragedy from happening.

On Trócaire boxes for its Lenten campaign of 2004 was the image of Josienne. Her father and three older brothers were murdered in a church during the 1994 genocide; she, her mother and her two younger brothers survived when neighbours hid them in their houses.

By 2004, Josienne was a healthy twelve year old and the picture on the boxes showed her skipping. She was attending one of the secondary schools Trócaire had supported and her brothers were attending the local primary school. The Trócaire programme officer in Rwanda at the time, Mark Cumming, said that Josienne was doing well, as was her mother, and that her schooling was progressing well. With Trócaire support, a soya-milk processing plant had been established in their community, giving employment to many of the survivors of the genocide. An adult-literacy programme was launched in the area in 2005.

Following the genocide, Trócaire and Caritas Rwanda funded a unique, parish-linked justice and reconciliation project, the only one of its kind in the country. Started by a Ugandan priest, Fr Jerome Nasizo, the work, which is ongoing, brings women widowed during the genocide together with women whose husbands were imprisoned for committing crimes during that time. The work allows neighbours, parishes and communities to heal and rebuild together.

Trócaire's programme in Rwanda continues to contribute to the restoration of normality there. Colette Craven, who has been back to Rwanda many times since her enforced evacuation from the country during the tragic summer of 1994, says that life has been returning to normal. 'We never forget what has happened,' she said. 'People live with the memory but move on; life has to move on and cannot be lived in the past.'

CHAPTER 13:
The Tragic Fate of Nigeria's Ogoni People

Early Trócaire initiatives in Nigeria

Trócaire was involved in development work in Nigeria since the 1970s, working through the Catholic Secretariat of Nigeria. Sister Nora McNamara, of the Holy Rosary Sisters, Killeshandra, Co. Cavan, spearheaded a development programme to help farmers in Kwara State. Climatic conditions, disease, lack of knowledge of modern farming methods and a failure to appreciate the cooperative ideal all served to hold these smallholders back. Trócaire grant-aided Sr Nora's development programme.

Sr Nora's programme involved 7,000 farmers by 1975 and aimed to reach 20,000 eventually. The idea behind the scheme was the establishment of farmers' councils. The scheme began with ten councils with an average of fifteen members each. The farmers retained their own individual farms but worked communally at the same time, where they learned modern farming methods. From ten initially, the number of farmers' councils had risen to 265 by 1975, and two local full-time social development workers had been employed, with Trócaire paying their salaries over a three-year period.

This one scheme alone showed what could be achieved in promoting the cooperative ideal among people who had never been aware of it before. Support for the Kwara prog -

ramme was part of a Trócaire allocation of £21,500 in 1975 towards sixteen projects in health, agriculture, education and training in Nigeria.

In that year also, Trócaire helped to tackle illiteracy in Kaduna, in northern Nigeria, where a media service centre, run by the Holy Rosary Sisters, was involved in an education programme for rural women. The project was for 100 sets of audio-visual programmes that were shown in health clinics, social centres, village halls and schools, and for the publication of a booklet in Hausa, the local language.

In 1977, Trócaire gave a grant to support a village industry programme in Nigeria, which provided better housing for people in rural areas. Most houses were made of mud block and seldom lasted longer than five years. Burnt-brick houses could be provided if the finance was made available to build kilns. The clay for bricks was available locally and so was the wood for fuel. Trócaire's grant supplemented the money raised by the people themselves to start a local burnt-brick industry. The project became self-supporting once the first bricks had been sold. As well as providing improved housing, the industry provided employment.

In July 1978, Trócaire allocated £10,000 towards a social development programme in one of Nigeria's poorest regions. The programme covered agriculture, health and adult education and was designed to assist people to develop these activities within their own communities.

The Nigerian Sr Bernadette Eyewan Okure was one of the speakers at Trócaire's tenth anniversary seminar in UCG in June 1983. She represented the Cardoso Community Project in the sprawling slum of Ajengunle on the outskirts of Lagos, where a fifty-strong team of Nigerians, along with an Irish and an English sister, ran a non-formal, voluntary aid prog - ramme for deprived slum dwellers. The project, a Catholic Church initiative, included a health programme based on prevention, a clinic for the handicapped, an adult-literacy club, a women's training unit and an employment guidance service.

Trócaire continued to fund many such development projects in Nigeria throughout the 1980s and into the 1990s.

Supporting the struggle for Ogoni rights

Nigeria was under military rule from 1966–1979 and again from 1983–1999. General Sani Abacha, who took power in yet another military coup in late 1993, was perhaps Nigeria's most brutal ruler; he employed violence on a broad scale to suppress any opposition.

Half a million of the Ogoni people lived in the Niger Delta, an oil-rich region in south-eastern Nigeria. The oil fields, which were run by Shell, brought severe pollution and environmental damage to the region. In 1990, after years of oppression, the Ogoni began to organise themselves, literally to ensure their own survival. The Movement for the Survival of the Ogoni People (MOSOP) was formed to force the oil companies to clean up the environmental mess caused by their operations and to pressurise the government to pass on a greater share of its oil revenue to the Ogoni.

The response from the Abacha military regime was one of widespread violence against the Ogoni. The leader of the MOSOP, the distinguished writer, campaigner and Nobel Peace Prize nominee, Ken Saro-Wiwa, was arrested many times in 1993. Arrested again in May 1994, he and eight col - leagues were charged with inciting the murder of four moderate Ogoni politicians. The nine were sentenced to death after a trial by a special tribunal that was condemned by international observers.

Amnesty International denounced the trial as politically motivated and blatantly unfair. Britain and the Common - wealth countries deplored the sentences and urged the Nigerian government to commute them, as did the Irish government.

Sr Majella McCarron, who was based in Nigeria, visited Trócaire around this time. She told the agency of the terrible things that were happening in Ogoniland where she had been working. She urged Trócaire to speak out on behalf of the

Ogoni and to give them whatever help it could. As a result of Sr Majella's visit, what was happening in the south east of Nigeria became one of Trócaire's priority campaigns.

Trócaire called on the Nigerian government to release the nine Ogoni leaders, saying that they should be tried fairly by an independent body. The agency ran a full-page advertisement in the Irish newspapers under the heading: 'Ken Saro-Wiwa's only crime was to campaign for his people. Now the Nigerian military regime wants to kill him for it.' The advertisement explained that the Ogoni were among twenty ethnic groups who made up the six million people living in the Niger Delta, that this oil-rich area provided more than 90 per cent of Nigeria's exports and 80 per cent of government revenue, but that the Ogoni had received no benefits from the natural resources of their land. Since 1958, when oil was discovered there, an estimated $30 billion worth had been extracted from Ogoniland, yet the people who lived there were among the poorest in Nigeria. There was no running water, no electricity, few roads or schools and just one hospital.

The daily oppression by the military government was adding to the poverty of the Ogoni, the advertisement said, and it quoted the following from an Amnesty International report: 'Members of the internal security taskforce were sent into Ogoniland to instigate attacks on villages. Troops fired at random, killing, assaulting and raping, setting fire to homes, destroying livestock and driving people into the bush … Many of these people are reported to have died from starvation, sickness or neglected wounds.'

Mary Sweeney, emergency officer with Trócaire, witnessed at first hand the destroyed villages and the degraded land. 'I was appalled at how many homes had been totally destroyed and concerned by the very obvious military presence,' she was quoted as saying. Trócaire was supporting the Ogoni in rebuilding their homes and villages, the advertisement said. Thirty-seven years after Shell had begun drilling for oil in the area, 400 square miles of Ogoniland were dotted with oil spills, contaminated water and gas flames.

The advertisement explained that Ken Saro-Wiwa and his co-accused had been held incommunicado for seven months before they were charged and that during the trial proceedings, members of the defence team and relatives of the defendants had been subjected to harassment, physical attack and detention. In addition, two prosecution witnesses had admitted that they were bribed. Any pretence of the tribunal being independent was made impossible by the fact that it was appointed by the military government and took place outside of both Nigerian and international standards of law. The sentenced had been given no right of appeal, the advertisement concluded.

On 10 November 1995, Ken Saro-Wiwa and his eight colleagues were hanged. The reaction worldwide was one of shock and anger. The Irish government condemned the killings and Irish NGOs called for the expulsion of the Nigerian ambassador to Ireland and economic sanctions against the military junta. Trócaire led a candlelight protest the following evening outside the Nigerian embassy in Dublin. Speaking at the protest, Annette Honan, newly appointed campaigns officer with Trócaire (the organisation's first full-time campaigns officer), said that although the international community would now issue statements of condemnation, after the event, their silence was deafening when the sentences were handed down 'by Abacha's kangaroo court'.

Trócaire called for 'more than words, more than diplomatic delicacies' to challenge the human rights abuses in Ogoniland. The role of Shell Oil in the region was condemned by many organisations. Ms Honan said that everyone knew that Ken Saro-Wiwa and the eight other Ogoni had been killed because they dared to protest peacefully against the ecological and social damage caused by the oil companies, and Shell in particular, to their land.

Following the killings, Trócaire and a number of other groups issued a joint statement making a number of demands. These included the release of the bodies of the nine for proper burial; that the oil industry pay a fair compensation to the people adversely affected by oil activities; that the oil companies clean up the environmental pollution; that the Irish government and all Irish companies with links with Nigeria use their influence to bring an end to the human and environmental abuses; that an international oil embargo on all Nigerian oil and gas products be put in place; and that there be an immediate ban on all arms sales to Nigeria.

Later in November 1995, Justin Kilcullen wrote to the newspapers expressing Trócaire's deep regret at the position taken by Shell in refusing to use its influence in defence of justice and human rights in Nigeria. Shell's official statement said that a large multinational company like theirs could not and should not interfere in the affairs of any large sovereign state, and referred to Shell's Statement of General Business Principles, issued to the press on 8 November. Among these principles, said Justin Kilcullen, was: 'The need is recognised to take a constructive interest in societal matters which may not be directly related to the business.'

He went on to say that the societal problems in Nigeria created by the military dictatorship there demanded a strong response from everyone. In the face of such blatant injustice and human suffering, every voice, especially those of influence, had to defend the weak and the defenceless, he argued.

The considerable influence of Shell International in Nigeria was indisputable, Mr Kilcullen contended; because it produced 50 per cent of Nigeria's oil and owned 30 per cent of the Nigerian National Petroleum Corporation, of which the Nigerian government was the biggest stakeholder, Shell had considerable power. He regarded the argument that it should not interfere in the politics of Nigeria as 'untenable and dishonest'. It was already politically involved by virtue of its strong economic relations and business partnerships with the regime, he maintained.

Mr Kilcullen contended that in the climate existing in Nigeria, economics and politics were deeply intertwined. He thought it 'particularly unfortunate' that in the same week as the Ogoni campaigners were sentenced to death, Shell chose to strengthen its ties with the dictatorship further by proceeding with a major gas deal.

He said their claim that such investment would benefit the people was 'highly questionable' because Trócaire knew from its partners on the ground that the profits from oil revenue had not benefited the ordinary people. Instead, there was spiralling poverty for the majority and no social services, with schools, hospitals and communities in ruins. Contrary to what Shell said, it was the case that the oil revenue enabled the military regime to survive despite mismanagement at every level.

Therefore, Trócaire called on Shell to withdraw completely from Nigeria until democratic government was restored. Its partners in Nigeria had told Trócaire that the current oppressive government would not give up power willingly and that the most effective way to bring about its demise was through a Nigerian oil embargo.

In January 1996, Justin Kilcullen again wrote to the newspapers to remind people that three years before, at that time of year, over 300,000 Ogoni people celebrated their national day in song, dance and peaceful demonstrations. The Ogoni Day march of 4 January 1993 was a milestone in the Ogoni movement, he said, bringing together more than half the Ogoni population in one place in peaceful protest against the environmental and social change caused by the oil companies operating in their lands.

Since that time, he explained, the Ogoni had been the target of a brutal reign of government repression, resulting in the deaths of thousands of them and the destruction of villages and livelihoods. Shell had insisted, he said, that it was not its role to get involved in the political situation of any country in which it operated, yet reports in the *Sunday Times* and other newspapers contradicted those claims and alleged a close relationship between Shell Nigeria and representatives of the brutal military dictatorship.

That particular week, he continued, the Ogoni were unable to assemble to mark national Ogoni Day. There were around 4,000 troops deployed in Ogoniland, an area the size of Co. Louth. All assemblies had been banned and even children going to school suffered intimidation and beatings. He finished by saying that Trócaire believed that Shell held considerable influence in Nigeria and that it was not too late to use it in the promotion of human rights.

Early in 1996, Trócaire joined with Action from Ireland (AfrI) and the Body Shop to form Ogoni Solidarity Ireland (OSI). Annette Honan was Trócaire's representative in the organisation and her work at political level led to the appearance of a Shell representative and an Ogoni environmental campaigner before the Oireachtas Foreign Affairs Committee of the Dáil in early February 1996. OSI had been calling for a boycott of Shell petrol and other products to focus attention on the degradation of life for the Ogoni. It wanted people to use their consumer power.

The Shell representative told the committee that the company was being used as a lever to influence the campaigners' real enemy, the dictatorship of General Abacha. But OSI challenged a Shell assertion that it did not get involved in politics by saying that it had been propping up corrupt and dictatorial Nigerian regimes for the majority of its sixty years of operation in that country. It also said that if Shell were to pull out of the entire Niger Delta, it would be of huge benefit to the Nigerian people.

The Ogoni environmental advocate said that Shell had a private army of up to 2,500. It was called the 'Shell Police' and wore Nigerian police uniforms, while it also, he said, supplied arms to the military in Nigeria. The Shell representative denied this although another Shell spokesperson had apparently admitted as much to the *Observer* newspaper the previous week.

Although Shell claimed it preferred dialogue when local problems arose, Annette Honan denied this and said that too often the response had been to use the regular Nigerian police or the Shell police.

Both Shell and a briefing document from the Nigerian embassy in Dublin referred to the company's work in building hospitals and schools for the Ogoni but OSI said that a sense of perspective should be kept on this. The Shell representative before the Oireachtas committee referred to a programme to build 'cottage hospitals'; six had been built and this was to increase to twelve, but there were six million people living in the Niger Delta. As to how much money allocated to community projects actually got to the projects, OSI said that the big issue in Nigeria was corruption and mismanagement, and that included Shell.

In a recent interview for this book, Annette Honan commented on what good partners Trócaire had on the ground in Nigeria. She recalled Fr Kevin O'Hara, who was particularly informative about the destructive impact of Shell's presence on the Niger Delta. (Fr O'Hara was a Trócaire partner for many years and did much vital work on behalf of prisoners and their rights.) These witnesses on the ground and the information they provided enabled Trócaire to organise an effective campaign, safe in the knowledge that it had its facts right, Ms Honan remarked.

In May 1996, she and Eamonn Meehan planned to go to Nigeria with three members of the Oireachtas Foreign Affairs Committee: Therese Ahern (Fine Gael), Pat Gallagher (Labour) and Michael Kitt (Fianna Fáil). Trócaire was organising the trip and they intended to spend a week in Nigeria meeting government representatives as well as human rights and pro-democracy groups, Irish missionaries, religious leaders and political detainees. The Nigerian embassy in Dublin was informed of the planned visit on 4 April and formal visa applications were made on 30 April, but by mid-May they still did not know if they would be granted visas.

In a press release, Eamonn Meehan said that at that critical time in Nigeria's history, it would be of great significance if Ireland could be the first EU country to succeed in sending a parliamentary delegation on a fact-finding mission. He said that the Nigerian government had undertaken to implement a transition to democratic rule but that Trócaire continued to receive different signals from opposition groups and human rights activists within Nigeria concerning the absence of basic freedoms.

When the Nigerian government decided to block the visit, on the grounds that it had 'previous commitments and a tight schedule', the decision was strongly criticised by Trócaire and the three public representatives involved. Mr Meehan said that the blocking of the visit was 'disappointing and incomprehensible' in the light of the repeated claims by the Nigerian government that its position had been misrepresented. He said that a visit of Irish parliamentarians would have served as a means of opening dialogue between Nigeria and the international community, especially in the context of Ireland assuming the presidency of the EU a few weeks after that time.

Mr Meehan pointed out that Ireland had strong cultural, humanitarian and missionary links with Nigeria. The decision posed serious questions about the Nigerian government's claim that the transition to democracy was proceeding as planned, including the claim that the ban on political activities had been lifted, he said. He added that it also called into question the claim that Nigerians enjoyed freedom of speech, movement and association.

Trócaire, he said, was particularly concerned about the conditions in which 'the Ogoni 19' and more than 100 other political detainees were being held. The Oireachtas delegation had hoped to meet with detainees, including imprisoned trade unionists, human rights lawyers, journalists and pro-democracy leaders, many of whom were remanded without trial and without access to legal or medical assistance.

In her recent interview, Annette Honan pointed to the massive publicity generated by Trócaire's attempt to organise the visit of the parliamentary delegation. She said it made major news at the time and she recalled being on national news bulletins on the day that the Nigerian government announced that they would not be allowing the visit. It was not a wasted effort trying to organise the trip, she said, because the Nigerian government's action simply highlighted the fact that it had something to hide.

In July 1996, Justin Kilcullen wrote to the *Irish Independent* in response to a correspondent who had decried the lack of 'courtesy' and 'respect' shown by those campaigning in Ireland on human rights abuses in Nigeria. The correspondent had claimed that the rulers in Nigeria at that time were trying to build a stable nation where all of its people would live in harmony.

Mr Kilcullen said that Trócaire very much regretted that information coming to it from Nigeria indicated a very different picture. Rather than building stability, it appeared, he said, that the military regime there was intent on holding on to power and wealth at the expense of the majority of the Nigerian people, and was causing enormous economic and political turmoil in the process. Numerous human rights organisations, such as Amnesty International, testified to a breakdown of law and a gross abuse of human rights, he continued, and he quoted Bishop Adelakun, chairman of the Episcopal Commission for Justice, Development and Peace, as describing the Nigerian leaders as 'greedy, power-hungry and self-centred, using their position and power to enrich themselves at the expense of the people'.

Justin Kilcullen referred to the suggestion of the *Irish Independent* correspondent of letting Nigerians find their own solutions. He said Trócaire very much agreed that the Nigerian people were well capable of identifying solutions to their own problems. However, the solidarity of the international community, both through humanitarian support and political advocacy, was crucial at that particular time in Nigeria's history, he maintained.

He explained that Trócaire had been supporting the people of Nigeria since 1973, through its long-term development projects, and would continue to support them in their struggle to build a better future and restore democracy. If the world sat by and left all the suffering people to 'find their own solutions', dictators and despots could freely rule and the international community would never raise its voice in favour of justice and human rights.

Remembering Ken Saro-Wiwa and continuing the campaign for Ogoni rights

Trócaire marked the first anniversary of the death of Ken Saro-Wiwa by taking out a full-page newspaper advertisement in Irish newspapers, with the headline: 'Ken Saro-Wiwa, thinking of you ...' The advertisement had a central picture of a noose with a candle at the end of it and eight similar pictures on the left-hand side of the advertisement with the names of the eight other Ogoni activists hanged with him.

The advertisement said that one year after the brutal execution of Ken Saro-Wiwa and eight other Ogoni by the military junta that ruled Nigeria, the oppression against the Ogoni had increased. Detentions, harsher prison conditions, increased poverty, repression of journalists, torture and death were the order of the day, said the advertisement, yet incredibly the EU and world governments sat back and waited for the democracy that the notorious General Abacha promised. Trócaire reminded people that nineteen more Ogoni awaited the same military tribunal that had condemned Ken Saro-Wiwa to death and that they faced a similar fate unless the world acted.

If the Nigerian military government did not listen before, why would they now, the advertisement asked. It went on to say that Trócaire believed that they had not listened before because the world did not shout loudly enough, and it did not use the powerful weapons it had – strong political and economic sanctions.

The advertisement pointed out that although Nigeria was the most populated country in Africa, with more than 100 million people, and although it had rich oil deposits, it was one of the most oppressed and impoverished. The Niger Delta, where the half million Ogoni lived, was once known as the 'food basket' of Nigeria. Since oil was discovered in 1958, the Ogoni oilfields had yielded Shell $30 billion. In return, the Ogoni had their air, water and land polluted and poisoned and themselves made impoverished. Shell International, in a joint oil partnership with the Nigerian government, relied on the military to stifle opposition in the oil-producing areas. Shell gave the military $10.8 million per day in oil revenue but still claimed it had no influence to save the Ogoni 19.

The advertisement concluded with the message that the Ogoni had suffered enough and it urged people to support Trócaire's campaign by writing to the Irish government to ask it to put pressure on the EU to impose tougher political, economic and trade sanctions on Nigeria. The advertisement also urged people to write to the Nigerian ambassador, demanding the release of all political detainees and the Ogoni 19, and to send a donation to support Trócaire's work with the Ogoni.

Since the MOSOP's very effective campaign had caused Shell to leave Ogoniland in late 1993, the company had been seeking an opportunity to return. It relied heavily on a public-relations campaign to create a more caring image of the corporation. Early in 1997, Environmental Rights Action (the Nigerian branch of the Friends of the Earth organisation) published a report, 'Shell in Nigeria: Public Relations and Broken Promises', which concluded that the company did little more than engage in 'sophisticated perception manage-ment' rather than clean up its act or do many of the socially beneficial things it claimed to have done.

In addition, a MOSOP leader who visited Ogoniland in early 1997 passed on his testimony to Trócaire. He detailed how Shell were attempting to bribe and cajole residents of the area into declaring publicly that they wanted Shell to return to their area. (The army used more robust methods than bribery or cajolery.) Shell would then use such declarations as proof to convince a sceptical world. As part of their approach, payment of compensation for spillages was made conditional on the litigant producing a passport photo of himself and being caught on video supporting Shell's return, the testimony of the MOSOP leader said.

In late October 1997, Trócaire called for the expulsion of Nigeria from the British Commonwealth over human rights violations. Along with the Irish Missionary Union and Ogoni Solidarity Ireland, it also called for trade sanctions, including an oil embargo.

Nigeria had been suspended from the commonwealth following the execution of Ken Saro-Wiwa and the eight other Ogoni leaders, but Justin Kilcullen said that there had been no significant change in the country since then and that it was now time to exert the strongest possible pressure on the Nigerian government. He added that basic human rights were consistently violated by the police, military and judiciary in the country. 'Lengthy detention in inhuman conditions, unfair trials and torture continue to occur. Pro-democracy activists, journalists and human rights defenders are the most common victims,' he said.

Komene Famaa of the MOSOP was in Ireland at the end of October 1997 and said that an oil embargo could not hurt the ordinary people of Nigeria (an argument often trotted out in opposition to an embargo) because they received no benefits from the industry anyway. He said that the military police in the oil-rich delta area terrorised innocent civilians so that they did not have the courage to speak of the environmental devastation and social injustice that resulted from the oil industry.

In mid-January 1998, Trócaire called on the Department of Foreign Affairs to take urgent diplomatic action to press for the release of the scores of Ogoni arrested and detained without charge by the Nigerian military. The arrests, accompanied by widespread beatings and sexual assaults, had occurred in the run-up to the celebration of Ogoni Day on 4 January.

Justin Kilcullen said that these most recent mass arrests and incidents of torture proved that trade sanctions, especially an oil embargo, should be imposed immediately on the Nigerian regime. 'In Nigeria, it is cheaper to bury environmentalists and democrats than oil pipelines,' he said, adding that 'civilised values, civil society and international standards' had no place in Nigeria, where it was the agents of the state who were acting like terrorists and the human rights activists who were acting peacefully.

Ledum Mitee, president of the MOSOP, addressed Trócaire's twenty-fifth anniversary conference in late February 1998. He said that the UN's Universal Declaration of Human Rights meant very little when there were no official sanctions against multinational corporations who violated human rights.

The Ogoni had suffered gravely since 1958 when Shell discovered rich oil wells in their lands, he said. Pollution had left locals unable to fish or farm, yet anyone demanding basic rights for the Ogoni was targeted by a 'security force' funded by Shell. This security force had instigated a 'scorched-earth policy' since 1993 that had left more than 2,000 dead, fifteen villages and communities destroyed and around 10,000 homeless.

He went on to say that their experience raised questions about the seriousness and credibility of the international community's commitment to human rights, especially where profitable economic resources were involved. He considered the issue vital in a world where the nation state was being eroded while transnational corporations were becoming extremely powerful, to the point where they had become quasi-governments in developing countries.

Early in May 1998, Trócaire called on the Irish government to lobby for a complete oil embargo on Nigeria at the EU foreign ministers' council meeting at the end of that month. Trócaire made the call at an event marking World Press Freedom Day where the agency highlighted the continuing attacks on the media by the Nigerian military regime. It pointed out that that year a Nigerian journalist, Christina Anyanwu, was due to receive the 1998 World Press Freedom Prize but was unable to collect it because she was serving a fifteen-year prison term in a Nigerian jail.

At that time, the EU was enforcing an arms embargo on Nigeria and was refusing to issue visas to members of the country's military. In 1995, the EU had given Nigeria a three-year deadline to move from military dictatorship to democracy, but there was no sign that that deadline would be met.

Justin Kilcullen said that 'the right to the truth is the foundation of all other freedoms and rights' and he asked what message did it send to other repressive governments if the world sat back and allowed journalists in Nigeria to be hunted down, tortured and murdered for simply doing their work.

The military dictatorship of General Abacha came to an end in 1998 and Nigeria became a democracy again in 1999. The situation in Ogoniland did gradually improve as a result of the transition to democratic rule. Annette Honan said that people who were doing human rights work on the ground, many of whom were missionaries, now found themselves under much less pressure. Arbitrary arrests, being thrown into prison and not being brought to trial also came to an end, she said.

She described the campaign against Shell in Ogoniland as a 'wake-up call' to the entire oil industry that it could no longer go into communities, despoil the environment and ignore the wishes of the local people (or indeed, in some cases, have people killed who got in the way of or threatened their profit-making prospects). If anything good came out of the terrible things that happened to the Ogoni, Ms Honan believed it was that oil companies (including Shell) have put in place independently verifiable systems and procedures to ensure that what happened in Ogoniland can never happen again.

However, no attempts have been made by the Nigerian government to bring about justice by investigating and prosecuting those involved in the violence and environmental degradation that have occurred in Ogoniland.

CHAPTER 14:
North Korea: The 'Slow-Motion' Famine

In July 1995, horrific flooding swept through North Korea, wreaking havoc, destroying food crops and grain stores and laying the ground for what was described as a 'slow-motion' famine over the subsequent years.

In mid-March 1996, Trócaire announced that the first £10,000 that came in from its annual Trócaire 2FM 24-Hour Fast had gone to North Korea to help with the worsening situation there following the serious flooding of the year before. Marie Smith, Trócaire's Asia Officer at the time, had just returned from the region. She said that due to a lack of information coming from North Korea (a one-party, communist state where the media is tightly controlled), it was unknown exactly how many of the twenty-three million inhabitants were starving but the signs were not good, with a country full of empty warehouses and the next harvest many months away.

Ms Smith said that children were unable to attend school because of the bitterly cold weather (there was also a serious shortage of firewood and coal) and lack of food. She added that schools reported that many of the children were sick, suffering from malnutrition. Rice, soya soup and pickled cabbage were the sole foods available but in very limited quantities. Reports reaching her suggested that, despite the frost, thousands in the countryside were busy clearing and preparing the fields for the following spring.

The unprecedented floods seriously damaged North Korea's vulnerable agricultural sector and the trend worsened in 1996 and 1997. In late May 1997, Trócaire launched an appeal for £500,000 to help provide emergency food aid for more than five million North Koreans who were facing starvation. Kathi Zellweger of Caritas, a sister agency of Trócaire in Hong Kong, came to Dublin to launch the appeal. She described the catastrophe unfolding in North Korea as 'a famine in slow motion', and was one of the few Westerners allowed into the country. At the launch, she poured a handful of rice into a glass, saying that this was all the average North Korean had to eat each day.

On her most recent visit to North Korea, Ms Zellweger found schools and nurseries abandoned. The economy was collapsing; the roads were empty because of the lack of petrol and most trains had stopped running. Because the communist regime had sealed the country off, the famine had attracted little notice. The foreign media had been denied access and only a few observers and relief workers had witnessed the disaster.

Ms Zellweger said that a monitoring system had been established to ensure that food provided did not fall into the hands of the army. She believed that it was better to help North Korea through that critical period while pressing for greater liberalisation, rather than risk an outbreak of famine, which would cause great suffering as well as destabilising the region.

Also speaking at the launch, Justin Kilcullen compared the situation in North Korea to the Great Famine in Ireland. He said that when the potato failed in Ireland for the third time in 1847, there was nothing left to eat, and with the failure of the rice crop in North Korea for the third time, people there were on the brink of starvation. He expressed the belief that turning our backs on North Korea would have disastrous effects, not only on that country itself but on the whole region. He said that humanitarian organisations feared that a sudden collapse of the regime in North Korea could trigger massive outflows of refugees to South Korea and China.

While other Western governments had generally treated North Korea as a pariah, the Irish government had given £100,000 earlier in 1997, and the German and Canadian governments had also changed their minds and given relief aid. Trócaire up to that time had given £150,000 through Caritas Hong Kong.

In June 1997, Justin Kilcullen paid a four-day visit to North Korea. On his return, he told the Irish newspapers about a visit to a kindergarten in Sunchon city, in the south west of the country. The kindergarten was half-empty, with no noise or play in the classrooms, none of the life associated with a school. The children were thin, with vacant faces and runny noses, and were clearly unwell. His group asked about the other children and were told that some were at home, too weak to go to school, some were in hospital and others were dead. Many of its twenty-three million population were slowly starving to death, he said.

Mr Kilcullen went on to say that North Korea had no food left. People told his group that they had last received their ration four weeks before and nothing since. International aid had been promised but none had reached the areas he visited and he was told that the machinery to unload the ships at the port had broken down.

He referred to one woman who told them that she knew which grasses were nutritious, and which tree barks were edible and which poisonous. She mixed seaweed into a brew and when they asked her how many she was feeding from the small pot – no more than a snack to a Westerner – she replied six.

Justin Kilcullen had seen many African famines but he said that he had never seen anything like that in North Korea. He described it as an urban famine – people relied completely on state handouts and these had stopped. 'They are stranded on the twentieth floors of grim concrete housing blocks without the means to help themselves,' he said. The extraordinary thing was that the fields were all planted and people came out from the cities to help with the weeding now that there was no petrol to run the machinery to do that.

However, the harvest was five months away and the rainy season was due in July; if there were floods on the scale of the previous two years, the crops would be destroyed, he said. He explained that the experts had said that flooding was inevitable because so many trees had been felled and the topsoil would be washed away.

Travelling between his base in the capital, Pyongyang, and the countryside, Mr Kilcullen and the government officials who accompanied him had had the roads to themselves – the shortage of petrol had taken almost all cars off the road. There had not yet been mass starvation because the misery was shared equally but it had reached a critical point, he warned.

A photograph that Justin Kilcullen took of children in a kindergarten was one of the first images to emerge from North Korea at that time, bringing the world's attention to what was happening there. It featured in the American current-affairs magazine, *Newsweek*, and was chosen as one of the magazine's pictures of the year.

In July, Trócaire held special church collections for North Korea. The agency had reached its first aid target of £500,000, which provided rice and grain for 100,000 people until the next harvest. The aim was to raise a further £500,000 by the end of July to increase the numbers who could be helped. Trócaire had bought 2,500 tons of Vietnamese rice and the church collections were expected to fund another shipment the following week.

Trócaire was one of the few Western agencies with access to North Korea through its link with Caritas Hong Kong. By mid-August 1997, it had contributed £400,000 worth of food aid and announced a further £200,000 at that time. All the aid sent was monitored by the WFP of the United Nations to ensure that it reached the people most in need.

Early the following month, Trócaire's Mary Healy and Niamh O'Carroll went to North Korea to assess conditions.

They found an urgent situation, with the general hospital in Pyongyang full of dying children but with no food, water, medicine or electricity. At the port of Nampo, they saw thousands of bags of rice arriving by ship, but with the approach of winter the weakened people would have to contend with temperatures as low as minus forty degrees Celsius, while fuel shortages continued.

More rice was needed urgently, they said, but measures to ensure people's survival throughout the winter were most necessary – multivitamins and blankets needed to be delivered before winter set in. In addition, they spoke of the need to supply seeds for the harvest to be sown the following March and April.

Ms Healy held the position of Trócaire emergency officer at the time and was responsible for organising Trócaire's response to what was happening in the country. In a recent interview for this book, she said that she visited North Korea some six times within a relatively short period. She described it as an 'extraordinary' place to visit, like 'another world', one that was almost 'inconceivable' to most outsiders. To visit a country where the people did not have to make a decision from the day they are born to the day they die was a unique experience, she felt. She found the level of state control over the people's lives to be oppressive. Even the language outsiders used about visiting the country reflected this, she said. One did not speak about going 'to' North Korea but about going 'into' it, and it was only when one came out of the country that one realised how oppressed one felt while inside, Ms Healy remarked.

She recalled visiting kindergartens in North Korea and noting that the earlier the propaganda machine starts, the more effective. She watched the children doing relay races, where the object of the exercise, when they ran with the baton, was to beat a model of a US soldier at the end of the track. Such indoctrination at such an early age is regretfully very powerful, Ms Healy said.

Helping the people but not supporting the regime

Mary Healy observed that working in a country like North Korea, where the government is so controlling and oppressive, presents a dilemma about what the role of an NGO can be in such circumstances. Trócaire's view was always that people have the right to assistance and solidarity no matter where they lived in the world or under what sort of regime they found themselves. Ms Healy said that Trócaire's perspective was that people should not have to suffer for the wrongs of their rulers. The agency took the twin-track approach of supporting the people and meeting their needs while at the same time doing some advocacy and lobbying work to try to get the communist government to loosen, to some extent, its iron-tight control.

As part of the latter approach, Trócaire took a delegation consisting of Eamonn Gilmore TD of the Labour Party, former West Belfast MP Dr Joe Hendron of SDLP and Bernie Malone, Labour MEP, on a fact-finding mission to North Korea.

Justin Kilcullen accompanied the delegation on its five-day mission. On their return, he said that they had been shocked by the combination of state decay and in some cases neglect that they had seen. He added that they had been absolutely convinced that there was a major humanitarian crisis in North Korea. Because of the shortness of the visit and the limited access allowed, it was very hard to be definitive about the scale but, combined with the insight of other delegations, it helped to build up a picture.

The approaching winter threatened to be a tragedy, he said, given the overall state of health and nutrition in North Korea. The country appeared to have ground to a halt and they had difficulty seeing how the more vulnerable would get through the sub-zero winter when there was little coal or other energy sources in the country.

He said that Trócaire estimated that some five million people – more than one-fifth of the country's population – faced starvation. But North Korea's communist government was trying to keep the food shortages under wraps and aid agencies were some of the few sources of information about the true extent of the impending disaster. The delegation had met the Communist Workers Party Central Committee and had criticised a number of the ways they were handling the disaster.

Mr Kilcullen speculated on the possibility of some opening up of the system in North Korea, saying that he hoped they had given an opportunity to those of a more open mind to speak out against it. However, he pointed out that in the end, the NGOs were not in a position to deal with the North Korean food crisis on their own.

Also in September 1997, Trócaire launched a newspaper advertisement with the controversial heading: 'Let them starve – they're only Communists.' The advertisement said that the North Korean famine was turning into one of the worst human disasters of the decade but that, incredibly, some countries were reluctant to help. 'It seems that because the country is one of the last bastions of communism, their people are being forced to pay the price,' the advertisement continued, and it explained that in the meantime, millions were moving towards the brink of hunger, sickness and death. The advertisement also explained that Trócaire had already spent £1 million on aid and vital supplies but it said that much more needed to be done.

In early October, the Irish government gave Trócaire £100,000 in funding for North Korea. During that month, the agency purchased £400,000 worth of food, mainly rice, for the country. Trócaire also bought £250,000 worth of multivitamins that were used to try to build up people's strength before the winter set in.

Early the following month, Justin Kilcullen wrote to the papers to thank the Irish people for their extraordinarily generous response to Trócaire's North Korean appeal, which up to that time had raised £2.3 million. He pointed out that there had not been an equivalent response from any other European country. He said he was very aware of the responsibility that Trócaire, and he personally, had in being accountable to all those who had contributed funds, especially so in the case of North Korea, because of the lack of access given to journalists and others. They would normally be the ones to keep the public informed and ask the awkward and hard questions if they needed to be asked.

He said that following his most recent visit to North Korea in September, he could report now in November that while the situation remained precarious, there was no doubt that the arrival and distribution of food aid had prevented mass starvation. Trócaire had sent 6,000 tons of rice, along with high-energy biscuits, palm oil, vitamin tablets and blankets. Despite this and the efforts of agencies worldwide, many thousands of children, the sick and the elderly had already died.

The rice harvest was then taking place in North Korea but they knew that it would be a poor harvest and that by April 1998 the country would again be virtually dependent on food aid until the October harvest of that year. So international efforts had to continue to build food stocks, rehabilitate agricultural production and help North Korea to reform its economy if it was willing to do so.

At the same time, Trócaire was acutely aware, he said, of the nature of the North Korean regime, especially its human rights record. Trócaire had confronted that issue by bringing a parliamentary delegation to address the authorities there on questions such as human and political rights and economic reform. That debate would continue, he remarked.

Justin Kilcullen explained that of the £2.3 million given to Trócaire, £1.7 million had been spent on three shipments of aid and a fourth shipment would include seeds and fertiliser for a supplementary crop of barley to be planted in March and harvested in June 1998. Trócaire would retain around £100,000 in reserve to begin some form of development process the following year in North Korea, if appropriate.

In December 1997, Trócaire ran another full-page newspaper advertisement with the headline, 'Christmas dinner in North Korea', with underneath an image of a pair of hands holding a small quantity of rice. The advertisement said that in the following year, the country would have only half the food it needed to sustain its people. It also said that the already weakened and malnourished people were then in the grips of a vicious winter with fuel in short supply. Houses had only plastic sheeting on them to resist the sometimes merciless climate, and as well as the need for food aid, there was also an urgent need for supplies such as soap, blankets, winter linen and shoes.

In February 1998, Eamonn Meehan paid a week-long visit to North Korea. On his return, he said that famine seemed to have been averted due to a combination of a mild winter and international food aid. He had seen no evidence of widespread deaths as a result of food shortages, he said. However, he warned that the harvest stocks and international food aid would run out by April and that the country would then enter a critical period.

By that time, Trócaire had raised £4 million for aid for North Korea. Mr Meehan, accompanied by Mary Healy and Kathi Zellweger, had spent two days in Pyongyang and almost four days in the south east, inspecting food-distribution centres and other facilities. They had seen evidence of serious malnutrition on visits to orphanages and children's centres and had noted a health service in major decline. They had also seen that water supply would be a problem after the prolonged dry weather.

With the prospect of having to supply food from March until the October harvest, all involved in the aid operation had said that there was a need to ensure food security by 2000, Mr Meehan added. He recommended that Trócaire should continue providing aid through 1998 and should also help to provide fertilisers, support agricultural development and continue the dialogue with North Korea about reform.

In a recent interview for this book, Eamonn Meehan said that the strongest impression that remained with him from that visit was the sheer level of control exercised by the North Korean regime over ordinary people in the country. That control reached into every facet of their lives and orchestrated how they spent their time on a daily basis, even down to deciding what time they got up at in the morning. Where they went to work and what kind of work they did, what time they went to bed and, especially, what they watched on television or listened to on the radio – all these were regulated by the state, he remarked.

Mary Healy recalled that Trócaire facilitated a visit by a North Korean delegation to Ireland around this time. One of the main interests of the delegation was looking at the possibilities for crop diversification in their country and in particular how the potato might be worked into that diversification. Ms Healy took the delegates to visit some potato farmers in Co. Louth. They also met with Teagasc (the agriculture and food development authority that provides research, advisory and training services to the agriculture and food industries in Ireland) and other similar bodies.

What Trócaire found most interesting about the visit, said Ms Healy, was that the North Koreans were open to sending a delegation and that the delegates they sent were open to listening and taking advice while they were in Ireland. It was a huge step forward for the North Koreans to be open to other opportunities and other ways of doing things, she believed. She saw it as a real indication that they had recognised and were now admitting the need for change.

In mid-April 1998, Médecins sans Frontières claimed that aid shipments to North Korea were being diverted to feed troops. Trócaire assured its supporters that supplies were getting through to the people who needed them most. A spokesperson said that the agency had made frequent visits to North Korea to monitor the situation and that the people there were benefiting fully from the £3 million worth of aid that Trócaire had sent so far. The spokesperson pointed out that Trócaire's partner, Caritas Hong Kong, had complete access to the Trócaire supply lines and aid projects at all times and that its representatives would report if anything was going astray.

Since the time that Trócaire had launched its North Korean emergency appeal, the agency had sent food aid on an almost monthly basis. But after three years of drought, floods and tidal waves, North Koreans still faced severe food shortages. The pressing need at that particular time, said Trócaire, was for food, fertiliser and plastic sheeting.

Early in August 1998, Marian Cadogan, who had worked for Trócaire in Asia before but was at that time a monitoring officer for the CI consortium, had just returned from North Korea. She found that there were signs of hope in the famine-hit country. She said that in 1997, the WFP had estimated that North Korea's grain shortfall was 1.9 million tons and that a disastrous situation had been contained because of a massive humanitarian effort. Food shortage continued, she said, and in 1998 the shortfall was estimated at just over 0.5 million tons. More food aid was needed but the situation was under control, she added.

One of the real signs of hope was that Caritas had introduced a new crop, barley, into North Korea. Ms Cadogan explained that because the land was frozen during four months of the year in winter, North Koreans had a very short growing season for their rice. Even in the best of times, before the September harvest, stocks were usually running low, she continued. Now for the first time, people were planting barley, which grew between March and June and which could help them through the lean period.

While she had been in North Korea, she monitored the distribution of aid and found no evidence that emergency supplies were being siphoned off by the military, as had been reported earlier in 1998 in some newspapers. She added that the barley seed was treated with fungicide and chemicals, so it could be used only for planting. She had found no sign of aid being diverted.

Increasing obstruction from the regime
In late December 1999, Trócaire and Concern Worldwide signed a joint statement criticising the North Korean govern-

ment for obstructing the humanitarian effort to save its famine-hit people. Aid agencies had been denied access to many famine-hit regions for 'security reasons' and the North Korean authorities had refused efforts to evaluate the effectiveness of the relief efforts. As millions still faced starvation after repeated harvest failures, the North Korean government was still spending millions on their military, especially their missile programme, which led to suspicions that aid money was being diverted to fund the military.

Earlier in 1999, the British agency, Oxfam, withdrew completely from North Korea because of the obstruction. Médecins sans Frontières also pulled out, protesting at the non-cooperation and claiming that food aid had been diverted to senior officials and arms factories.

Although they had signed the statement, Trócaire and Concern said that they would stay in North Korea. A Trócaire spokesperson said that the agency had signed in solidarity with other development agencies and in recognition of the problems they faced but pointed out that, working through Caritas Hong Kong, Trócaire itself had experienced few problems. The spokesperson said that many of the difficulties caused were not deliberate but resulted from the political system in North Korea; there were restrictions on movement and everything had to be arranged in advance. In addition, local aid workers were recruited from government nominees mainly because government officials were the only people who spoke English and because that was the way the system worked.

Trócaire gave £200,000 worth of aid to North Korea in 1999 and said that it would continue its aid programme there. In her recent interview, Mary Healy said that access was becoming increasingly difficult and that more and more counties were becoming out of bounds. Food aid was not sent to those counties that were off limits and, as the number of those counties was growing, the point of supporting such a small number of counties began to be questioned. She said that Trócaire's involvement in North Korea diminished gradually and ceased altogether from 2002. However, some Caritas agencies are still involved, she said, and Trócaire maintains contact with them.

Because of the closed nature of North Korean society, it is impossible to be definite about how many people died during the famine there. Estimates vary between three and 800,000 per year, during the three-year famine, peaking in 1997. One estimate puts the total number of people who may have died at two million. It is most likely that many died from famine-related illnesses such as pneumonia, tuberculosis, and diarrhoea rather than starvation.

But for the efforts of Trócaire and other international aid agencies, doubtless the numbers dying would have been much higher.

CHAPTER 15:
'Death of a Nation': The Indonesian Occupation of East Timor

Keeping the world mindful of a cruel military occupation

In 1975, Indonesia, a military dictatorship at the time, invaded the eastern part of the tiny island of Timor, known as East Timor. In the subsequent twenty-five-year military occupation, it is estimated that between one-third and a half of the 600,000 East Timorese population died violently. The continuing oppression led to ongoing campaigns by organisations around the world, including the East Timor-Ireland Solidarity Campaign (founded in Dublin in 1992) and Trócaire, to end Indonesia's cruel occupation.

Throughout the latter half of the 1970s and the entire 1980s, Trócaire supported humanitarian work in East Timor. For example, at the end of 1975, through CI, Trócaire gave a grant of £3,000 to help victims of the war in East Timor. The money went to a programme initiated by Australian Catholic Relief to provide food, medicine, shelter and clothing to refugees. Near the end of the 1980s, in early February 1989, Trócaire announced funding for a human rights group working in East Timor.

In 1991, a demonstration in Dili, the capital of East Timor, against the cancellation of a visit by a Portuguese parliamentary delegation (the island is a former Portuguese colony) ended in the infamous Santa Cruz massacre, committed by the Indonesian armed forces. The atrocity left 528 people dead or 'disappeared'.

Bishop Casey called on the Irish government to make representations to the UN and the EEC to investigate urgently alleged massacres and human rights abuses by Indonesian forces in East Timor. The bishop said that Trócaire sources in East Timor indicated that the atmosphere of terror there at that time was worse than at any time since the 1975 invasion, and he referred to the Santa Cruz massacre where he said hundreds of young Timorese, including schoolchildren, had been gunned down by the military.

In June 1993, Maura Leen, Trócaire Asia Projects Officer, said that recent media attention had done a great deal to raise public awareness of the very grave situation in East Timor. She remarked that the sharp contrast between the swift reaction of the international community after the invasion of Kuwait by Saddam Hussein and the continued cooperation of some countries with Indonesia's ruling forces, which added to that government's unwillingness to surrender its illegal prize, had been nothing short of shameful.

Ms Leen pointed out that for many years Trócaire had been supporting initiatives to raise awareness of the genocide and gross human rights violations inflicted on the East Timorese people, and she said that the Catholic Church in East Timor had been to the fore in condemning these abuses, as evidenced by the speeches of Bishop Carlos Belo of Dili. She praised the media for drawing the attention of the Irish public to the facts of the terrible crimes committed by the Indonesians since their 1975 invasion, most notably the massacre of an estimated 200 peaceful mourners at a memorial ceremony in November 1991. A year and a half later came the trial and harsh sentence of the East Timorese leader, Xanana Gusmao.

The International Red Cross had recently announced that it had suspended all prison visits in East Timor because of the lack of compliance with its conditions by the Indonesian authorities, Ms Leen explained. In addition, pressure had been increasing for the Red Cross to have uninterrupted and unfettered access to Mr Gusmao, who had been on hunger strike since being sentenced to life imprisonment on 21 May. Despite repeated requests, his family had been refused permission to visit him. Ms Leen said that the difficulties encountered by the Red Cross could only be reversed by intense pressure (including sanctions and other deterrents) from governments around the world that maintained close relations with the military regime in Jakarta. The Irish, she said, had shown their deep concern over human rights abuses in the former Yugoslavia, in Somalia and in many other countries. The time had come to focus far more attention on East Timor and to lobby TDs and MEPs to push for peace and self-determination for the people there.

At the end of February 1994, Justin Kilcullen spoke publicly about John Pilger's documentary, *Death of a Nation*, which had just been screened on a number of television channels and which graphically illustrated the tragedy of East Timor. Mr Kilcullen said that since the illegal Indonesian occupation in 1975, the major powers (the US, Britain, Australia and Japan) had behaved shamefully towards the people of East Timor. The Indonesian military had killed hundreds of thousands and many more had died from epidemics and malnutrition, he said.

He pointed out that in 1991 the oil fields of Kuwait had evoked a speedy international offensive against Iraq. He thought it unfortunate that the rich oil potential of the Timor Gap together with the lucrative Indonesian arms market had drawn studied indifference from the British, Australian and Japanese governments, each of which had opted to ignore the very serious human rights abuses being perpetrated by the Indonesians.

He also considered that the parallels drawn by John Pilger's documentary with Cambodia were stark but saw one crucial difference: the UN had passed many resolutions condemning the invasion of East Timor but no practical actions had been taken to back them up.

However, signs of hope existed, Mr Kilcullen said. The US Senate Foreign Relations Committee had decided to make the sale of US arms to Indonesia conditional on improvements in human rights in East Timor. In numerous countries, including Ireland, solidarity campaigns and the efforts of development agencies were raising public awareness of East Timor. He said that it was vital that the Irish government spoke out on the tragedy in East Timor at the EU and the UN.

In July 1995, Bishop Belo paid a short private visit to Ireland as a guest of Trócaire. He had been nominated for the Nobel Peace Prize in 1993, 1994 and 1995 and was awarded the prize the following year. Since 1983, when he had returned to East Timor, he had been an outspoken critic of Indonesian brutalities there and an unceasing world advocate of the rights of his people. In Dublin in July 1995, he met President Mary Robinson and the Minister of State for Foreign Affairs, Joan Burton.

He concelebrated Mass at Dublin's Pro-Cathedral with Archbishop Desmond Connell, where he was welcomed as a visitor from a country 'deprived of freedom', where torture and other human rights abuses were widespread. Fr Pat Carroll, the cathedral's administrator, described the East Timorese as 'a suffering people' and he said it was a privilege to welcome the bishop, who had survived two attempts on his life.

Bishop Belo also met Bishop Kirby, chairman of Trócaire. Referring to the previous week's World Court decision on the Timor Gap oil exploration treaty between Australia and Indonesia, Bishop Belo said that he saw the court's affirmation of East Timor's right to self-determination as positive. He was also seeking support for the building of a new seminary in East Timor, which was necessary because of the huge increase in vocations there. He said that the church in East Timor was seen as the protector of the people, as a church that was 'ready to defend them'. With just seventy-two priests for more than 700,000 people, many parishes were without priests for weeks on end.

Intensifying the pressure at national and international level

In March 1996, Fionnuala Gilsenan, Trócaire project officer, went to East Timor to observe what the situation was like on the ground and how Trócaire's projects were progressing there. The following autumn, the agency announced plans to fund a project working with farmers who were returning to the valley areas from the mountains where they had lived since the invasion. The mountainous areas were deforested and, with soil erosion, had become increasingly infertile.

These farming families needed basic farm implements and training in rice production in order to farm successfully in the valley areas. An agricultural training college was set up to train farmers' children and help was given settling students in their villages as a follow-up to their training. There was a 50:50 ratio of men to women and the farm attached to the college was developed to a high level, complete with dairy cows and goats for self-sufficiency.

In November 1996, Trócaire urged the EU to stop selling arms to Indonesia. Justin Kilcullen pointed out that while the EU had hundreds of regulations restricting trade in a myriad of goods, the controls on the arms trade were not being implemented. According to EU regulations, arms should not be sold to countries that violated human rights, yet both the Swedish and British governments had sold arms to Indonesia, where human rights abuses were commonplace.

Calling on the Irish government to use its EU presidency to address the issue, he said that the government had a vested interest in ensuring that the arms controls were enforced, given its commitment to peace building and dis-armament at home on the island of Ireland.

In December 1996, Bishop Belo and Jose Ramos-Horta (a leader of the resistance to the Indonesian occupation and current president) received the Nobel Peace Prize in Oslo. The award was given to them for their unceasing efforts to find a peaceful solution to the crisis in their homeland. A number of Irish people were present at the award ceremony in Norway, invited as guests of Bishop Belo to mark his

'DEATH OF A NATION'

appreciation for the support given them. Among the invitees were Justin Kilcullen, the former Taoiseach, Garret FitzGerald, and the former Nobel Peace Prize winner, Mairéad Maguire.

Tom Hyland, the founder of the East Timor-Ireland Solidarity Campaign, said that the award represented a call from the international community that the issue of East Timor should not be forgotten. Justin Kilcullen said that East Timor was an occupied territory where there was no rule of law, no court of appeal, no freedom, and where power was in the hands of extra-judicial bodies that controlled life and liberty at will.

The Irish Bishops' Conference praised the work of Bishop Belo and Mr Ramos-Horta and supported the call made by the Nobel Committee for greater efforts to find a diplomatic solution to the conflict in East Timor based on the people's right to self-determination. The bishops urged the Irish government to work with its EU partners to implement the EU Common Position on East Timor with concrete actions. They said that that position expressed an explicit commitment to encourage dialogue towards a fair settlement. They added that it also pledged to improve the human rights situation and that a vital first step to achieving that was to stop the supply of arms from EU countries to Indonesia, which were being used as instruments of oppression in East Timor. The bishops also called on the Irish government to demand the withdrawal of the Indonesian military from East Timor.

In early June 1997, Bishop Belo paid a brief visit to Ireland to thank the Irish people, and especially the East Timor-Ireland Solidarity Campaign, the Irish Catholic Church and Trócaire for their support. During the visit, he briefed President Robinson on the human rights situation in East Timor at that time.

He told a press conference that the East Timorese people did not enjoy the traditional freedoms enjoyed by European people. He said that Europeans had the freedom to speak out but that if the East Timorese did this, they were arrested and beaten. However, he said that a military solution to the

Indonesian occupation was not an option – the solution had to be a negotiated one from round-table meetings.

Eamonn Meehan, overseas director of Trócaire at the time, said that the human rights situation continued to deteriorate in East Timor despite the attention that resulted when Bishop Belo and Mr Ramos-Horta won the Nobel Prize the year before. He said that this was partly because of the violence linked with the elections going on in Indonesia at the time and partly because the Indonesian authorities were angry at the decision to award the prize to the two men.

On the occasion of Trócaire's twenty-fifth anniversary in 1998, Bishop Belo sent the following message: 'To its everlasting credit, Trócaire has supported efforts to bring the East Timor situation to international notice when few knew or cared. I myself have experienced the generosity of the Irish people, have been comforted by their prayers and strengthened by their solidarity. May a strong and visionary Trócaire continue in the years ahead.'

In the first week of July 1999, it was announced that Bishop Kirby was paying a solidarity visit to East Timor. The following month, the country was due to hold a referendum on independence, ending the Indonesian occupation. However, the violence had continued and the referendum had already been postponed once at that stage.

Before his departure, Bishop Kirby said that a systematic campaign of repression had been unleashed by pro-integrationist militias (favouring the integration of East Timor into Indonesia), armed and controlled by the Indonesian army. People in remote areas in particular had been tortured, beaten and murdered, he said. The bishop said that he was travelling to East Timor to express solidarity with the work of the church there, which had continually highlighted and condemned human rights atrocities. As well as providing protection for the people, the church had been to the fore in promoting peace and dialogue, he added.

When Bishop Kirby returned, he wrote a newspaper article about what he had experienced on his trip. He expressed his doubts about a free and fair referendum taking place. He explained how, on 5 May 1999, an agreement had been reached involving Portugal, Indonesia and the UN to allow a consultation process with the people on the political future of East Timor. However, despite the agreement to hold a ballot, everyone he met there, including Bishop Belo, said that nothing had changed and that in fact things had got worse despite the visible presence of the UN.

Civilian militias, supported and armed by Indonesia, were engaged in a systematic campaign to stop the referendum being held in August, Bishop Kirby said. He had heard stories of widespread intimidation, ranging from verbal threats and warnings to physical assault and murder. The UN itself, he added, had come under attack and had been regularly forced to withdraw its personnel to the relative calm of the capital, Dili.

He said that no one was safe in East Timor and that almost everyone he met had a story to tell. One teacher told him about teenagers finishing their final exams in secondary school but being killed before they could collect their certificates, and that every family in East Timor had lost at least one close relative. While he was there, an aid convoy bringing much-needed relief to thousands of internally displaced people was attacked by a militia group. Caritas East Timor, a Trócaire partner, was part of the convoy and witnessed the brutal attack – some members of the convoy were still unaccounted for, he reported.

What he found truly frightening about visiting East Timor was to hear how well orchestrated the campaign of terror had been. Much-needed resources for health and education were being diverted and invested in the campaign of terror, thus undermining the consultation process, he said. One school he visited faced the prospect of not being able to reopen after the summer holidays because teacher salaries and student subsidies were being diverted by the military.

When Bishop Kirby visited the town of Baucau, seventy kilometres east of Dili, Bishop Basilio do Nascimento of Baucau explained to him that the most acute impact of this situation was on health. Vital medical staff were fleeing the country to escape the insecurity. The exodus was also prompted by their wages being stopped. Baucau, a rural area on the northern part of the island with a population of 94,000 and in an area where malaria and TB were rampant, had been left with just one government-paid doctor.

Indonesia had a deliberate policy of making people weak and dependent, Bishop Kirby explained. Most of the professionals in East Timor (doctors, nurses, teachers) were from Indonesia; before the most recent escalation in the violence, only 18 of the 197 doctors in East Timor were Timorese and only 3 per cent of teachers. This policy was especially apparent in the agricultural sector; East Timor depended on Indonesia and its sea lanes for a supply of rice, the staple diet of the populace. Bishop Nascimento told him there was only one month's supply of rice in the territory at any given time and to cut off the supply routes was a powerful threat hanging over the people of East Timor.

With teachers fleeing, 80 per cent of the seventy-five schools in Baucau diocese would not open at the beginning of the new school year in August. This was the situation even though teachers knew well that leaving so many young at loose ends would put their lives at risk because many would be drawn into politics and would become targets of the militias and the military.

Bishop Kirby said that his visit to East Timor had been an act of solidarity with the people of East Timor. The people there had placed great trust in the Catholic Church, which was a well-respected voice for the oppressed and had struggled to promote peace through dialogue. It was the only institution in East Timor where people could gather in large numbers, offering physical protection from persecution and the advocacy of human rights and values. Priests and nuns had continually offered shelter and protection to the oppressed and provided humanitarian assistance to the internally displaced. The church would continue to play a

'DEATH OF A NATION'

central role in East Timor but unfortunately there were still many people who had taken refuge in the mountains and no organisation could reach them.

The bishop said that during his visit, the glaring weaknesses in the UN-brokered agreement had been starkly revealed. The deal gave responsibility for security to the Indonesians but every Timorese he met despaired of that decision; for them it was like the fox looking after the chickens. No one believed that Indonesia would live up to its promises and implement the agreement. The government there was presenting one face to the international community while continuing to direct and support the militia, undermining any hope of a free and fair ballot.

Bishop Kirby called for a UN peacekeeping force to be deployed to ensure the peace and security of the people before the ballot on their political future. He felt that the international community had abandoned East Timor since the 1975 invasion and its support was now necessary to restore confidence in democracy and the rule of law. They had to insist that Indonesia lived up to its obligations, that the militias be disarmed and that humanitarian organisations had access to the internally displaced to look after their basic needs.

The consultation ballot had initially been scheduled for 8 August but had already been delayed until 22 August and would have to be postponed if the atrocities continued, Bishop Kirby said. He expressed the hope of one day returning to a free East Timor. In the midst of all the terror and atrocity, he had been continuously inspired by the courage, resilience and warmth of its people, he concluded.

At the end of the first week of August 1999, the *Irish Times* quoted Bishop Belo as saying that the Indonesian military was openly and clearly distributing guns in the eastern towns of Baucau and Laga and in other places. The bishop said that they were turning Timorese against Timorese and that the situation there was 'like hell'.

The same *Irish Times* article said that, with nearly 440,000 voters registered so far, the registration had clearly been the success the anti-independence militias had tried to prevent. Reliable Catholic Church sources were cited as claiming that attacks by those militias had claimed three to 5,000 lives, and Bishop Belo was again quoted as saying that in remote areas, special forces and militias were still threatening people.

Trócaire warned that the distribution of guns signalled 'a crisis point'. Spokesperson Fionnuala Gilsenan said that if action was not taken, it could be the prelude to a massive bloodbath. Tom Hyland urged the sending of a UN-armed peacekeeping force (which the UN was then considering) to help prevent the expected heavy violence after the voting.

Post-referendum violence and eventual independence

Widespread violence did indeed follow the vote, which took place on 30 August 1999. That vote gave overwhelming support in favour of East Timor breaking away from Indonesia. Just before the violence was unleashed, Fionnuala Gilsenan and Annette Honan of Trócaire visited the country. In a recent interview for this book, Ms Honan recalled that there was a widespread feeling of elation among the people they met following the successful holding of the referendum. Little did they know, she said, that only a short time after they returned to Ireland they would hear of such atrocities being committed against those same people who were on such a high while they were there.

Even during the short time she and Ms Gilsenan were there, they heard stories of some of the terrible things that had been done during the decades of the occupation. They stayed in Dili with Bishop Belo for some of their visit and then went to Baucau, where they stayed in a school run by the local church. This was a boarding school and the main reason it was boarding, according to Ms Honan, was for the safety of the children, being one of the principal ways that parents could secure the safety of their children. The parents could not afford to pay the boarding fees and the local church supported the children by keeping them in the school.

'DEATH OF A NATION'

Ms Honan described the area as extremely poor and said that the conditions in the school were primitive. Rabbits were bred behind chicken-wire enclosures in various places and the children were fed rabbit meat as their primary source of protein. The people in the school told them that all of the local villages around them had been attacked at different times. When they drove around the area, sites of massacres were pointed out to them.

Shortly after the Trócaire workers returned to Dublin, pro-Jakarta militias roamed through Dili, killing and terrorising people and destroying property. Thousands fled to West Timor, which was part of Indonesia. But despite warnings that the people of East Timor would be slaughtered, the UN continued to hold off intervention in early September. Japan, the biggest country donor, and Britain both refused to freeze aid to Indonesia.

The Irish branch of Amnesty International urged the Irish government, on behalf of the EU, to redouble pressure on the Indonesian authorities to disarm the militias. Bishop Kirby said that he had never been so dismayed at the inaction of the international community and he called on the Irish government to state publicly if they had sought the suspension of loans to Indonesia or if they had sought the earliest possible deployment of UN military personnel to East Timor.

He warned that the people of the country were facing genocide. Pointing to the example of Rwanda in 1994, he said that the UN had stood by and watched people being slaughtered there. The Indonesians had learned that lesson very well and were forcing the UN and the international media to leave East Timor so that they could continue their awful project of overturning the result of a free vote and making the territory ungovernable, he said.

On 11 September 1999, Trócaire and the East Timor-Ireland Solidarity Campaign held a protest outside the US embassy in Dublin. They also took out a full-page advertisement in Irish newspapers that day under the heading, 'East Timor betrayed again'. The advertisement referred to the shock, dismay and deep disturbance felt over the previous week at the brutality unleashed against the defenceless people of East Timor by the Indonesian army and the militias. It had been a week of unmitigated terror, cold-blooded murder and slaughter of the innocent, the advertisement said.

It had also been a week of broken promises and false assurances by the Indonesian government, it continued, and a week of betrayal by the international community. The advertisement listed the promises the UN had made to the people of East Timor: to hold a ballot, to count the votes and to remain in East Timor after the vote. The people had trusted the UN to protect them; nearly 99 per cent went to the polls and almost 80 per cent voted for independence. The advertisement accused the UN of breaking its promise to the East Timorese and of standing by and doing nothing as people were being murdered.

It was another betrayal of East Timor, the advertisement declared. When the Indonesians invaded in 1975, the international community did nothing; when 200,000 people were killed during the genocidal Indonesian occupation, it did nothing; at that particular time, as a second genocide was taking place and tens of thousands were being forced out of their country, it still did nothing. The permanent members of the UN Security Council with the powers of veto were refusing to act. The US, Britain and other countries were putting their national self-interest before the lives of innocent men, women and children, the advertisement accused, and it asked readers was this the type of world they wished to live in. If it was not, they were urged to act, and to join Trócaire's and the East Timor-Ireland Solidarity Campaign's protest outside the American embassy in Dublin if they could and to let US President Bill Clinton and British Prime Minister Tony Blair know how they felt.

Trócaire and the East Timor-Ireland Solidarity Campaign called on the Irish government and Ireland's EU partners to live up to their moral and legal obligations under the UN

Convention on the Prevention and Punishment of the Crime of Genocide by taking immediate action to prevent genocide happening in East Timor. Trócaire and the East Timor-Ireland Solidarity Campaign also believed that it was both legally and morally imperative for the UN to intervene. The annexation of East Timor by Indonesia was illegal and the UN had never recognised the occupation; therefore, it was legitimate for the UN to intervene and to send a regional force immediately to disarm the militias and establish peace.

The advertisement said that it was imperative that Ireland, the EU, the US and the international community imposed sanctions on Indonesia, conveying that it had become a pariah. The specific actions the advertisement called for were: all IMF and World Bank loans to be suspended immediately; international aid programmes, including EU aid, to be suspended; EU ambassadors to be withdrawn except that of Finland, which had the EU presidency and would continue to liaise with the Indonesian government; and the ending of all arms exports to Indonesia.

The advertisement concluded by reviewing Trócaire's work in East Timor since 1975 and it told how, over the previous week, Trócaire's partner, Caritas East Timor, had paid the price for its support of the Timorese people with the murder of most of its forty staff. The global CI network was appealing urgently for funds to provide food and shelter to the 200,000 people fleeing to West Timor.

Bishop Kirby, Justin Kilcullen and Tom Hyland met the Taoiseach, Bertie Ahern, and proposed to him that Ireland invoke the UN convention on genocide. Trócaire also sent a letter to President Clinton calling for the convention to be invoked. The President replied positively, saying that he agreed with Trócaire's view on the issue.

A few days later, Justin Kilcullen wrote an article for the *Irish Times* saying that the Irish government seemed to have accepted the legal case for invoking the convention. He asked, now that Indonesia had accepted UN peacekeepers, should the issue be dropped. He said that Trócaire believed that it should not for three reasons: (i) there was a very real threat of a second genocide against the 100,000 refugees who had been forcibly removed to Indonesian territory; (ii) the world had to recognise that a genocide had taken place and its perpetrators had to be punished; (iii) the phenomenon of impunity, enjoyed by perpetrators of past genocides, must not recur.

Mr Kilcullen said that it was clear that President Habibie of Indonesia was not in control of his own military. There was a massive loss of face for the generals in having to accept the international peacekeeping force and they were quite capable of taking out their anger on their captive East Timorese population, he believed. The Indonesian authorities were thwarting attempts by the aid agencies to reach the refugee camps, he said. He felt that all that had been achieved up to that point was a possible end to the violence in East Timor and he argued that prevention of further genocide against the 100,000 disappeared was now the priority.

Justin Kilcullen contended that it had also to be recognised that genocide had taken place and the perpetrators had to be brought to justice. There should be no question of an amnesty for the perpetrators under the terms of acceptance of the peacekeeping force, he said. He pointed out that the UN High Commissioner for Human Rights, Mrs Mary Robinson, had already made the case for the establishment of an international war-crimes tribunal to deal with punishment and he said that it would strengthen her hand greatly if the Irish government invoked the convention, thus forcing the appropriate bodies within the UN to act to punish those involved.

They should be careful not to allow a repeat of the impunity witnessed in the cases of Cambodia and Rwanda, he said. He went on to argue that, until the international community made it clear that the crime of genocide would no longer be tolerated and that those responsible would face the full weight of international justice, it could only be assumed that it would continue to be perpetrated,

'DEATH OF A NATION'

especially in parts of the world where ethnic tensions were strong.

He speculated that the Irish government might be tempted to pull back from invoking the convention lest it antagonise nations whose vote Ireland was at that time seeking to obtain a seat on the Security Council. But he thought that could be hypocritical in Ireland's approach to the UN because there was little point in aspiring to a Security Council place unless it itself vigorously implemented the UN's own conventions. He maintained that by proceeding with invoking the convention, Ireland would have established a precedent, which the world could not ignore and which would earn it its seat on the Security Council.

A week later, Trócaire published an 'update' on the situation in East Timor in the newspapers. It referred to UN peacekeepers going into the country nearly two weeks after the genocide had begun. This was welcome news, it said, for the more than 300,000 people who had survived by hiding in the mountains and were now sick and hungry. The update said that Trócaire was also concerned that the 100–200,000 people held hostage in refugee camps in West Timor and in eastern Indonesia would be forgotten. Their lives were in danger, it added.

The update explained that Trócaire, as part of CI, had organised relief supplies for people in East Timor and in West Timor but it said that many more were in need. The update made a number of demands: the UNHCR, the UN's refugee agency, and all other agencies to have full access to all areas including the camps in West Timor; the militias to be disarmed and disbanded; the Indonesian military to leave East Timor immediately; a humanitarian corridor to be created from West Timor to East Timor to help the refugees to return home safely; all EU, IMF and World Bank aid and loans to Indonesia to be suspended until there was peace and security; the UN genocide convention to be invoked to compel the UN to take action against the perpetrators of the genocide.

By late September, Trócaire had sent £120,000 from its emergency fund to support the desperate, starving and traumatised people who had fled to East Timor's barren mountainsides or across the border into West Timor where food supplies, medicines and shelter were available. Justin Kilcullen told the *Irish Catholic* that the refugees had no water, food, shelter or medicines and that Trócaire staff would go to East Timor as soon as the peacekeeping operation allowed.

In a letter to the Irish people, Bishop Belo appealed for Irish support. He said he had but one message: to stop aid to Indonesia and to send in troops immediately. What was happening he described as genocide and he said that if Xanana Gusmao (leader of the independence movement) ever became president, he would lead a country of trees, weeds and animals but would not find any Timorese there. East Timor, the bishop said, was 'a scorched country'.

In a submission to the Oireachtas Foreign Affairs Committee in late October 1999, Trócaire said that Indonesia had to make reparations to East Timor. The agency also called on Ireland to recognise East Timor's independence as a nation state and to make it a priority country for Irish aid. Justin Kilcullen said that it was also vital that other countries did not 'go soft' on Indonesia and that East Timor must not fall down the EU's priority list as states became anxious to restore normal relations with Indonesia.

The submission also argued that the UN commission investigating human rights abuses and killings in East Timor should be given active political support. And it said that any assistance for East Timor from international financial institutions should be in the form of grants so that the new state did not start its existence mired in debt. Given that Indonesia was responsible for the destruction of East Timor, a mechanism should be set up to ensure that Indonesia contributed to the cost of reconstruction in the country, the submission maintained.

Trócaire also called on the Irish government to ensure that UN troops entered the isolated East Timorese enclave of

Oecusse. Justin Kilcullen told the Oireachtas Committee for Foreign Affairs that Oecusse had been particularly hard hit by the activities of the militias and the Indonesian military. The mainly flat landscape there meant that people were unable to flee to the mountains as in other parts of the country. Trócaire said that of a total population of 50,000 in Oecusse, at least 40,000 had been displaced – fleeing as refugees or lost among 'the disappeared' and dead.

From December 1999 to May 2002, East Timor had a UN Transitional Administrator and the country became the first new independent state of the twenty-first century on 20 May 2002.

Trócaire had long been working in East Timor and was joined by other aid agencies after independence. Irish Aid made the country one of its seven priority countries in the world, with some €6 million of aid per year spent on a wide variety of assistance, covering food security, civil society and job creation.

In 2006, Trócaire set up a small office in Dili, which is run by Kathryn Robertson, and indicates the agency's continued commitment to East Timor.

CHAPTER 16:
Hurricane Mitch Devastates Honduras

Scenes of horror

Hurricane Mitch, which struck in late October/early November 1998, was one of the deadliest and most powerful hurricanes on record. It dropped historic amounts of rainfall on Honduras and Nicaragua. More rain fell in two hours, when the hurricane was at its worst, than falls in Ireland in three years. The hurricanes killed up to 11,000 people and left more than 8,000 missing by the end of 1998. Flooding and mudslides caused enormous damage, destroying tens of thousands of homes.

On the first day of the hurricane, as she walked out her front door in Tegucigalpa, the capital of Honduras, Sally O'Neill was confronted with a scene of horror: a car, with a family inside, being swept away by a runaway swollen river. The occupants were beating the windows in a frantic bid to escape. But the car was swept onwards and its hapless occupants were most likely buried under a mountain of mud.

'The sense of helplessness I felt, watching this happen before my eyes and knowing that I could do nothing, was horrific. It really was terrible,' said Ms O'Neill, Trócaire's Central America director.

Following Hurricane Mitch, Trócaire mounted a major relief operation, coordinated by Sally O'Neill, in five departments of Honduras, providing food, water, medicine and essential cooking stoves to 85,000 people who had lost their homes and crops because of the hurricane. At least one million people were affected, one in six of the population. More than 100 villages and communities had disappeared. People who had very little had now lost everything. It was a humanitarian disaster that unleashed human suffering on a massive scale and ruined the fragile economy of what was already one of Latin America's poorest countries.

Sally O'Neill quoted the Honduran vice-president as saying that it could take the Honduran people forty years to get back to where they had been before the hurricane struck. She reported that ten days after the start of the floods, entire communities in Tegucigalpa, most but not all poor, had been swept away. They had no electricity, little food, petrol had run out, phones functioned in only one district and one-third of all homes had been swept away. At least one-quarter of a million families were displaced in Tegucigalpa alone. Half the country was submerged by floods.

Assessing the damage in Tegucigalpa, she found that only one of the five bridges over the massive Choluteca River that bisected the city was standing, and that the water had reached the third floor of the main public hospital. She met a man carrying his three-year-old daughter, dead, wrapped in a plastic tablecloth – he had been turned away from the morgue, which had no electric power and was packed to the ceiling with dead bodies.

The walls of the central prison had collapsed and 2,000 prisoners tried to jump into the river below, resulting in the police opening fire on them. Ms O'Neill was trapped on the other side of the river and she said that it looked like a scene from a horror movie as bodies of dead prisoners were carried along in the swollen river together with fridges, TV sets, wood, pick-up trucks and bits of houses.

Assessing the damage

Honduras was one of the poorest countries in Latin America, with 82 per cent of the population living below the poverty line. A typical monthly shopping bill for a family of five came to £280, while the monthly minimum wage was only a quarter of that. And that was before Hurricane Mitch struck.

Honduras was a country where everyone worked because work meant survival – there was no dole or state-funded safety nets. Shoe-shiners, newspaper boys and women and children selling sweets and snacks were everywhere on the streets of the major cities. Entire rural villages moved to coffee plantations in the harvest season. Hundreds of thousands of families depended on employment on plantations where bananas, citrus, sugar cane and melons were grown for export. They also worked on shrimp farms and in 'maquillas' – clothing assembly plants for the US market but in essence sweatshops.

However, as a result of the hurricane, 70 per cent of these key exchange earners had been wiped out. The free-trade zones on the coast had been flooded and were swamped in mud. The foreign-owned companies would mostly go to other countries and leave 100,000 Hondurans jobless.

The damage to infrastructure was huge, with up to ninety bridges destroyed and five airports out of operation. This damage was so extensive that only massive international commitment and technical assistance could have enabled Honduras even to return to where it was, let alone continue to develop. While emergency aid was needed to solve the immediate problems, the scale of the disaster called for long-term structural aid and the cancelling of Honduras's foreign debt.

The cost of the damage to roads and buildings was put at some $2 billion. Electricity and water systems were down in 70 per cent of the country and it was impossible to move around from one city to another. All of this destruction had occurred in a country which was already burdened by a massive debt and which had been struggling to get on its feet after the horrors of the 1980s when all of Central America was hampered by civil wars.

For Trócaire, the disaster meant that a decade of work had been lost and hundreds, if not thousands, helped by the agency and the Irish people had been killed. Some twenty-nine Trócaire projects had been destroyed and another thirty in health and agriculture made meaningless. This meant loss of hope for the poor and most vulnerable communities.

Before Hurricane Mitch had wiped out so much of the country's infrastructure, Honduras had featured on the list of the world's most indebted countries hoping to get debt relief from the World Bank and its international creditors. If its external debt of $4 billion was unpayable before the disaster struck, the only way the country could survive was for the world financial community to write off the debt. Long before Hurricane Mitch, the Honduran government, ruling a country so poor that some of its inhabitants used hammered-out Coca-Cola cans to build houses, repaid $1 million a day to the developed world. As one journalist remarked at the time, even the most stony-hearted could understand the complete injustice of asking a country to repay loans on roads and bridges that no longer existed.

Trócaire's response

Trócaire called on the Irish government to play a key role in motivating the EU to take a coordinated response to the destruction in Central America. It urged the Irish government to engage in serious discussions with the EU and the inter - national financial institutions at the highest level on recovery and reconstruction, debt cancellation and disaster prepared-ness in the region.

Trócaire had earmarked £400,000 for the Hurricane Mitch disaster by the end of the first week of November 1998. It received £100,000 in funding from the British government. A few days later, the Irish government announced a second allocation of £200,000 for disaster relief in the region. The money was channelled through Trócaire and the Agency for Personal Service Overseas (APSO).

An *Irish Times* article on the disaster, in mid-November 1998, said that Trócaire was 'delivering assistance in a fashion that is markedly different' from many other international agencies that came into the region to offer aid. Despite their intentions, the article said, it became immediately obvious to observers that many of the big international agencies were unfamiliar with Honduras. They were struggling to become familiar with the chaotic terrain and in addition were dealing with their own bureaucratic and communications difficulties.

Trócaire, the article said, had huge advantages. People like Sally O'Neill, who had first arrived in the 1970s, were Central America experts and had lived there for years before the hurricane struck. Most importantly, Trócaire was small enough to be fast and efficient. While some American-based agencies were still trying to find trucks to rent and to clear the paperwork to get the money to do so, Ms O'Neill had already cleared an emergency budget approval of £200,000 from Dublin. Bags of rice were already on their way in trucks rented from local Honduran contacts by the time the rain subsided, the *Times* article remarked approvingly.

Another person mentioned in the article, Annalisa Murphy, was coordinating a distribution of emergency food and medicine to some thirty remote villages in an area outside El Triunfo in southern Honduras, to which Trócaire had sent three trucks. She had a master's degree in rural development and Trócaire had a total of 160 rural develop-ment projects in the region, all based on training people to help themselves. Trócaire had a network of local workers and volunteers to distribute food, medicine and water – this was especially important in getting vital supplies to remote villages that had been cut off because roads had been washed away or covered by mudslides. In Central America, Trócaire's involvement had been mostly in long-term development including health clinics, agriculture projects and community rebuilding projects.

Epidemics became a major threat in the wake of the flooding and infections claimed an increasing number of victims, particularly among children. The vast quantities of stagnant waters left by the floods provided ideal breeding grounds for malaria-carrying mosquitoes. In the slums around Tegucigalpa alone, some 50,000 children were exposed to malaria and many more were threatened across the country.

In mid-November 1998, Emma Bonino, the European Commissioner for Humanitarian Affairs, visited Central America. She said that in Nicaragua the damage was more localised but that the entire country of Honduras had been turned upside down. Sally O'Neill met with Commissioner Bonino and described the meeting as very positive. They talked about the difficulty of delivering the aid and Ms Bonino had said that she would intervene with the Honduran authorities if the aid agencies needed help.

Later that same month, Trócaire chairman Bishop Kirby, as well as Bishop Bill Murphy of Kerry and Bishop Ray Field, an auxiliary Dublin bishop, visited Honduras and Nicaragua. Before they left Ireland, they criticised the government's cut in ODA. Bishop Kirby said that the cut was coming at a time when the people of Central America were destitute and totally dependent on outside assistance to survive. He said that during their visit they would be meeting the people behind the statistics, displaced and forced to live in overcrowded shelters, and that they would be hearing the stories of the bereaved.

They spent eight days in Central America, and upon their return called on the government, the Catholic Church and the Irish people to help the victims of the hurricane. They expressed shock at the conditions they had witnessed and called on the government to press for the relief of the major debt burdens faced by Honduras and Nicaragua.

Bishop Kirby condemned the Irish government's decision to freeze the ODA budget for a year. He said that Ireland had advanced considerably because of development aid from the

EU, yet we lacked generosity in what should be a caring attitude to developing countries. The government itself, he said, had set its own ODA target of 0.45% of GNP by 2002, but it was slipping back on that promise.

Bishop Murphy said that they had been 'shocked, appalled and almost frightened' by what they had seen in Honduras and Nicaragua, which was far worse than what they had expected. But he had been very impressed by the resilience of the people and humbled by the depth of their gratitude to them for visiting and by their gratitude to Trócaire and the Irish people for coming to their aid.

Bishop Field described the situation as 'an appalling tragedy on a number of levels'. He said that Honduras already had a foreign debt of $4.5 billion, while flood damage was estimated at $4 billion. Some 7,000 people had died, at least 12,000 were missing and some 300,000 were at that time in makeshift shelters, he said.

Mary Sutton, Trócaire's director of communications and education, and also on the trip, said that there was a great fear of epidemics in the region. Cases of cholera had already been reported and mothers worried about malaria and TB. She saw children and women walking up to their ankles in mud – mud contaminated with sewage. She said that Trócaire had hired extra local staff and had been assigned other workers by APSO. By that time, Trócaire had 1,000 people working in the region and had raised more than £1 million for the relief operation.

Sally O'Neill came back to Ireland for a week in December 1998. In a newspaper interview she gave before she returned to Honduras, she said that the cost of the damage in financial terms would be huge; 3,000 metres of bridges had been swept away and it cost £30,000 to replace, even temporarily, each metre with a portable, pre-fabricated bridge (known as a Bailey bridge), giving some idea of the costs involved.

A lot of the land that had been covered by mudslides would not be suitable for rebuilding, so other land would have to be made available, she said. A large number of people were homeless and did not have ready access to clean drinking water, so they would not be in a position to go to work. And even those who would be able to work could not do so because their places of work no longer existed.

Ms O'Neill gave a very specific example of the crippling burden of debt on Honduras. In 1978, the Hondurans borrowed £90 million to build a hydroelectric dam. By 1997, they had repaid £263 million without having made any inroads into repaying the actual debt. They would not have that £90 million debt paid off until 2046.

In late March/early April 1999, President Mary McAleese visited Honduras. She met President Carlos Flores who thanked her for the efforts of the Irish aid agencies. He said that the Irish presence in his country had been an inspiration.

President McAleese toured Trócaire and APSO aid projects, one of which was the makeshift settlement of El Pantanal in the hills above Tegucigalpa. It had housed hundreds but mudslides had destroyed their homes. They wanted to rebuild there, feeling safe on the higher ground well above the river but the government wanted them to move to an adjacent lower area of land where it was cheaper to supply water and electricity.

The president was accompanied by the Honduran Minister of Development. The people had been trying to get him to visit the site for some time or at least to respond to their concerns. Trócaire had been working with the community and Sally O'Neill told the minister that her agency and others could bring electricity and water to the people there. He was defensive, saying that they did not even know where the original houses had been located but she replied that they had a map of exactly where the houses had been and could start straightaway, work to which he agreed.

Rebuilding and restoration work

In mid-February 2000, in advance of the annual Trócaire 2FM 24-Hour Fast, the *Star* newspaper ran a number of articles on the restoration work taking place in Honduras almost eighteen months after Hurricane Mitch had struck. One of the articles told of the village of Guacamaya, where more than half of the 730 families who lived there had been affected. The women of the village had fought back with the help of Trócaire. By February 2000, they had already built eighty houses, with the women making concrete blocks with an obsolete machine that manufactured six-inch blocks two at a time. They built a community centre where twenty-eight women formed a sewing group to learn tailoring and dressmaking. All this they started with £500 seed capital from Trócaire.

Their men folk were working on farms – or what was left of them – so it was the women who designed and built the houses. These were solid, concrete structures with at least three rooms, all built for around £370 each. By that time, Trócaire had injected £13,000 into this development. Sally O'Neill explained that they had an agreement that Trócaire would pay for a building supervisor and any raw materials.

They had started by dealing with the worst cases in the village – single or abandoned mothers or those with large families. Each family housed had to repay 40 per cent of the cost of their house over three years; the first twelve families to be housed after Mitch had helped more than fifty others to have their homes repaired. The profits from the scheme were ploughed back into it; at that time, they were being used to build toilets beside each completed dwelling.

Many problems had yet to be overcome in Guacamaya, however. Young girls still worked in the maquillas for seven pence an hour. But at least this community owned its own land and was building solid homes that would withstand the inevitable winter floods. In a country as poor as Honduras, that was progress beyond most people's dreams.

Another *Star* article of mid-February 2000 told of how many agencies had swept into Honduras when Mitch had happened, how their efforts had been well intentioned but often ineffectual, and how many of them had left when the publicity had died down. But, the article pointed out, Trócaire was at the forefront of those still involved. It said that the people whom they worked alongside were grateful but did not wish to rely on handouts. They had quickly formed community groups again and had tried to organise themselves. They decided that after a month they would not simply accept aid and instead they made people work to help repair the damage before they could qualify for aid. Maintaining the dignity of communities was vital for the future development of the people and the article regarded Trócaire's approach as very progressive and extremely effective.

Sally O'Neill told the paper that Trócaire felt it was more effective to go into partnership with people on projects that were sustainable and permanent. The approach was not paternalistic and did not throw big sums of money at projects, she said. Instead, people were asked what their needs were and Trócaire tried to make things work so that the people themselves did the work and learned the skills; Trócaire provided the finance to help buy the materials.

Honduras was the original 'banana republic' – so called because the entire northern coast depended on the fruit for its livelihood. Two giants, Chiquita and Dole, carved up the north of the country between them and the plantation workers earned between $2 and $3 a day. Hurricane Mitch wiped out an entire crop and, by February 2000, just half the twenty-two banana plantations owned by Chiquita had been rebuilt. One week had cost 4,000 workers their jobs and 2,500 more union members were in what was known as permanent suspension.

The Coordinating Body for the Unions of Banana Workers in Honduras (COSIBAH) was trying to band workers together in seven Latin American countries so that they could not be divided and conquered. Hurricane Mitch resulted in a huge migration of workers and left the union with as much work in providing emergency food relief and the provision of social housing as in its normal workers' rights brief.

Trócaire worked with COSIBAH on its food and housing projects and with helping the former workers to survive but it was a situation with no easy solution. The agency sought to work with consumer groups in Europe to produce a banana that was justly produced, safe and organic, and that would still offer value by comparison to giant operators in the region.

Campo Cielo, about twenty minutes from the busy centre of Tegucigalpa, was the area worst affected by Hurricane Mitch. In one part of the sprawling slum, at a place called Le Soto, thousands were killed when a massive landslide ripped a hole in the side of the mountain. Almost one and a half years after Mitch had struck, Campo Cielo still had no sanitation or running water. The people, who were mainly poor, uneducated countrypeople who had come to the city in the hope of finding work, were living in deplorable conditions. Their homes were built precariously on the very steep mountainsides and streams of raw sewage ran past their homes.

Trócaire worked hard to try to change things in Campo Cielo. Sally O'Neill told the *Star* that the first thing the agency had done was to ask the people what was their priority – she had thought that it would be food or housing, but it was sanitation that they wanted first. Trócaire worked in partnership with local people who were trying to organise their community.

One of these was Sergia Vazquez, who had used Trócaire funding to build concrete steps to help people get up the mountain. In the wet season, the place was a mud bath so the steps were vital. They also built concrete latrines to take the sewage away. Her community also worked on small-scale, job-creation projects and better housing with the help of Trócaire funding.

However, a lasting solution to the problems of Campo Cielo needed massive government or outside intervention, neither of which was likely. The key to the problems was that the people did not have their own land and work was either hard to come by or woefully underpaid.

Trócaire has continued with its steady and vital restoration work in Honduras. In March 2006, Cardinal Oscar Andres Rodriguez Maradiaga of Tegucigalpa visited Ireland as a guest of the agency. He said that Hondurans were grateful for the help they had received following the devastation of Hurricane Mitch. They had recovered almost everything, he said, which he likened to a miracle thanks to solidarity and working together. One unresolved problem was housing but this was a long-term problem, he said, and the church had been helping a lot with it.

He told of his own involvement in building a small town with 540 houses but he said that it was not a case of just giving a house but of inculcating a new way of being a citizen, with civic education. He said that the people would be responsible for their town, keeping it clean and making a commitment not to have drugs in the community, where there were many young people. He also referred to a congregation of religious sisters who held workshops in the town in baking, computer technology, mechanics and sewing, and the workshops were doing well, he said.

Cardinal Rodriguez spoke of the importance of community to human beings and said that this had been obvious in the aftermath of Hurricane Mitch. They were grateful in Latin America for what people in Ireland had done for them, and remarked on how they had Irish soldiers helping them and that President McAleese had visited to see the damage. Honduras was a small country and it was very important to have had that kind of solidarity, Cardinal Rodriguez concluded.

The southern part of Honduras suffered terrible devastation at the time of Hurricane Mitch. Nothing much grows there in an area that borders Nicaragua and El Salvador because the earth is dry due to temperatures that rarely drop below thirty-five degrees Celsius, and are frequently in the mid-forties all the year round. However, when farming proved futile, Trócaire found the solution for more than ninety rural communities. The climate could not be more perfect for cashew nuts, grown organically and, thanks to Trócaire seed capital, sold directly to a supermarket chain in Albuquerque through the fair-trade company, Just Cashew.

But the enterprise does not only involve cashew nuts. Trócaire provides seed capital in the nearby rural area of San Bonaventura to help women make colourful hammocks, sleeping mats woven from rushes and clay tortilla plates, which are for sale there and across the border in Nicaragua. Now an area where little grows is seeing real progress – thanks to Irish money that created the opportunity for real well-being to flourish.

Sally O'Neill says that Trócaire has built almost 8,000 houses in Honduras in the years since the hurricane devastated the country – probably one of the biggest housing programmes undertaken by the agency. She recalled taking President McAleese to see some of Trócaire's housing projects and how amazed and impressed the president was at the widespread involvement of women in these projects. Ms O'Neill also expressed her gratitude to the Irish government for the financial support it gave her agency in undertaking the vital reconstruction work following the hurricane.

She also paid tribute to the Irish radio and television personality, Gerry Ryan, whose radio show took a particular interest in the aftermath of Hurricane Mitch and aroused the sympathy and support of the Irish people for the victims. Once the lines of communication were restored after the damage done to them by the hurricane, the Gerry Ryan radio show made frequent telephone calls to Honduras to find out what was happening and this evoked a strong response from the Irish public. The show sent an ordinary Irish person, one of the many who had got in touch with the programme, out to Honduras and she reported back daily on the devastation that had occurred and the rescue and restoration work that was under way. Ms O'Neill said that this provided huge publicity that benefited Trócaire's work on the ground.

She said that the effects of Mitch are still being felt in Honduras, especially in terms of the repair to infrastructure, which is still going on.

CHAPTER 17:
The 'Jubilee 2000' Campaign Against the Indebtedness of the Developing World

The inception of and the reasons behind the campaign

The Vatican, in the 1980s, was already well aware of the problem of Third World debt through its network of papal nuncios and justice and peace workers. In 1986, the Pontifical Commission for Justice and Peace published *An Ethical Approach to the International Debt Question*. The Debt and Development Coalition of Ireland (DDCI), of which Trócaire was a leading member, was founded in 1993. The credit for linking the campaign against debt to the Jubilee year 2000 goes to two Anglican theologians, Martin Dent and Bill Peters. In April 1996, they brought together Christian Aid, CAFOD and the Tearfund (a UK Christian relief and development agency, working with a global network of local churches) to found the Jubilee 2000 campaign. The DDCI saw the value of the idea and in 1997 adopted Jubilee 2000 as the name for their campaign.

Early the following year, Trócaire joined with the Jubilee 2000 coalition in Britain, CAFOD, Christian Aid, SCIAF (the Scottish Catholic International Aid Fund of the Scottish Catholic Bishops' Conference) and a wide range of inter-national organisations to give the more than one billion people, living in countries with high levels of debt owed by their governments to rich Western governments and banks, something to celebrate when the new millennium arrived. Their quest was for a new world in which balance, order and justice were restored.

One of the greatest world disorders the Jubilee 2000 movement perceived was the crushing weight of international debt. People in the West were generally unaware how it seriously damaged the lives of people in countries affected by it. Even if countries such as Sierra Leone, Rwanda or Burundi became bankrupt, the debts and interest on those debts continued to pile up. Scarce resources needed for health, education and safe water had to be diverted to pay the debts to rich creditors such as the US, Germany, the UK and Japan or to institutions dominated by them.

For every £1 the West as a whole gave to developing countries, £3 came straight back in the form of debt repayments. People in the West might not like having to repay loans they have taken out but at least they signed a contract. The poor of Zaire, for instance, were never asked if they agreed with any of the £5 billion-plus loans made to their corrupt dictator Mobutu (ruler of Zaire, now the Democratic Republic of the Congo, from 1965–1997) by the well-dressed bankers and civil servants of the IMF, the World Bank, the US Finance Department or the British Treasury. But those same poor were the people who were being forced to repay the debt in 1998.

The value of the commodities that earned poor countries money to pay off their debts fell dramatically in the 1980s. International debts could not be paid off in Zambian Kwacha or Mozambican Metical – they had to be paid in dollars or sterling. These 'hard' currencies could be obtained only by exporting goods to international markets. But when the prices poor countries were paid for products such as tea, coffee, copper and sugar fell dramatically, many got into serious difficulties and the IMF moved in. It imposed 'Structural Adjustment Programmes' that required cuts in government spending, cuts in jobs and services and the removal of subsidies. It also forced governments to privatise

THE 'JUBILEE 2000' CAMPAIGN

national assets such as airlines or communications, which were often snapped up by powerful foreign companies. The process was basically a new type of colonialism.

Trócaire and its fellow international agencies were calling for a one-off cancellation of the unpayable backlog of debts of the poorest countries by 2000. They also wished to change the way that loans were given and to impose discipline, honesty and transparency on the lenders as well as the borrowers.

They were collecting signatures for what they hoped would be the biggest petition in the history of the world. The aim was to take that petition to the annual meeting of the leaders of the G8 (the name given to the richest creditor countries), which was due to be held in Birmingham on 16 May 1998. The intention was to surround the meeting with a massive human chain of thousands of people. The theme was, 'Make a chain to break the chains' (of debt and slavery). They were also prepared to take their petition to Berlin in 1999 and Tokyo in 2000.

Contacts had been made and supporters found in sixty countries around the world, with the Jubilee 2000 movement encouraging people to join their coalition wherever they lived.

Trócaire initiatives in 1998

In mid-April 1998, Justin Kilcullen launched a joint policy document with CIDSE and Caritas, 'Putting Life Before Debt', in the US at an international conference that coincided with the spring meetings of both the World Bank and the IMF. By this time, he had been elected president of CIDSE, which was urging world leaders to take into account the human cost of the debt burden. 'Children are now pulling ploughs in Zimbabwe because farmers cannot afford to replace cattle which have died,' he said at the launch. He went on to say that the children carrying the burden of the debt in Zimbabwe, Zambia, South Africa or Bolivia would not be mentioned at the World Bank and IMF meetings; a crisis in

Africa was a crisis for Africans but clearly not for the rest of the world.

He said that the world's debt crisis was almost twenty-five years old by that time, with little respite for the forty-one severely indebted countries, and it had escalated to the point where every person in the developing world owed £250 to the rich countries, more than a year's wages for many of them. 'Putting Life Before Debt' proposed the cancellation of unpayable world debt by 2000 so that those developing countries could begin the next millennium with a fairer chance of making progress.

Trócaire and the DDCI were in Birmingham for the G8 meeting in mid-May 1998. In an event organised by Jubilee 2000, more than 30,000 people formed a human chain around the building where the G8 leaders were meeting as an act of solidarity with the Third World.

Justin Kilcullen pointed out at the time that cancelling the debt owed by Zambia would cost £6.3 billion – less than the cost of one US-made Stealth bomber. He rejected the assertion that cancelling the Third World's debt would be 'utopian folly', and pointed out that already a European precedent existed, because in 1953 the debt of the Federal Republic of Germany (West Germany) was substantially cut.

In September 1998, Trócaire launched the policy document, 'A Human Development Approach to Debt Relief for the World's Poor', which argued that highly indebted, poor countries should be allowed to set aside funds for basic health and educational needs, as well as investment in productive capacity, before they were asked to make debt repayments. The document criticised a Third World debt-reduction initiative introduced in 1996 by the World Bank and the IMF. This initiative aimed to bring poor countries' debts down to realistic levels. However, the Trócaire document argued that the definition of what was a realistic level was flawed, because it measured countries' ability to repay debt in relation to their export income, irrespective of the level of poverty and the investment required to fulfil basic human needs such as primary education and healthcare.

Trócaire's document set out an alternative approach to the debt issue, which it said was consistent with the OECD's target of halving the number of people living in extreme poverty by 2015. At the launch of the document, Justin Kilcullen said that the world had to take into account the human cost of the debt burden on poor countries, when it cost only $16 per year to provide healthcare for every person, and a comprehensive primary education cost only $12 per pupil per year. Yet even those paltry figures were too much to pay, he said, when countries were heavily in debt.

Jubilee: the basis for three Trócaire Lenten campaigns

Trócaire made the cancellation of the debt of the world's poorest countries and giving those countries a new start in the new millennium the theme of its 1999 Lenten Campaign. The agency took the biblical Jubilee idea and decided to make it the basis of its three Lenten Campaigns for 1999, 2000 and 2001. Annette Honan, Trócaire's education and campaigns coordinator, devised the three campaigns and provided the educational and campaigning material for each of them. A particular country focus was adopted as well as a particular theme.

In a recent interview for this book, Ms Honan said that the Jubilee campaign was very much trying to speak to a church audience as well. The education materials went out to the schools and would have been used there mainly, though not exclusively, by religion teachers, she said, but she also wrote a booklet for each year with homilies for each Sunday in Lent and the themes of the campaign were woven into those homilies. These booklets were sent to priests all over the country and gave them the option of basing their homilies for their Sunday Masses on the material in the booklets.

Ms Honan felt it was a very effective way of getting Trócaire's message out about the Jubilee campaign. She described that campaign as very inclusive and said that large numbers of signatures supporting the aims of Jubilee 2000 were gathered at Masses. Throughout the Lenten Campaign, leaflets giving information on Third World debt were distributed to every church in the country. She said that each Sunday in Lent the message was coming from the pulpit, the leaflets were at the back of the churches and very often a Trócaire worker was present at the Masses and asked people to sign the Jubilee 2000 petition as they left the church.

At the launch of the 1999 Lenten Campaign, Bishop Kirby said that one half of the world would be cracking open bottles of champagne on the stroke of midnight that year, while millions in the developing world would be drinking stagnant water. He blamed the debt crisis for the death of a child almost every minute in the developing world.

Bishop Kirby described the world's unpayable debt crisis as 'a silent holocaust' and said that Trócaire wanted a once-off cancellation, by the year 2000, of the unpayable debt owed by the world's poorest countries. He went on to say that the cost of cancelling the debt was estimated at £100 billion – just over 4.3% of the total debt of developing countries. Tackling the debt issue by the end of 1999, which was possible and should happen, he said, would mean that the dawn of the new millennium would be a global celebration.

The Lenten Campaign was launched with the release of fifty-seven helium-filled balloons with Trócaire boxes attached. The balloons symbolised the fifty-seven children who died each hour in the developing world because of famine, starvation and misery, most of it the result of the debt burden.

A full-page newspaper advertisement calling for 'a fresh start for the poor' accompanied the start of Trócaire's Lenten Campaign in February 1999. The advertisement explained how the Third World debt came about, how early in the 1970s, the oil-producing countries raised oil prices, made a fortune and put this money mainly into US and European banks. In turn, the banks gave loans to the poorer countries, in many cases not checking where this money was going. Lots of it was wasted on projects that failed due to bad management and planning. Some dictators stashed the money in foreign bank accounts. However, some countries spent the loans on health, education and genuine development.

Then at the end of the 1970s, interest rates rocketed and those countries had huge interest bills to pay; this coupled with the fall in the price of their export produce led to a situation spiralling out of control. The IMF and the World Bank then stepped in to give new loans and thus ensure that the countries would continue to meet their debt repayments. The impact of this was devastating on healthcare, education, the environment, women and children as these countries continued to borrow just to meet their interest bills. This situation had to end, the Trócaire advertisement declared.

It called on its readers to imagine a really new millennium – one that heralded a new world order, a world of fairness, equality and peace. In contrast was the existing world of war, slavery and oppression, where in some countries even the most basic of needs (water, food, sanitation) were not being met. The advertisement said that the world was on the threshold between these two opposing visions, and the decisions that the world governments would take in the following years would shape the next millennium. It was too important to leave it only to them and all must play their part, the advertisement urged, and added that there was a powerful new movement growing around the world to deliver a more enlightened millennium – a new beginning for the world's poor and oppressed.

The problems of the world could seem overwhelming: more than a billion people survived on less than a dollar a day, while 225 rich people lived on the same combined income as half the world's population. The advertisement gave some startling statistics: for example, while Europe spent $12 billion on ice cream, $9 billion would provide water and sanitation to those who did not have them in the developing world; while the US spent $8 billion on cosmetics each year, an extra $6 billion would provide basic education for all children unable to attend school at that time.

The advertisement pointed out that ten million children each year – 230,000 per week – died because of malnutrition and preventable diseases, such as measles, pneumonia or even diarrhoea. Many countries in Africa, Asia and Latin America were caught in this 'life or debt' trap, the advertise - ment explained. It urged that, in order to launch the new millennium, a solemn contract should be made with the world's poorest countries, and it called on its readers to intensify the powerful movement worldwide for a once-off cancellation of unpayable debts.

The advertisement referred to the active role Trócaire was playing in the international Jubilee 2000 campaign, and declared that it was time to dump the debt, along with slavery, torture and oppression, on the scrapheap of the abominations of the old millennium.

People could make exciting plans about how they would mark the new millennium, or they could say there was nothing they could do about world injustice, or they could take action, the advertisement continued. It reminded its readers that most positive change came about because many people took small steps. It described how, by supporting Trócaire, Irish people were already helping the debt-ridden people of Zambia and other countries.

In the village of Luansobe, in the copper-belt province of Zambia, working through a local organisation called the Koloko Trust, Trócaire helped with the construction of housing and with farm-management courses, also ensuring that essentials such as a clean water supply, farm equipment, crops, livestock and food stores were in place. As a result, a thriving community began to develop and, by 1999, an area that was once a wilderness was home to 15,000 people, all with access to education, healthcare and food within their own community – an inspiring model of what could be done when the poor were given a fresh start.

At that crucial time in history, the advertisement declared, Trócaire believed its role was to help people to take those small steps: to speak out and name injustice; to support organisations toiling for positive change; to stand beside human rights defenders, and to foster partnership. That meant people in Ireland and local people in the developing world all working together, partners in a new millennium, the advertisement concluded.

The G8 summit in Cologne, June 1999

In June 1999, leaders of the G8, meeting in Cologne, agreed to write off $71 billion of the debts owed by the world's poorest nations. They claimed that this would reduce the poor countries' total debt burden by one-third and they also agreed to increase the number of countries eligible for debt reduction from twenty-nine to thirty-six.

However, Trócaire's Caoimhe de Barra, in Cologne to take part in Jubilee 2000's demonstration in which more than 50,000 people formed a human chain around the centre of the city, criticised the decision to include $20 billion of aid-related debt in the package. While welcoming the reduction, she said that it was not actually as generous as it appeared and would not substantially change the problems that developing countries faced.

Justin Kilcullen, also in Cologne, said that the DDCI was bitterly disappointed that the G8 commitment fell far short of even the limited expectations that they had had but that they would continue to rally public support for the alleviation of the debt. He pointed out that the money freed up amounted to $27 billion over a number of years, dramatically less than what was needed to provide a permanent release from the debt crisis for poor countries.

He emphasised that while the G8 also noticed the vulnerability of developing countries to 'exogenous shocks', the biggest shock remained the burden of unpayable debt. The G8 summit had earmarked $70 billion in write-offs for struggling Third World economies, but the cumulative debt of sub-Saharan Africa alone stood at an astronomical $250 billion. For the countries worst affected, repayments added up to approximately 40 per cent of government budgets, and

Tanzania, for example, spent nine times as much on debt servicing as it did on health, with 40 per cent of its people dying before the age of thirty-five.

Bishop Bill Murphy, also in Cologne, said that he was especially heartened by the public response to the issue of Third World debt during the summit. He spoke of the pride he felt when the crowd cheered loudly in acknowledgement of Ireland's achievement in gathering more than 800,000 signatures to add to the Jubilee 2000 global petition of twenty-two million. How could the leaders of the West ignore those millions of voices, he asked; if they did, their attitude was not only anti-poor but also anti-democratic.

At the end of September 1999, President Bill Clinton announced that he wanted to write off the total debt to the US of the poorest countries, and Jubilee 2000 warmly welcomed the announcement. The British Chancellor, Gordon Brown, also welcomed it and indicated that Britain would consider following suit. Irish anti-debt campaigners criticised the Irish Minister for Finance, Charlie McCreevy, for failing to call for more radical debt cancellation at the annual joint meeting of the World Bank and the IMF.

Trócaire initiatives in 2000
Throughout 2000, the Jubilee 2000 campaign in Ireland focused on lobbying Japan, which was to host the G8 summit in July that year. The link between debt and environmental destruction was also highlighted – the world's indebted nations were destroying their rain forests, fisheries and other sustainable resources, trying to raise debt-repayment revenue. Indeed the environment and environmental degradation became the focus of Trócaire's 2000 Lenten Campaign.

In late May 2000, Justin Kilcullen wrote an article for the *Irish Times* in which he argued that Ireland had a vital role to play in the EU's relations with Africa. He pointed out that some 85 per cent of people throughout Africa were impov-erished; of the 590 million in sub-Saharan Africa, 205 million lacked access to healthcare and 220 million survived on less than $1 a day. He also pointed out that the global epicentre of the AIDS epidemic was in the same area, yet money vitally needed for treatments was being diverted to the West to pay for unpayable debts.

Each year, the area paid around $12 billion to the West in repayments, yet only $9 billion would pay for health, education, and other basic regional needs. Things were getting worse, not better, he added, because that was the only region in the world where the number of malnourished people was expected to rise in the period to 2020. It was the only area where average incomes were lower in 2000 than they had been in 1970, he pointed out.

The leaders of Europe and Africa had met for the first ever EU-Africa summit in Cairo in early April 2000 to look at their shared responsibilities in promoting sustainable development, eradicating poverty and fostering peace in Africa. The leaders promised to intensify efforts to meet internationally agreed targets for ODA (0.7% of GNP – the UN target set back in the 1970s) and, as part of their action plan, they expressed hope for the creation of a world-solidarity fund to address Africa's development. As a first step, Justin Kilcullen contended that EU members should strive to set a specific timeframe to reach the UN target as against their average at that time of 0.34%.

He went on to show how the unpayable debt crisis was crippling Africa. He gave the example of Mozambique, where the economy had been booming before the recent floods hit the country, with average annual growth rates of 10 per cent; however, its debt burden was a major obstacle in translating that growth into poverty reduction. He lamented how some of the decisions reached by the EU leaders at the summit were at best minimalist and at worst likely to be ineffectual.

At the beginning of the new millennium, he said, the EU was a shining example of a region overcoming past legacies of conflict and rebuilding devastated economies. Within the EU, Ireland had a proud tradition, spanning many decades, of solidarity with Africa. As the rest of the world exploited the continent, Ireland was providing support, he said, and he stressed the vital importance of Ireland working within the EU to transform Europe's relationship with Africa.

The September 2000 meeting of the IMF became the next focus of the Jubilee 2000 campaign. Many thought that the G8 meeting in Cologne the previous year had seen a real breakthrough in the debt campaign, but Justin Kilcullen remarked in late July 2000 that while it had been announced in Cologne that debt relief would be granted in a matter of weeks, a year later only one country, Uganda, had received any form of relief. He added that as the world's poorest countries waited for debt relief, lives were being sacrificed, opportunities wasted and hope was fading for millions.

Slavery the theme of the 2001 Lenten Campaign

As the third prong of its three-year Jubilee 2000 campaign, Trócaire made 'slavery' the theme of its Lenten Campaign 2001. Its full-page newspaper advertisement for the campaign began with the shocking statistic that there were twenty-seven million slaves in the world at that time: men, women and children held against their will, forced to work under the threat of violence and paid a pittance, if anything at all. The different types of slaves were listed: chattel slaves, bonded labourers, sex slaves and child soldiers. Slavery was big business in the world at that time, the advertisement avowed.

It referred to some of the crucial differences between 'old slavery' and 'new slavery'. One difference was that old slavery was legal and slave-owners were held legally responsible for their slaves but now, while slavery was officially abolished in almost every country, no one took responsibility for the millions of slaves, and many governments were unwilling to enforce their own laws. Another difference was that in the nineteenth century, slaves were in limited supply, expensive to buy and generated low profits, but in the twenty-first century, they were cheap, plentiful and hugely profitable. New slaves were treated like dirt; extremely vulnerable children, women and men were controlled, abused and thrown aside

– treated like disposable commodities with no rights, no hope and no future.

The most common form of this new evil, the advertisement said, was bonded labour or debt bondage. Poor, vulnerable people were tricked into taking a loan for as little as £25 – the cost of medicine, for example, for a sick child. To repay the debt, they were forced to work long hours, seven days a week, year after year. They became trapped, under the threat of violence, and remained in bondage long after the original debt was cleared. In other situations, people could be lured away from extreme poverty in the hope of finding a better life – only to be tricked and enslaved.

Trócaire was fighting the shame of slavery worldwide because it was time this obscenity was abolished forever, the advertisement declared, and it went on to describe three ways in which the agency was working against slavery. One was by supporting local groups in developing countries battling to liberate slaves and to hold governments and slave-owners accountable. A second was by offering a fresh start (with education, training and grants) to people who had been enslaved. And a third was by campaigning, on an international level, for an end to all forms of modern slavery.

The advertisement featured a picture of a four-year-old girl called Priya, who was born a slave. To her mother, the advertisement said, she was precious but to her slave-holder she was next to worthless. It went on to explain that for generations her family had been enslaved as bonded labourers on estates in Tamil Nadu, India, and that her father saw both his father and grandfather tied to and flogged at the same tree. He knew people who had been beaten to death and that everyone lived in constant fear of beatings and abuse.

The advertisement told how one of Trócaire's local partners had begun to help Priya's family three years before that, how they entered the estates disguised as relatives, giving the workers the knowledge, confidence and support to be liberated. Priya was saved along with her three brothers.

But it was too late for her fourteen-year-old brother. Priya's father was forced by abject poverty to sell him into bondage for just £25 a year before the family was freed and now he could not be found. His father felt pain and regret for losing his eldest son, but since emancipation he had become a strong voice for other families still enslaved. Priya was lucky. Her family was free at last of a cruel world that trapped generations into slavery and forced parents to sell their own children.

The advertisement argued that low-cost, high-profit slavery was big business and declared: 'When you're greedy and ruthless, profit has a greater value than any human life.' Human slaves, it continued, had become a cheap, disposable and lucrative source of income for greedy and powerful people throughout the world. Across south-east Asia, India, Pakistan, north and west Africa and Brazil, large-scale slavery thrived on corruption and the complicity of governments and the police.

The advertisement pleaded with people not to say there was nothing they could do, and asked them, if there was nothing else they did, to help with these two actions: one was that from 5–21 June 2001, the annual conference of the International Labour Organisation, governments, trade unions and employers from 175 countries would be examining the problem of forced labour. A plan of action for the subsequent four years was to be agreed and Trócaire wanted the Irish Minister of State for Enterprise, Trade and Employment, Tom Kitt, to ensure that practical action would be taken at that meeting to fight slavery worldwide. The first action people could take to strengthen the minister's hand was to sign a cut-out coupon provided at the end of the advertisement and to send it to the minister, care of Trócaire. This would be part of Trócaire's biggest postcard campaign ever.

For almost thirty years, Trócaire had supported enter - prising human rights groups that were fighting slavery and injustice in the developing world. It was difficult and dangerous but absolutely vital work. Countless courageous groups urgently needed Irish people's support and, as their second action, people were being asked to give that support.

On 8 March 2001, Trócaire organised a public meeting in Dublin on 'Slavery in the Modern Economy'. The main speaker was Professor Kevin Bales, an adviser to the UN working group on slavery. He called on Ireland to take a leadership role on the UN Security Council (of which Ireland was a member in 2001 and 2002) on the issue. He said that slaves were cheaper at that time than they ever had been in human history and compared them to biros, 'things that can be bought cheaply, used intensively for a limited period and then discarded easily'.

Keeping the pressure up on the G8

In advance of the G8 finance ministers summit in Genoa (21–23 July 2001), Trócaire called the promises of the world's richest nations to relieve Third World debt 'hollow'. Deputy director Mary Sutton said the G8 countries were misleading public opinion when they pretended they had given 100 per cent debt cancellation. She said analysis of actual debt cancellation revealed that heavily indebted poor countries had had on average one-third of debt-servicing payments cancelled. This meant that the world's poor were still paying more on debt repayments than on healthcare or education, she said, and added that Trócaire was waiting for the G8 'to see the job through'.

Zambia showed the reality of poverty more than most poor countries. Its national external debt was $6.3 billion but most Zambians lived on a dollar a day and many died from disease or hunger because they lacked even that means of survival.

Trócaire gave the example of Caroline Mumba. Her experience gave a glimpse of the reality of Zambia's debt and indeed that of many other African countries. She lived in Masisi 'compound', a collection of ramshackle huts between a railway line and a disused limestone mine – a terrible place of open sewers, drunks and children orphaned by AIDS. Her hut, shared with her unemployed mother, her grandmother and her cousin, was the size of a coal shed and just as dirty. Like the other huts in Masisi, it had no electricity or running water.

Caroline, a sixteen year old, sat on a dirty blanket, her legs stretched out in front of her. Despite the squalor, she looked smart in her checked blazer, and was dignified greeting visitors with a shy smile. But when the cloth covering her legs was pulled back, the sight was heartbreaking: her right foot was a disfigured mash of raw flesh and metal pins. To horrified visitors she explained that it had been like that for four months. She had been knocked down by a lorry and rushed to Lusaka's main hospital.

Under normal circumstances, she might have been released in a week and have made a full recovery. But Zambian hospitals could not afford surgical gloves, let alone expensive surgery. The doctors cleaned the wound, with Caroline's mother having to go out to buy some of the medicines from a nearby pharmacy because the hospital shelves were bare. The makeshift job they did with pins and wire did not work and eventually they sent Caroline home, telling her mother to wash the wound with water mixed with Jik, a caustic powder used to scrub sinks and toilets. Since then, she sat in the half darkness of the shack, going to the toilet where she sat and fearing the inevitable amputation. But she bore the wound uncomplainingly; 'at night it is painful,' was all she said.

Caroline's case was highlighted by Declan Walsh in the *Irish Times*. Readers responded generously and donated the money that enabled her to have the medical treatment that saved her leg and that helped her family to move to better living conditions (as confirmed in the *Irish Times*, 14 September 2002).

This young girl's case, repeated many times over through - out Africa, illustrated the terrible burden of Third World debt. For example, in 2000, Zambia spent $76 million on propping up its ramshackle health system. During the same period, it spent $89 million on servicing its enormous national debt.

Forty-eight sub-Saharan African countries carried this impossible burden, paying $13.5 billion in annual interest. Most of these countries had collapsing health and educational systems and were being ravaged by AIDS.

Still, Western creditors insisted the debt had to be paid, a stance the Jubilee 2000 campaign had been battling as deeply immoral and economically crazy. The campaign achieved some, if limited, success, with the IMF and World Bank agreement, at the end of 2000, to cancel a large part of the debt of twenty-two countries under the Highly Indebted Poor Countries (HIPC) initiative. In Zambia's case, this involved cancelling or rescheduling 60 per cent of its national debt.

However, half way into 2001, the benefits of the HIPC initiative were difficult to see. Debt relief came with an extensive array of conditions, and the actual benefit for the twenty-two countries was much smaller than it might have seemed. Zambia benefited by just $35 million per annum over the subsequent five years and, ironically, because of the oddities of the IMF loan structures, its interest bill in 2001 was higher than in 2000.

Therefore, in late July 2001, campaigners descended on the G8 summit in Genoa, calling for the unconditional cancellation of the entire Third World debt.

Concerns about accountability and transparency caused the IMF and the World Bank to demand that the beneficiaries of debt reduction draw up poverty-reduction programmes that clearly showed the debt-relief money being funnelled into health and education. But such requirements could be overly bureaucratic and slow moving, and by July 2001 only Uganda and Mozambique actually managed to fulfil the stringent conditions and receive full debt relief. Campaigners wanted political reforms to follow debt cancellation and not vice versa.

The debt debate also opened up a wider argument about the hold the West had over African economies through the IMF and the World Bank, and whether enforced globalisation was the solution to the problems of the world's most under - developed continent. Zambia was an example of where a country had accepted liberalisation in the past yet slid further into poverty. Hospital fees were introduced as part of 'cost-sharing' to reduce health spending but the result was that many could not afford treatment. Copper mines, once Zambia's main foreign-currency earner, were privatised, with many losing their jobs, although some mines subsequently did well. Inflation fell significantly throughout the 1990s but people had less spending money.

Luanshya, in northern central Zambia, was once one of the biggest mining areas in the copper-belt but a bungled privatisation in 1997 led to disaster. Debt campaigners pointed to it as symptomatic of the havoc caused by Western economic recipes. They admitted that corruption and mismanagement were endemic and that debt cancellation would not be the panacea for poor countries' problems, but they argued that it would at least give them a chance to get off their knees.

Trócaire was one of the fourteen members of the Catholic network of development agencies that met in Genoa to coincide with the G8 summit. At the summit, only £13 billion of the £100 billion debt reduction promised in Cologne was written off. Trócaire said that Genoa was an example of a golden opportunity that had been missed. Policy analyst Maura Leen told the *Irish Catholic* that the cost of holding the summit could have removed the debt of Ghana. She said that the global economy had taken off at a pace that had not ensured fair play and that many countries were moving in the wrong direction on their overall aid budgets.

Difficulties over debt relief for poor countries were fundamentally about power and accountability, she said, adding that the G8 accounted for nearly half the shares and votes of the IMF. She pointed to the example of Uganda, which had received debt cancellation and now had universal primary education, and she said this should spur on further relief.

The Jubilee 2000 campaign achieved some success and the experience gained and lessons learned from participation in it fed into the 'Make Poverty History' campaign, which began in 2005.

CHAPTER 18:
'The Gardeners of the World, Not Its Plunderers': Making Poverty History

Postcard campaign launched, January 2005

When it became known, in late 2004, that the Irish government was going to renege on its promise, made by Taoiseach Bertie Ahern at the UN Millennium Summit in September 2000, to reach the UN target for ODA of 0.7% of GNP by 2007, Trócaire participated in the 'Make Poverty History' campaign. In December 2004, it called on the Irish people to support its bid to wipe out world poverty. It announced it was launching a postcard campaign, in January 2005, in an effort to press world leaders to stamp out hunger and poverty around the globe.

Trócaire believed that the postcards, which it wanted people to send to the Taoiseach would put pressure on the Irish government to stick to the promises it had made about the MDGs (Millennium Development Goals). There were a set of eight internationally agreed development targets to be reached globally by 2015, including reducing child death rates, wiping out extreme poverty and hunger, and tackling diseases such as HIV, AIDS and malaria. A G8 summit was due in the summer of 2005 and Trócaire wanted to drive home the message in time for that gathering.

But it needed the support of the Irish public if pressure was to be put on all the governments who had signed up to the MDGs to reach the agreed international targets on time. A Trócaire spokesperson explained at the time that many MDG campaign organisations from all around the world were joining forces to establish a global network and collectively call on all governments to 'Keep Our Word'.

Trócaire wanted people to pick up the free postcards, which it was making available from January 2005, sign the back and send them to the Taoiseach as well as the British Prime Minister, Tony Blair, endorsing Trócaire's campaign. The intention was that this would be the first step into a decade that would make poverty history. The Trócaire spokesperson said that Ireland was one of the 189 countries to agree to the MDGs at the UN Millennium Summit in New York in September 2000. The Irish government had also made the MDGs a priority when it held the EU presidency in 2004.

The postcard to Bertie Ahern urged him to reinstate Ireland's commitment to spend 0.7% of national wealth on overseas aid and to ensure that this commitment was enshrined in legislation before the end of 2005. The card to the British Prime Minister, Tony Blair, urged him to use the G8 summit in July 2005 as an opportunity to double aid, cancel debt and commit to measurable reforms of international trade – all of which would help make poverty history.

In late January 2005, Lara Kelly, Trócaire campaigns officer, said that the Asian tsunami disaster of 2004 had led to an outpouring of compassion and generosity from all sectors of Irish society. She added that Trócaire hoped that that spirit of compassion would remember not just the victims and survivors of the tsunami but also those who lived through the daily disaster of poverty and hunger worldwide, 24,000 of whom died needlessly of hunger each day. The public had led the way in the tsunami response, she said, digging deep and giving generously. Now Trócaire was asking the ordinary people once again to take the lead in demanding from their politicians that 2005 be the year that we 'Keep Our Word' and 'Make Poverty History'. She asked people to send those postcards to Bertie Ahern and Tony Blair.

The *Star* newspaper covered the annual Trócaire 2FM 24-Hour Fast appeal in February 2005 by sending a reporter to Malawi to look at a Trócaire-funded project there. The reporter's article began by asking its readers to think about the fact that one billion people in the world lived on less than 75 cent a day, that most of them had to walk more than a mile every day just to collect water and firewood, and that they suffered and died from diseases that had been eradicated from rich countries decades before. In addition, reported the article, in some of the poorest countries, less than half the children went to primary school and less than one in five to secondary. This meant that 114 million children in the world did not get even a basic education and 584 million women were illiterate.

The article took the example of Maria Dimba (forty-three years old), who lived in Lilongwe, Malawi and who knew all about the problems just outlined. She could not read or write, had five children and was five months pregnant. But she was attending a literacy class in Lilongwe run by the Medical Missionaries of Mary (MMM) with Trócaire funding. She wanted to learn to read and write so that she could start a small business and make some money for her family. She said that she needed to know how to count and give change to her customers. She believed that learning to read and write would be a start in the process of setting up a business.

Her teacher was Teresa Changaluca (forty-two years old), who came to teach her and other women every Tuesday and Friday afternoon. Although she had five children and taught in the primary school in Divanga during the day, she took the time to help these women because she knew how important it was for them to learn to read and write. She said that with the help of Trócaire and the nuns, the women and their families were being given the chance of a better life.

Sr Mary Donovan, a dynamic MMM nun from Co. Louth, worked with Trócaire to help the families there to grow crops, become literate and get basic healthcare. She had gone to

Malawi in 1988 and had worked as a lab technician in the tropical hospital in Mzuzu. Her mission was to make hospitals safe and hygienic and to start testing for HIV/AIDS in blood transfusions. She said a little education with help in agricultural training and healthcare made a huge difference to those families.

The country focus of the Trócaire Make Poverty History 2005 Lenten Campaign was Ethiopia. Twenty years after the terrible famine of 1984/85, seven million Ethiopians were still dependent on food aid for their survival. The main image on the front of the Trócaire box for the 2005 Lenten Campaign was of a six-year-old girl called Dansa Kule, who lived in southern Ethiopia. 'Dansa' translated into English as either 'prosperity' or 'clean water', which probably reflected the deepest desires of the parents who named her in a country in which drought and poverty go hand in hand. On the back of the box was an image of her walking with her sixteen-year-old sister Badada in the desert where their family lived. The area had been hit by many severe droughts in the years up to 2005 and most families had seen their cattle die and crops wither when the water ran out.

Dansa's and Badada's father was a small farmer and provided for the whole family from his small herd of cattle. A few years before, no rains came and all of his cattle died under the raging sun. The family only just survived. Trócaire had been designing and digging large deep wells in the area so that when water was scarce, cattle could be driven to those wells to drink. Badada often walked the eight cattle that her family owned at that time over six miles to those wells. She often spent much of her day driving them to the wells and then back home again.

As a result, many children and young people did not get a chance to attend school. Taking cattle to water and carrying home enough water for the family became the most important tasks every day. So Trócaire set up 'night schools' in villages such as Dansa's and Badada's. Classes began at 8 p.m. and finished at 10 p.m. Students came eagerly to these schools that were lit only by a single oil lamp because there was no electricity in any of the villages in the area.

In its 2005 Lenten Campaign, Trócaire declared that the world needed a new sense of purpose and energy to help make poverty a thing of the past. In 1985, it said, the Irish people had stood by the people of Ethiopia in solidarity and compassion; twenty years later little Dansa was asking, on behalf of the people of Ethiopia, that the people of Ireland stand by them again. 'Stand by Me' was the theme of Trócaire's 2005 Lenten Campaign. It was a call to action, asking everybody to become involved.

Make Poverty History campaign launched, February 2005
In February 2005, Trócaire joined with other Irish NGOs, trade unions and campaigning groups to launch the Make Poverty History Irish campaign, the Irish contribution to the global campaigns against poverty that year. As well as free post-cards, white wristbands were also on sale online through Trócaire's website and from the agency's offices in Cork, Maynooth, Belfast and Dublin city centre for €1 each. Trócaire also urged people to sign its online petition on the MDGs at www.keepourword.org.

Campaigns officer Lara Kelly said the white wristbands helped to raise public awareness of the campaign and to get the message out to people that pressure had to be kept up on government politicians. She thought that the political will did not yet exist to make the required changes to meet the MDGs.

In an article in the *Irish Times*, shortly after the death of Pope John Paul II in April 2005, Justin Kilcullen argued that his successor could make his own mark on history by lending his moral voice to the campaign for the eradication of global poverty. He referred to how the late Pope had always cham-pioned the cause of the poor and how Trócaire had been greatly influenced by his approach and commitment to human rights. But he warned that unless the nations of the world were truly determined to tackle the problems of poorer countries, and especially those in Africa, the unjust status quo would remain.

Furthermore, he argued that in the modern world, human institutions were responsible for more suffering than so-called acts of God. As plans were under way for the long overdue reform of the UN, the moral authority of the new Pope should be a great advantage in compelling wealthy industrialised nations to tackle the issue of world poverty, Mr Kilcullen maintained. He asked the Irish people to remember that at the richest time in their history in economic terms, they were living in a world where more than 800 million went to bed hungry every night and where somebody, usually a child, died from hunger every 3.6 seconds. Almost three billion did not have clean water and sanitation, and more than thirty million in Africa were infected with HIV/AIDS. Poverty in the developing world meant that thirteen million children died every year because of malnutrition or preventable diseases.

Justin Kilcullen saw the issue of Africa and poverty as the leading moral and ethical question of the time and asked how could the world in good conscience stand by and let this man-made tragedy unfold while society in the north wallowed in consumerism. Catholic teachings on social justice demanded that the church lead the way in helping the world's oppressed, he said. Thus the new Pope had to confront, as did his predecessor, the issues of debt, unfair trade and levels of development aid. The new pontiff had to take up the call of John Paul II for solidarity with the world's poor and for the international community to (in John Paul II's words) 'denounce the existence of the economic, financial and social mechanisms that accentuate the situation of wealth for some and poverty for the rest'.

The UN's MDGs were unlikely to be achieved within the original target date of 2015, Mr Kilcullen thought. John Paul II had pointed out that governments repeatedly failed to honour their promises on aid for development, resolving the question of the heavy foreign debt of African countries and giving those countries special consideration in international trade. The new Pope had to face that reality, Mr Kilcullen ruefully remarked.

In early May 2005, Trócaire published 'More than a Numbers Game? Ensuring the Millennium Development Goals Address Structural Injustice'. Trócaire policy analyst Lorna Gold summarised the document in an *Irish Times* article. She said that by that time, the political haggling ahead of the Millennium +5 Summit, due for the following September, was in full swing at the UN. The purpose of the summit was to review the implementation of the Millennium Declaration, signed in 2000, and progress towards the MDGs.

The so-called 'quick wins' for development put forward by Professor Jeffrey Sachs in the Millennium Project report, 'Investing in Development', were receiving much attention in the media and in government negotiations at the time, Ms Gold pointed out. His idea was to rid the world of global poverty by rapidly improving basic service provision for the poor: providing more mosquito nets, expanding school meals' programmes and undertaking the massive replenishment of soil nutrients. All of this was eminently sensible and, if implemented, would no doubt make a real difference to millions, Ms Gold agreed.

But were 'quick wins' what the developing countries needed or wanted, she asked. Were these proposed solutions not 'easy wins' that the rich countries could take credit for without threatening the balance of power?

In the face of IMF-imposed caps on public spending, crippling external debt, stagnant economies and a lack of predictable finance for basic services, the most pressing challenges were not nets and school meals but avoiding national bankruptcy, Ms Gold maintained. In the first round of negotiations ahead of the September summit in New York, developing countries called for some alternative quick wins, she said, which would have a much greater impact on their development prospects. These were: cancellation of poorest countries' debts, an agreement on the end date for agricultural-export subsidies, full participation of developing countries in standard-setting processes, and in the governance structures of the World Trade Organisation, World Bank and IMF.

Lorna Gold argued that if these changes were implemented immediately, they could transform the balance of power globally. They would lead to more equal conditions for international trade, release additional finance for reducing poverty, and give developing countries a fair say in their own economic and social development. But she felt that, far from being regarded as quick wins, such essential reforms seemed to be slipping off the international development agenda. The global consensus, encapsulated in the MDGs, seemed to be leading the debate away from the difficult yet critical questions of structural reform. Such reforms were wrapped up in political processes that, by their nature, were complex, time consuming and often divisive, she continued.

For the time-bound MDGs, speed was of the essence, she believed. Instead, the focus was on easy solutions often based on a 'sticking-plaster' approach, which could not replace the quest to provide long-term cures. The MDGs were not bad in themselves, she agreed, because they had shown their power as an advocacy tool to put poverty on the global agenda at a time when security was dominating global politics. Yet, they could be interpreted in many ways. They represented a serious risk to the wider politics of development, she believed.

She warned that any proposed increase in aid could lead to new problems if it was not accompanied by reform of the international system. It could bring increasingly centralised dependence on the policy prescriptions of the World Bank and IMF. It was entirely plausible that their failed policies of rapid privatisation and liberalisation, coupled with decreased investment in basic services, could be further accelerated in pursuit of the MDGs.

Ms Gold feared that, in the run up to 2015, many developing countries could find themselves trapped in the paradox of being forced to fulfil IMF conditions in return for 'MDG aid', knowing that those conditions undermined the poverty-reducing impact of government expenditure, thus further increasing dependency on aid. She believed it was possible to avoid such a scenario but that required a more critical approach to the dominant MDG framework. More attention needed to be focused on the systematic blockages to development at a national and international level, she maintained.

At the end of May 2005, Archbishop Seán Brady joined the cardinals and archbishops from Ethiopia, Zambia, Nigeria, India and Honduras for talks with the British government aimed at reminding Tony Blair of his government's commitment to the MDGs. The church delegation delivered more than 177,000 Make Poverty History campaign postcards to 10 Downing Street after their meeting with Chancellor Gordon Brown. The meeting with the British government was only one on a rapid tour that included meetings with the governments of Germany, France and the European Commission in advance of the G8 summit, taking place in Edinburgh in July.

The delegation's objective was to remind the eight wealthiest countries of their commitment to achieving the MDGs. The delegation issued a statement saying the decisions made by the world leaders at the summit would be decisive for the lives of millions of the world's poorest people.

Eamonn Meehan of Trócaire accompanied Archbishop Brady. He said that the churchmen's tour was closely linked to the Make Poverty History campaign. The action demonstrated a global network collectively calling on all governments to Make Poverty History. It was a chance to let the politicians know of the public's strong feelings about overseas development before they met at the G8, he said, and in doing so, the delegation was showing solidarity with those most in need.

Preparing for the G8 summit in Edinburgh in July 2005
In the first and last weeks of June 2005, Trócaire and the other Irish agencies involved in the Make Poverty History campaign organised public rallies in Belfast and Dublin to demand global government action to rid the world of poverty.

Lawrence McBride, Trócaire's campaigns officer in Northern Ireland, said the Belfast rally was a resounding success and the focus was then on getting people to Edinburgh for a planned large-scale rally to coincide with the G8 July summit. He said that busloads of people from Northern Ireland were expected to travel there because people were beginning to stand up and take an active interest in the issue.

Towards the middle of June 2005, Bob Geldof and Bono were credited by the media with causing the G8 group to cancel the debts of eighteen African nations. But both they and the aid agencies warned that this historic step was the first of many needed to wipe out global poverty. And they urged no let-up in the support for the Make Poverty History protest march at the following month's summit in Edinburgh.

Bono called on Taoiseach Bertie Ahern to renew his pledge to commit 0.7% of Ireland's annual wealth to developing countries; the promise was to have been honoured by 2007 but the target date had been abandoned. Bono urged Mr Ahern to use that week's top-level summit of EU leaders in Brussels to reset his sights on a deadline. The aid agencies joined Bono in this plea and suggested the new target date should be 2010.

Caoimhe de Barra, policy analyst with Trócaire, said Ireland should also act as a watchdog to ensure that the eighteen countries due to benefit from the G8 decision would not pay for the waiver in loss of aid. She said that there was a long and dishonourable tradition of G8 leaders promising debt relief and taking money from aid budgets to pay for it. Trócaire's big concern was that essentially this new initiative would be another smoke and mirrors event, she said. After the first big debt write-off at Cologne in 1999, aid budgets were increased but the extra money was used to cancel debt, she recalled.

She added that the list of the eighteen countries chosen did not necessarily represent the countries in most dire poverty but those that it was felt would put their waived payments to best use. She warned that there was a risk of a two-tier system coming about where certain countries would be 'donor darlings and others would be donor orphans'. Ireland's job was to make sure that the countries that were in danger of becoming orphans were not forgotten, she said.

In an article in the *Irish Times*, on the day of the Make Poverty History campaign rally in Dublin (30 June 2005), Lorna Gold gave three reasons why people should join the rally. The first was that it was urgent that the Irish people send a clear message to the Irish government that this issue mattered. As the government dithered about announcing the new target date for meeting the UN target of 0.7% of GNP for ODA, she said the new date being mooted was 2012. But she pointed out that missing the 2007 target, as promised by the government in 2000, cost lives because this broken promise could represent a net loss of more than €1,300 million to the countries that relied on Irish support. According to a costing exercise carried out by the UN Development Programme, with that amount of money, MDGs on health, education and water could have been met in Uganda and Tanzania by 2015.

In addition, she saw a major fear that a future administration would also let this date slip unless there was continued pressure from the public. With so many departments competing for budget allocations, there was always a risk that aid would be put on the back-burner, which was why Trócaire was calling for a precise timetable of year-on-year commitments, she said. In political terms, she continued, it all boiled down to issues that won votes, not moral high ground, so that the Irish people needed to show that this issue was one that mattered to them as a people.

A second reason Ms Gold gave for people to attend the rally was because of the G8 summit taking place two days later. A clear message needed to be sent to the G8 that people worldwide expected results, not just those in the G8 countries themselves. The G8 might not be elected, she said, but millions had to live largely by what it decided. The injustice of this, she believed, should be enough to make people take to the streets, and the G8 leaders needed to know the world was watching.

Her third reason for attending the rally was that, on the eve of White Band Day, when people worldwide would be protesting on poverty, the Dublin rally was an important chance to show Irish solidarity with the world's poorest. She pointed out how mass demonstrations, events and concerts were planned all over the world that weekend to coincide with G8 and Live 8. Therefore, she saw it as an enormous opportunity to show that this was an issue that was not only at the top of the agenda of world leaders but also their own agenda as people.

An estimated 20,000 took part in the Dublin rally, which was led by Bishop John Kirby. Justin Kilcullen was one of the speakers who addressed the rally. He said the crowds gathered at the start of an historic week for relations between the world's poorest and wealthiest countries, and he called on the Irish government to play its part in history by making a fresh commitment to meeting the UN target on ODA. He went on to say that efforts were being made to put together a realistic and genuine response from wealthy countries to the poor and the rally wanted Ireland to be at the heart of that process.

However, all they had to show at that time was a broken promise, he lamented, and as the world leaders were gathering, there was no indication from the Irish government as to what role Ireland would play. He demanded a response from the government that reflected Ireland's position and the presence of so many on the street. What they wanted, he said, was a commitment to reach the UN target by 2010 at the latest and they wanted legislation in place to ensure there would be no reneging on that promise.

Trócaire was among the aid agencies and other organi-sations that organised buses to take people to Edinburgh for the demonstration to coincide with the G8 summit. More than 1,000 Irish travelled there and joined the 250,000 who marched through the city centre. Emer Mullins, communications coordinator for Trócaire, afterwards wrote about the event in the *Sunday Independent*.

She described it as the biggest demonstration in Scottish history, involving young and old, black and white, male and female, clergy and lay people, communists, socialists, ideologists, capitalists and campaigners of every hue. Their demand was clear, she said: Make Poverty History. She asked what would be the legacy of Edinburgh, of the Live 8 concerts in nine cities, of a global event designed to influence the G8 summit later that week.

Ms Mullins thought it beggared belief that in a Western society of such conspicuous consumption, where people were often judged by what they drove or where they lived, that a baby or a young child just a nine-hour flight away died every three seconds from poverty-related causes. While she wrote those few words, how many had died, she asked.

She said that her first trip to Africa the previous year had brought home to her how naive she had been in assuming that if something could be done to help Africa and the developing world, then surely it would be. That one trip had shown her the value placed on the lives of millions, she said. They were not worth 7c in every €100 that Ireland earned in GNP, according to the government then in power, she remarked and went on to say that the lives at stake in that monstrous game of global haggling over money were black lives. If they were not black or brown or yellow, it would not happen, she maintained, because the Western world would not allow a white child to die every three seconds from poverty.

Edinburgh's legacy would be apparent in the subsequent days and weeks, when the media had gone and the last strains of music from the concerts had died away, she concluded.

During the summit itself, Lorna Gold, who had remained in Edinburgh for its duration, said Trócaire hoped that the demonstrations of public opinion that had been witnessed over the previous week would be turned into concrete action. She specified $50 billion of additional aid to start the following year, 100 per cent debt cancellation for sixty countries that needed it and further progress on free trade.

The G8 leaders at Edinburgh pledged to double the amount of aid for Africa to $50 billion by 2010, as well as a $50 billion increase in funding worldwide. Trócaire expressed disappointment at the limited increase in aid to Africa announced, stating that it was not enough to make poverty history. Caoimhe de Barra told the *Irish Catholic* that delaying the increase in aid to 2010 would cost the lives of millions in Africa and affect the achievement of the MDGs. She said the new increase would not deliver immediate relief to the millions living in abject poverty in Africa, and she pointed out that $50 billion was needed in 2006 alone and only $10–$20 billion of the proposed $50 billion was new money. The remainder was merely a restatement of old promises.

However, Trócaire welcomed other announcements coming from the G8: universal access to HIV/AIDS treatment, moves towards a deal on debt cancellation and the introduction of a new peacekeeping force for Africa. But the agency said the detail of each of these proposals would have to be studied carefully.

Preparing for the UN world summit in September 2005
As the three-day world summit at the sixtieth session of the UN General Assembly in mid-September approached, which was due to review progress towards the MDGs, Justin Kilcullen said in an article published in the *Irish Times* in late August 2005 that the preparations for the summit had been the most acrimonious in recent memory. The real loser in that acri - monious debate had been the world's poor. He pointed out that the meeting was originally billed as the review of the millennium summit, where all member states would consider progress towards the MDGs that were designed, among other things, to halve extreme poverty by 2015.

Yet, he said, despite the millennium project's subsequent 60,000 pages of research into and recommendations on how to end world poverty, virtually no new commitments in the area had been discussed in the run-up to the summit. The lives of the poor seemed as distant as ever from the power politics of international institutions, he lamented.

He said the general view was that the financial issues had been substantially taken care of in the EU Council and at the G8 summit. (In April 2005, the EU had collectively pledged to raise the levels of spending on ODA to 0.7% of GNP by 2015. At the G8 summit in July, the US and Japan had also pledged to increase their spending on ODA, and the summit also pledged to cancel the debts of the eighteen poorest countries.) The consensus, he said, was that the deal had been done and there was no new money on the table; it was not even discussed.

However, Mr Kilcullen thought that the deal reached at the EU and G8 left much to be desired. He said the collective contribution of the international community still fell well short of the recommendations of the major international studies on the MDGs, and he believed a further push, in the context of the summit, would have been possible. Nor had trade reform been on the summit agenda either, he pointed out. Instead, that contentious issue had been postponed to the World Trade Organisation talks in Hong Kong that were coming up. He saw something incongruous about an international summit to review progress on the MDGs that had not negotiated any of the issues under Goal 8, which was building a global partnership for development.

Ireland, he said, had played an important role behind the scenes in the run-up to the UN September summit. Now that it was completed, Mr Kilcullen said that Ireland had a special responsibility to speak out forcefully and publicly in support of the multilateral system and especially the UN's central role.

He urged the Taoiseach to lead by example; when he spoke at the UN General Assembly Hall on 14 September, he had to demonstrate an unswerving commitment that Ireland wanted to be a leader in building a global partnership for development. For Mr Kilcullen this meant three things: a renewed promise to reach the UN target of spending 0.7% of

GNP on ODA by 2010, a reaffirmation of Ireland's commitment to 100 per cent debt cancellation for the poorest
countries, and an underscoring of Ireland's commitment to
reforming the world trading system to work for the poor.

He said that if the Taoiseach did these three things, he
would have the full backing of the Irish people and would set
Ireland apart as a country prepared to take risks and lead the
way in international affairs. Ireland's leadership in 2000 had
helped to bring about a shift in development thinking in the
years since, he said, and he expressed the sincerest hope that
the Taoiseach would find the strength and courage to lead by
example.

At a function in Dublin's Mansion House on 9 September
2005, the Irish Bishops' Conference launched a pastoral letter,
'Towards the Global Common Good'. At the launch, Bishop
Kirby said the Taoiseach had the opportunity the following
week (at the UN summit) to deliver a new commitment on
behalf of the Irish people, one that was realistic, achievable
and morally required. Archbishop Seán Brady said that the
bishops believed the poorest nations of the world continued
to look to Ireland to set the global standard for commitment
to development aid. He said they also believed there was
substantial support among the Irish people for a compelling
and world-leading target that would express their commitment to a more just and compassionate world.

The pastoral also called on Irish Catholics to avoid
branded products, to buy 'fair trade' tea, coffee and fruit, and
to do more to conserve energy in their homes in order to build
a more just world.

The Irish branch of the Make Poverty History campaign at
the same time urged the government to deliver on its
promise to poor countries. That night, supporters from up to
forty groups, including Trócaire, held an all-night sit-out at
Government Buildings where a giant digital counter stated
that a child died every three seconds in the Third World. The
campaign called on the Taoiseach to go to New York the
following week with a credible plan for delivering on the

commitment made to the world's poor and to announce that Ireland would reach the UN target no later than 2010.

At the summit itself, on 14 September 2005, the Taoiseach said that Ireland would reach the UN target by 2012, three years ahead of the EU target date of 2015. Justin Kilcullen, who was with a Trócaire delegation at the summit, said they had hoped the year would be 2010 but they had now been promised 0.6% by 2010 and 0.7% by 2012 – a very positive outcome.

The following day, in an article in the *Irish Times*, he said the final document issued by the summit fudged many of the issues. It fell far short of the 'global partnership for development' on trade, aid and debt that was needed to achieve the MDGs; for example, there were no new commitments on aid, simply a restatement of those made in other forums earlier in the year. On debt, he said there was an acknowledgement of a need for a resolution of the debt crisis but no agreement on how it could be addressed. Nor could governments agree on anything substantial on trade reform. Instead, decisions on trade were deferred to the World Trade Organisation summit in Hong Kong later that year.

It was tempting, he said, given these failures, to call the summit itself a failure but individual member states had set out their own initiatives and commitments to international cooperation. He said the focus now had to turn to the implementation of all these promises – both globally and nationally. The days of world leaders shelving promises made at summits were gone, he continued, because civil-society movements had demonstrated their willingness to hold leaders to account on their promises. He said that young people, especially, took those promises seriously. From Ireland's perspective, they now awaited the annual plan that would turn the solemn promise made into action, he concluded.

Trócaire was among the NGOs that sent representatives to the World Trade Organisation meeting in Hong Kong in mid-December 2005. They were there to push for greater access for developing-country agricultural produce to world markets. At the Hong Kong meeting, countries agreed to phase out all their agricultural export subsidies by the end of 2013. Further concessions to developing countries included an agreement to introduce duty- and tariff-free access for goods from the least developed countries.

Cardinal Rodriguez on globalisation and 'savage capitalism'
Cardinal Oscar Andres Rodriguez Maradiaga, Archbishop of Tegucigalpa, paid a short visit to Ireland with Trócaire in March 2006. The cardinal is widely regarded as one of the world's most charismatic campaigners for human rights and the poor. He has been an outspoken advocate of the cancellation of Third World debt and criticised the US administration under President George W. Bush for its overnight decision the previous summer to provide millions of dollars for the war in Iraq while money for development had been neglected.

In Dublin, Cardinal Rodriguez praised campaigns like Make Poverty History because they opened the eyes of the politicians to the rest of the world. In Belfast, he delivered a lecture on globalisation in which he said we must be 'the gardeners of the world, not its plunderers'. He urged that more be done to help the developing world.

He was impressed by the interest people had in participating in the campaign and making it a political issue. In the globalised world in which they lived, he said, there was a danger of globalising only the economy and the market – people were forgetting to globalise concerns. As regards the tendency to privatise everything, he said the worst thing that could be attempted was to try to privatise humanity because human beings had been designed in community and without community they could not develop and mature. This meant working together to make their world a better place, he said.

Cardinal Rodriguez was a former Vatican spokesman at the IMF and the World Bank on the issue of Third World debt. He said he would like to see Western governments do more to solve the problem but expressed his belief that ordinary people could make a difference by 'sharing their goods, their time, their concern and their prayers as well'.

Delivering the annual Trócaire lecture in Maynooth, he warned that 'a savage capitalism' was returning to the world, where poverty and social injustice were real 'weapons of mass destruction'. What he called this 'neo-liberal capitalism' he saw as creating a world where there was a desire to open up all frontiers to goods, while many obstacles hindered the free movement of persons from southern to northern countries. He went on to say that only the logic of the financial markets had been globalised and that the absolutism of this capital was creating havoc. 'We might say that only the rich are globalised,' he concluded.

Although the Make Poverty History campaign ran only for the year 2005, Trócaire continues to campaign for the issues that were central to that momentous year's activities. In a recent interview for this book, Eamonn Meehan recalled that there was a strong sense at the time that the MDGs were regarded as being very significant in terms of responding to world poverty. There was a strong sense around, he said – largely generated by Messrs Blair, Brown, Bono and Geldof – that one large global push to provide additional resources to end finally the debt burden, to increase aid and improve fair trade would support poorer countries and their development and bring about the delivery of the MDGs.

Mr Meehan contended that there was quite an amount of 'euphoria' around at the time that what was being done was valuable and that if a major effort were only made, that it would be a dramatic contribution towards ending poverty in the world. Looking back from the relatively short vantage point of only a few years later, he felt that the hopes then existing have not been fulfilled. While there was an increase in ODA for a time, the promises made have not been delivered on; most of the rich countries that promised dramatic increases in aid have not, regrettably, kept those promises, according to Mr Meehan.

What the Make Poverty History campaign has taught him, he said, is that there are political uses that can be made of poverty, injustice and international development that support politicians at particular times in their careers and can be used to mobilise people but which do not, by and large, seem to turn into positive outcomes for poor people. He has his doubts about a view of the world that is based on the belief that the solution to poverty will be delivered by the West to others. There is a lot of thinking to be done, he believes, about that particular viewpoint and about the whole development enterprise and what might need to be done to change approaches.

CHAPTER 19:
The Tsunami Disaster in South-East Asia

The early stages of Trócaire's response

As soon as news broke of the tragic earthquake and tsunami in south-east Asia on 26 December 2004, Trócaire immediately donated €100,000 for the relief of victims of the disaster and began to work through its local partners assisting people in the region. The following day, Mary Healy, Trócaire's emergency coordinator, said that the agency's local Caritas partners in India and Sri Lanka were assessing the situation so that they could ensure that the needs of the millions of homeless were met in the long term. She added that it was vital, however, that the emergency relief that was being distributed continued because there were still hundreds of thousands in dire need of temporary shelter, food and clothing.

Mike Williams, head of Trócaire's international department, said that Caritas India and Caritas Sri Lanka were already distributing essential relief supplies to those most in need. He said that thousands of families were being given temporary shelter in churches and schools, and being prov - ided with food, clothing and essential medical assistance. The distribution of this initial emergency relief was vital if the needs of the millions of homeless were to be met in the short term, he said. By 30 December, Trócaire had donated €500,000 to its Caritas partners.

Mr Williams also said that it was vital that the distribution of emergency relief was a jointly coordinated process among all the development agencies if aid was to be efficiently distributed and targeted at those most in need. He regarded it as essential that the UN and the EU took the lead in providing full support to highly qualified and experienced agencies on the ground who were experts in dealing with natural disasters. He expressed the fear that the subsequent weeks would bring further disaster as the risk of disease heightened. Mass burials were already taking place, but the risk of outbreaks of cholera and other water-borne diseases meant larger numbers of people could die, he warned.

On 30 December 2004, Trócaire ran a 'Disaster in Asia: Emergency Appeal' advertisement in the papers. It explained how the unprecedented natural disaster in Asia had claimed tens of thousands of lives and how the death toll continued to rise. In Sri Lanka alone, the advertisement said, more than one million had lost their homes and their livelihoods. Trócaire was working with local partners to provide urgent shelter, clean water, medicines and sanitation, and needed crucial relief funds immediately.

On New Year's Day 2005, Trócaire sent the first of its aid workers – Vicky Tindal and Deirdre Ní Cheallaigh – to Sri Lanka to assist the emergency-response support team made up of Caritas groups from across the world. Ms Tindal said that one of their priorities would be to establish the most urgent needs in the area, which she saw as clean drinking water, medical supplies, food and shelter. She said that since the tsunami, Caritas staff in Sri Lanka had been working round the clock to meet the needs of survivors, and that the reports that had come in from there confirmed the massive need for immediate relief. She added that hugely damaged infrastructure had made the relief workers' job doubly difficult.

They had seen the statistics and images on television and the death toll was rising, she said. More than one million were homeless and the priority was to meet the needs of those in camps. There was a need to move quickly, she continued, with both the UN and NGOs warning that disease among the survivors could double the death toll. She said that the task was much greater than any one agency could meet, so Trócaire had been coordinating a response with local partners. The best way she saw for the Irish public to help was to give what they could.

Ms Ní Cheallaigh spoke to the *Irish News* newspaper about witnessing catastrophic conditions in Sri Lanka a few days after arriving in its capital, Colombo. Sri Lanka was the second-worst affected country in the region – she said that the death toll at that stage had exceeded 30,000, with another 21,000 either injured or missing. The worst hit areas were in the north and north east of the island. Because it was the monsoon season, there had been several flash floods and many of the bridges still standing after the earthquake had been swept away, with some areas experiencing depths of water of six feet.

She said the main problem that faced the agencies trying to help the millions of affected people was getting the aid to them. Around 800 camps for displaced people had been set up but Ms Ní Cheallaigh said that the country was desperate to get itself back to normality. Many of the camps were in temples or schools but the school authorities did not want the likes of latrines built there, she explained, because they wanted to show the pupils that things were getting back to normal as quickly as possible. As a result, a way had to be found to try to get people into other camps. She believed that finding temporary shelter would be one of the most important tasks in the subsequent weeks.

As a number of NGOs met the Taoiseach and the Minister for Foreign Affairs to discuss how best the government's donation of €10 million should be spent, Trócaire called on the government to take the opportunity to press the Indonesian authorities to resume talks with the freedom movement in Aceh. Mary Healy said that until the tsunami, no one had been allowed into this heavily militarised part of

Indonesia. She said that Trócaire expected to be working in Indonesia for a long time, given the devastation it was witnessing, and she expressed the hope that the Irish government would be in for the long haul too.

Trócaire also called on the Irish government to use its recently established diplomatic links with Burma to secure access for humanitarian workers to that country. By that time, some ten days after the tsunami had struck, the Burmese military regime was still refusing to allow access and had issued disputed figures about the impact of the disaster.

Justin Kilcullen said that when Ireland set up diplomatic links with Burma in early 2004, the government said it would facilitate dialogue with the Burmese. He said that Trócaire was now calling on the Taoiseach to use those links to secure access for Trócaire and other NGOs to help respond to the emergency.

He also wanted the government to monitor the aid pledged to the affected regions and to ensure it was delivered. After Hurricane Mitch had devastated Honduras in 1998, only one-third of the aid pledged internationally had been delivered, while less than half of the €700 million pledged to Afghanistan after the fall of the Taliban in 2001 had actually made it there. Mr Kilcullen said that the stricken countries round the Indian Ocean rim should not suffer the same fate. He said the people and communities there would need adequate shelter and their healthcare and education systems restored, their livelihoods rebuilt and fishing communities supported in starting up again. It was a long-term and very expensive project that would take several years to complete, he concluded.

Anne Holmes of Trócaire reported back her initial impressions of Aceh, saying that the expression she met with most widely from the people was, 'Everything is broken; it is not enough to weep'. The Indonesian media constantly used the term 'crisis' which, she said, captured the general feeling of sadness and helplessness of the Indonesian people for what had happened to the people of Aceh. Therefore, practical commitments to provide relief, healing and the rebuilding of communities were vital, she believed.

However, she also met with many stories of humanity and hope. She found the dedicated efforts of volunteers, emergency and relief workers, army and police, medical staff and so many others were examples of the massive sympathy people held for those left homeless in the wake of the destruction.

She said that hundreds were still in the horrific process of gathering and burying the dead, and the numbers could reach up to 2,000 a day. Refugee camps for internally displaced people had appeared around the city to accommodate the 320,000 displaced who had been left homeless, she reported. She said the needs were great on the ground for so many basics – especially food for babies and small children, clean water for drinking, cooking and hygiene, sleeping mats and mosquito nets.

Children were the most vulnerable, she said. There were many whose parents had died or gone missing. Families, even whole communities, had been destroyed. Many were looking after the orphaned children who roamed the streets and she saw their care and protection as of deep concern. One woman who had lost all her family told her: 'This child is not mine but she too has lost all her family. Now our fates are entwined.'

A few days later, Ms Holmes told her local *Drogheda Independent* of the appalling scenes witnessed by aid workers in Indonesia. These were people, she said, who had worked in disaster areas all around the world but the situation in Indonesia was beyond anything previously experienced. It was impossible to escape the smell, she observed; with up to 10,000 bodies still trapped in the rubble, the stench of death was overpowering.

At this stage, she had put together an initial aid programme estimated at €1.5 million. She explained that a big aspect of the programme would be trauma counselling, alongside the normal work of sanitation, clean water supplies and helping people to re-establish their livelihoods.

The plight of the 35,000 who had been orphaned was one that really touched her heart, she told the paper. She said they were at huge risk because they were going back into their flattened villages looking for their parents and homes. They were coming across dead, bloated bodies in the rubble. Both the health risks and the psychological impact of such experiences were terrible, she said.

She found things like the dispute between the only remaining relative of a five-year-old boy and the woman neighbour who rescued him to be just as heartbreaking. The woman had lost her husband and two children; the child she rescued had lost all his family. Then an uncle of the boy had been found but the woman did not want to give the child up because he was all she had. Ms Holmes described this harrowing situation as an everyday tragedy in Indonesia.

Deirdre Ní Cheallaigh, who was in Sri Lanka, reported that tensions between the government there and separatist rebels were hindering some aid efforts in the north east of the country. Since the 1980s, the Tamil Tigers had been fighting for independence from Sri Lanka. A ceasefire had been brokered in 2002 but tensions between the two sides had simmered since then. The Tamils, together with the government and the NGOs, had founded a group to help distribute aid in the north east of the country; the group was to ensure and coordinate national and international relief for the Tamil region. But it was slow in starting up because the two warring parties could not agree on the name the organisation's speaker should use.

The representatives of Caritas, Trócaire's partner in the area, had been infuriated at the political manoeuvring by the two sides. Fr Jeyakumar was the director of Caritas Jaffna in the north. His word had some weight in the region and both parties took him seriously, but he told Ms Ní Cheallaigh that they were behaving like children and people were suffering as a result. She said the Tamils had had some success in coordinating aid in the areas that needed it most.

The village of Mullaittivu in the north east had been virtually swept away by the tsunami. More than 2,000 of its inhabitants were dead with a further 1,000 missing. Villagers became trapped between the wall of water surging towards them and a flooded lagoon, which lay at the back of the village. The Tamils had mobilised quickly to begin the aid effort, Deirdre Ní Cheallaigh said. They had brought a generator, bulldozers and trucks to clear the streets, and they had started to pump out the salty water from the wells.

However, she reported that in a camp about twelve miles outside Mullaittivu, aid agencies were having some problems with the separatists. First, they refused entry to Russian doctors; then word was spread that no patient records were being kept in the camp hospital. In many cases in the area, no aid had arrived at all, she said.

Trócaire announces its long-term programme

On 18 January 2005, Trócaire announced that it was winding down its tsunami fund-raising appeal. By then the agency had raised an amazing €20 million. Of that, some €15 million had by this stage been counted from the amount collected at Masses the previous Sunday in dioceses all over Ireland. This far surpassed the previous record collection for the agency when more than £6 million was raised for Ethiopian famine relief in 1984, in a nationwide, church-gate collection. (It should be remembered how much more difficult economic circumstances were in Ireland in the 1980s, however.)

With the government pledging a further €20 million, Trócaire and three other leading Irish aid agencies decided to wind down their fund-raising activities for this particular disaster. Trócaire said it would focus from that time on spending the money raised, and would also resume other projects. It said that it was important to keep a balance in its programmes. The reality was that the same number of people who died in the tsunami was dying every two weeks in Africa from hunger and disease. Trócaire said it would concentrate from then on on giving tsunami survivors a new start.

It announced that the money would be spent on a three- to five-year €35 million programme with local partners in the affected regions, aimed at rehousing millions of homeless and displaced people and rebuilding communities and livelihoods. Justin Kilcullen said that it was not enough to return people to the poverty they had known before and that an investment of that magnitude gave the opportunity to lift entire communities to a new level in terms of income and liveli- hoods. He acknowledged that it would take years to rebuild those devastated areas but said that there was enough money to tackle long-term problems as part of the rebuilding.

He thanked the public, the bishops and the clergy for supporting the appeal so strongly, saying that the unprece- dented disaster seemed to have struck a chord with the people of Ireland and that they had shown a special solidarity towards the people of Asia. But he also warned that other global crises should not be overlooked because of the tsunami disaster. He said 2005 was designed to focus on Africa in terms of development and that it still needed special attention to break the cycle of poverty.

By late January, fears were growing among aid agencies that aid operations might be cut short because of political or military pressure in the countries worst affected by the tsunami disaster. Burma had denied access to the agencies and the military junta there played down the effects of the disaster. The Indonesian government was also reluctant to allow foreign aid workers or military personnel a prolonged stay in the war-torn region of Aceh. It seemed that the Indonesian government wanted to get on with the war there and it was very difficult for the agencies to plan long-term projects when they were working off short-term visas.

Relief efforts in Sri Lanka were being hindered by the government's insistence that members of the military accompany food convoys travelling into areas controlled by the Tamil Tigers. The Irish government appointed a special envoy to travel to the region for six months to monitor the relief efforts funded by Irish donations.

For the 2005 St Patrick's Day parade in Dublin, the organisers decided to appoint as grand-marshals four representatives from the aid agencies Goal, Concern, the Irish Red Cross and Trócaire. This was to pay tribute to them for the way they organised the tsunami relief and to express gratitude to the Irish people for their extraordinary generosity. The *Irish Times* pointed out that by mid-March 2005, the Irish people had contributed €75 million to nine aid agencies who had been collecting money for tsunami relief since 26 December 2004. Up to mid-March, Trócaire had raised the largest amount, €27.19 million, of which some €20 million had been raised in parishes throughout the island at weekend Masses in January 2005.

Trócaire was working through Caritas Sri Lanka, which was based all over the island. Temporary housing was going up at that time to help the families who were in the camps to move into more private space. In the north of the island, they were working with fishing cooperatives to replace boats that had been lost. Trócaire was also preparing to train community leaders in trauma counselling and confirmed that aid was filtering down but was not always necessarily visible. Trócaire's policy was to work through local people – they had plenty of capacity and just needed support, which Trócaire was providing. The agency envisaged being in Sri Lanka for around five years.

In late June 2005, the Irish *Daily Star* sent a reporter and photographer to Sri Lanka to see how the survivors were coping in the aftermath of the catastrophe that had engulfed their island. They reported that the focus of Trócaire help was on empowering people to rebuild their lives by tackling such issues as shelter, livelihood, the needs of women's groups and psychosocial health. More than 1,200 temporary shelters had been constructed by Caritas Sri Lanka to provide victims with basic accommodation, clean water and sanitation. By this time, attention was turning to permanent housing.

The *Star* article acknowledged that Trócaire and other NGOs had been criticised for the slow progress in starting construction of permanent housing but pointed out that the reality was that this could take between five and ten years. There were a number of reasons for this. The Sri Lankan government had forbidden the construction of permanent structures within a 'buffer zone' between 150 and 300 metres from the beach, depending on the area, so many families could not rebuild where they had lived before. The government had allocated alternative sites for those who had owned their land but many of these sites were found to be unsuitable by Trócaire/Caritas and the local community. In addition, the vast majority of fishermen were opposed to moving inland to shelters and wanted to remain living on the beach where they had access to their boats.

The push for permanent housing may also have been premature because the consensus among those living in transitional shelters was that permanent housing was not a priority. Income was their chief priority at that particular time. Tools and equipment were necessary so that people could resume their livelihoods. Trócaire/Caritas had delivered new boats to 400 fishermen who had lost their boats in the tsunami.

An *Irish Times* article, also in late June, referred to the many well-meaning people who had collected money and gone to the disaster area after the tsunami and sought quick-fix solutions to very complex problems with long-term implications. The article argued that the problem with quick fixes was that they could cause harm. Some examples were: boats given out indiscriminately, some to people who did not even fish; large sums of cash given out, with the minimum of research into how needy the recipients were; buildings rushed up and sited inappropriately – for example, too close to the shoreline; and work such as installing water-supply systems being replicated, and then being replaced the next week.

A result of the early uncontrolled largesse, especially in Sri Lanka, was the tensions evident by June 2005 between those who had benefited and those who had not, or who perhaps received less.

The massive attention the tsunami got and the incredibly generous response it provoked was a mixed blessing for the agencies, this *Irish Times* article pointed out. In particular, they did not want attention distracted from other needy areas of the world, especially Africa. Justin Kilcullen had just returned from El Salvador, where he witnessed shocking scenes of suffering. He told the *Irish Times* reporter that Trócaire tried to focus on long-term development and justice but that it was very difficult to get money for long-term work.

Six months to the day that the tsunami struck, Trócaire told the *Sunday Tribune* that its tsunami relief programme would last three to five years, with €6 million of its €27 million budget spent by that time on various projects. It said that it had been most heavily involved in Indonesia, which was the hardest-hit area; €3 million had been spent on thirteen different projects there, mainly rebuilding homes and establishing safe sanitation and water supplies.

Trócaire set up a new web section to mark the six-month anniversary of the tsunami. Www.trocaire.org/tsunami paid tribute to the groups who had been working alongside Trócaire since the disaster struck, helping to rebuild the lives of millions affected by the tsunami. Justin Kilcullen said that it paid tribute to the Irish people's fund-raising efforts. The unprecedented number of fund-raising activities by individuals, businesses and clubs had helped Trócaire's work tremendously, he said.

Some Trócaire tsunami projects
A series of articles in the Irish *Daily Star* (19–21 July 2005) looked at some Trócaire tsunami projects. An hour down the coast from Banda Aceh in Indonesia is the sprawling area of Lhoong, where twenty-six villages were rendered wasteland within minutes by the tsunami. Trócaire and Caritas Germany undertook the reconstruction of the area and by this time, 150 of a planned 800 permanent houses had been built. The

project was established in consultation with local people, who made their own decisions on design and location. However, the first *Star* article pointed out that progress had stalled in most other areas due to the complex land ownership and other issues, and Trócaire estimated that it could take five to ten years to rehouse all the victims.

The second *Star* article described how in Sri Lanka, Trócaire/Caritas had opened children's welfare centres in Mullaittivu and Jaffna to accommodate children who had been affected by the tsunami. Fr Jude ran the Boys' Welfare Camp at Mullaittivu, which at the time was home to forty-three boys. There were not only orphans there, he told the newspaper. Many one-parent families were finding it difficult to raise their children in temporary camps. Some parents had been injured and could not work to support their families. At least in the welfare centre, the children could go to school, Fr Jude said.

He added that the boys were all traumatised in the begin - ning but were by that time becoming more settled. Caritas ran a counselling programme and the children did drawings and activities with counsellors so that they became able to talk about their experiences. The *Star* reported that trauma-counselling programmes and psychosocial activities, aimed at the most vulnerable women and children, were being estab - lished to target more than 4,000 families, as part of the Trócaire/Caritas two-year rehabilitation programme.

In late August 2005, a peace accord was signed between the Free Aceh Movement and the Indonesian government, ending thirty years of conflict in which some 12,000 people had died, mostly civilians. Orla Fagan of Trócaire told the *Daily Ireland* newspaper that the first thing that had struck her about the people of Aceh was their resolute inner strength and their determination to overcome a disaster of such colossal proportions.

Slowly Aceh had started to recover from the destruction, and the signing of the peace accord represented a bright new promise for the area. Ms Fagan said that peace and development had to go hand in hand, and without peace any invest-ment in development was worthless. She pointed out that the conflict in Aceh had religious, cultural, economic and political aspects and she said these facets needed to be tackled for the peace agreement to succeed. There were still many challenges to be faced but hope was high that the restoration of peace would bring a much-needed respite and better economic development for the people of Aceh, she concluded.

From 20 December 2005 to the end of January 2006, Trócaire ran an exhibition called 'Tsunami: Natural Disaster to Sustainable Recovery' to mark the first anniversary of the south Asian tsunami. The purpose was to inform the public how the €29.1 million donated to Trócaire by the Irish people was being used. The exhibition included information and photographs from the four main countries affected: Sri Lanka, Indonesia, Thailand and India. It was held in Trócaire's Dublin resource centre in Cathedral Street and was replicated in the agency's Belfast and Cork centres, as well as in various public libraries around the country.

In mid-December 2005, Orla Fagan, Trócaire's communi-cations officer in Indonesia, had an article published in the *Irish Medical Times* on how Trócaire and other agencies were helping to rebuild community health services following the devastation caused by the tsunami. She showed from her interviews with healthcare workers how slowly things were returning to normal but how it would take some time yet to return to full capacity. Gradually equipment was being replaced and new units were being built, designed to ensure they were earthquake proof.

Ms Fagan said that another major issue for healthcare professionals in the tsunami-affected regions was the trauma experienced by the survivors. She referred to Sr Roselyn, who was coordinator of a psychosocial programme run by Trócaire partners in India. She said Sr Roselyn believed that sup - porting people's social needs was every bit as important as their psychological needs. Thus, a major focus of her team's work had been on the renewal of livelihoods. Sr Roselyn said that the worst affected were the poor, who would not normally seek the help of a psychiatrist or psychologist. They normally relied on their community and that was what her team had been trying to support, concentrating on encouraging people to share their problems and providing them with a social outlet to do so. They had trained local counsellors to identify the more severe cases of depression, and potential cases identified were referred to medical staff for treatment.

As well as being involved in replacing equipment, re-building units and offering trauma counselling, Trócaire-funded organisations were training midwives, with courses in general obstetrics and in management to ensure the proper supervision of midwives. Ms Fagan concluded her article by saying that Trócaire and its partners in the Caritas confederation would continue to assist those who had suffered the immense physical and psychological damage caused by the tsunami in long-term development.

A few days later (18 December 2005), the *Sunday Tribune* reported from Batticaloa, on the east coast of Sri Lanka, an impoverished and war-torn coastal community destroyed by the tsunami, where people lost their homes and all their belongings. Trócaire/Caritas Sri Lanka had given this community good-quality transitional shelters and the means to restart their crafts and livelihoods. By this time, the paper reported, Trócaire-supported partners had moved into the second phase of their long-term rehabilitation programme, which took an integrated approach to rebuilding the lives of the most vulnerable, regardless of religion or ethnicity, with substantial support for creating sustainable livelihoods as well as house construction. Vital assets had been restored, such as boats and nets to 3,000 fishermen and 2,000 toolkits to traders and farmers, and the project encouraged the opening of joint savings accounts to ensure that small businesses and craftspeople had a fund for the future.

The article reported that by the end of 2005, Trócaire's partners would have built 700 permanent houses, with a target of more than 20,000 over the subsequent three years.

Also in the *Sunday Tribune*, Orla Fagan reported from Trócaire's other projects. She said the challenges of rebuilding Aceh post-tsunami could be captured under two different but closely related headings of livelihoods and communities. In many areas, before any reconstruction could be contemplated, she said that roads and bridges had to be repaired and replaced just to gain access to communities. Materials could not be transported without proper infrastructure in place. For example, Trócaire's partner, CRS, had to build the road on the island of Pulo Aceh just to connect villages. At the time she was writing, she said that many more men, women and children had returned – there were temporary schools, a ferry had been provided and there was a bustling life there once again.

She said that Trócaire's long-term ties with Caritas India proved valuable when the tsunami struck the coast of south-east India. Local capacity among the dioceses was well established, she observed, so the generous response of the Irish public was invaluable in helping the affected people. The main challenge in India was sustainability in livelihoods. Many organisations arrived in the initial stages to help in the emergency phase and then departed leaving nothing behind, she said. The focus of Caritas India was to improve the lives of those affected by the tsunami. Communities were consulted about their needs, aid was designed to achieve sustainable improvement and Trócaire's challenge was to ensure that these changes would continue over a long period.

Turning to Thailand, Ms Fagan remarked that with that country's booming tourist trade, it was difficult to imagine that there were many challenges faced by Trócaire's partner, Caritas Thailand. Before the tsunami, the Catholic Church had worked within its own community but had afterwards got involved outside and there was no going back, she said. Bishop Joseph Prathan told her the church had been insular before the tsunami, rarely moving outside the Catholic community but all that had now changed. He said that while no one had control over natural disasters, the challenge remained to build stronger, more durable structures, so that the effects of another tsunami or earthquake could never be as bad again.

On the third anniversary of the tsunami, Trócaire revealed the amount it had spent in the four countries worst hit. Affected most of all, Indonesia had received the most funding; €11,397,291 up to that time had been spent on programmes ranging from house building to education and sustainable agricultural programmes. Sri Lanka had received €8,208,851 by the end of 2007, which had helped build more than 6,000 houses and many health centres, market buildings and playgrounds, among other projects. In India, having helped 60,000 families receive food, medicine and water, Trócaire was now committed to continued support of the affected communities with special focus on marginalised groups. Up to that time, €5,160,538 had been spent in India.

The tsunami affected so many millions in so many different ways but lives are slowly being rebuilt. Trócaire's focus has moved on to long-term development and helping communities build themselves back up and be more resilient in the face of future disasters.

Assessment and lessons learned

In a recent interview for this book, Mary Healy pinpointed three aspects in particular of Trócaire's response to the tsunami. One was that the agency had a fairly long-estab-lished history in most of the countries that were affected, which enabled it to respond rapidly to the emergency. A second was that Trócaire had been doing a lot of work with its sister agencies within the Caritas network in relation to joint and collective response to disasters and the tsunami provided an opportunity to put that preparatory work into action. Ms Healy believed her agency's response was thus a more collective one than some of Trócaire's earlier emergency responses had been.

Thirdly, she said that what is most memorable about the response to the tsunami was the sheer scale, not just of the emergency itself but also of the response to it. Analysing the latter facet, she said she found it difficult not to allow a certain amount of cynicism to creep into her attitude. She felt that much of the response was motivated by the time of year, the number of Europeans affected (many were holidaying in the area when the tsunami struck), the familiarity of Westerners with the locations involved and the extent of the media coverage of the disaster. When she compared the response to the tsunami with the responses to other conflicts and disasters around the world, not just in terms of finance but also as regards level of engagement, Ms Healy considered it 'unfortunate' and observed that it shows that there is still much work to be done in raising both media and public awareness and understanding of the issues.

On a more positive note, she said that a lot of work has been done, especially by Trócaire but by other agencies as well she believes, in analysing and learning lessons from how they responded to the south-east Asian tsunami.

Ms Healy saw the result of the response the tsunami provoked in Aceh in Indonesia and in Sri Lanka as contrasting. The natural disaster served to open up and make Aceh accessible and also move it much more towards peace and reconciliation; in other words, the tsunami had a really positive impact on the conflict there. On the other hand, it had a really negative impact on the conflict in Sri Lanka and worsened the already bad situation existing between the Tamils and the Sri Lankan authorities.

Why it had an opposite effect in those two regions would make an interesting and useful study, Ms Healy believed. Her own view of the Sri Lankan situation was that those who had been affected by the conflict over the years received little or no support, while those affected by the tsunami, by contrast, received enormous support. This was very wrong, she said, and simply added to the injustice. Trócaire's attitude (and that of Caritas Sri Lanka, which had been working on the conflict there for many years) was that those affected had to be supported in an integrated manner: funding could not be restricted only to those affected by the tsunami. Many other agencies, Ms Healy said, were rigid in insisting that help must go only to victims of the disaster, without taking cognisance of the wider community. The result of this approach was that sometimes people who had lost a fishing boat in the tsunami got three new ones, while those affected by the war still had none.

Mary Healy expressed the hope that the peace agreement that was reached in Aceh will hold but she referred to a difficulty there that aid to tsunami victims gave rise to, and that is the proselytising activities of some Western NGOs in what is a strongly Muslim context. The insensitivity shown and the unease it caused led to the authorities demanding that all faith-based NGOs leave the region. Some NGOs were forced to leave but not Trócaire/Caritas, although at times the situation did become tricky enough for their activities. It is an unfortunate aspect of disasters that some people see them as an opportunity to proselytise, Ms Healy remarked.

She recalled that, overall, the aftermath of the tsunami was an extraordinary time in terms of public response, with people wanting to do fund-raising events all over Ireland. Indians, Sri Lankans and others from the affected countries who were living in Ireland came forward in great numbers wanting to send container-loads of needed materials to their native countries and help in whatever other ways they could. How to channel this public willingness was a challenge for the aid agencies, Ms Healy said, and Trócaire got together with the other Irish NGOs to produce a resource called 'Good Giving' as a result of the whole tsunami experience.

One of the most interesting things that emerged from Trócaire's response to the tsunami, according to Ms Healy, developed from the determination to 'build back better', make buildings earthquake proof and educate people in disaster awareness. The agency worked with communities in the region to improve their preparedness for future disasters

– not just constructing the buildings better but preparing the people better as well.

To achieve this, Trócaire collaborated with a group called No Strings, which had been set up by people who used to work on *The Muppet Show* on American television. The result of the collaboration was the production of a number of DVDs, in various languages, using puppets to tell about natural disasters. The DVDs cover tsunamis, earthquakes, volcanoes and so on, and Trócaire trained people to show these DVDs in communities and to work with those communities to increase their understanding of the risks involved and what they should and should not do in disaster situations.

Ms Healy described this approach as innovative and said it has been hugely successful. It was started in Indonesia and translated for use in Sri Lanka. Based on its success, Trócaire is now seeking to expand it for use in other parts of the world, particularly Africa.

Trócaire aims to have wound down its main programme activity in the tsunami-affected region by late 2009/early 2010; it will continue some involvement in the area but expects that the bulk of the work will be completed by then.

CHAPTER 20:
Gaza: 'The World's Largest Open-Air Prison'

Since the establishment of the state of Israel in 1948, the Palestinian people have continued to live under occupation of one kind or another. Before 1967 the occupying powers were Egypt in the Gaza Strip and Jordan in the West Bank. Israel captured both territories as a result of war in 1967 and has continued to occupy them ever since.

In 2005 Israeli forces withdrew from the Gaza Strip but invaded the following year and again in late 2008. Since 1994 Gaza has been surrounded by a separation barrier that enables Israel to control all overland entry and exit from the strip, except for the border that Gaza has with Egypt.

In 2002 Israel began to build a 'wall' (the term used by the International Court of Justice) around the West Bank and it is still under construction. According to an advisory opinion issued by the International Court of Justice in 2004, this wall is a violation of international law. Most countries and international bodies refer to both the Gaza Strip and the West Bank as 'occupied territories'.

Trócaire has been working with local partners in the Palestinian territories since 2000. In a newspaper article in mid-August 2005, Justin Kilcullen argued that Gaza was in danger of becoming the world's largest open-air prison. He told how, the previous December, he had turned up at a border crossing leading from Israel to the Gaza Strip as part of a delegation of Catholic development agencies. He had been looking forward to the visit, he said, to seeing at first hand the situation in which thousands of Palestinians were living. But four hours later he walked away, he said, together with half the group – they had been refused entry by the Israeli security forces because their papers did not have the required approvals. While the Palestinians living within this small piece of land could not get out, he could not get in, he remarked.

However, three other members of the delegation did get in and their subsequent reports of the poverty and deprivation suffered by the Palestinians were bleak and harrowing, according to Mr Kilcullen. He pointed out that the UN had established that 68 per cent of the residents of Gaza lived on less than a dollar a day – poverty levels akin to the poorest African states. He found it hard to believe, driving through Israel to reach the frontier, that people were living in such appalling circumstances beyond the barbed-wire fence.

He quoted from a recent UN review on the Occupied Palestinian Territory (OPT): 'Living conditions have further been eroded by the substantial decline in the quality of health and education services, and the inability of Palestinians to access them.'

He said the Palestinians were poor and getting poorer because they could not get jobs. They could not get access to adequate healthcare, to education or to employment because of the internal controls imposed by Israel. They needed permits from the Israeli authorities to gain access to land and crops, medical facilities, schools and universities, and even to visit family and friends.

Mr Kilcullen pointed out that the World Bank had acknowledged that poverty in the OPT was due to the loss of employment and the drop in economic activity resulting from the closure of the Israeli border and other internal borders. The construction of the 670-kilometre long wall encircling the occupied territories was the most visible aspect of those closures, he added.

He remarked that more than 3,000 journalists were expected to descend on the Gaza Strip in the subsequent days to watch the dismantling of seventeen settlements that had been occupied by roughly 8,000 Israelis since the 1967 war. When the Israeli army and settlers withdrew from Gaza, what would it really mean to those Palestinians trying to find work, go to school or access health services, he asked. Gazans might feel relieved that there would be no more Israeli military checkpoints inside the strip, but he said that little else would change because the Israeli authorities would continue to have ultimate control over all exit points from Gaza to Israel, the West Bank and abroad.

He referred to an example from the previous year of how Israel controlled the internal borders, which showed that there was cause for serious concern. For a total of 156 days, the main crossing into Israel, Erez, was closed completely to all workers. Rafah, the exit point on the Egyptian border, was closed for eighty-two days in 2004. All Palestinian males between sixteen and thirty-five wanting to leave, even for hospital treatment, were barred from crossing from 17 April 2004 to February 2005.

Justin Kilcullen acknowledged that the removal of the 8,000 settlers from Gaza and four West Bank settlements was an important political event, but he said that it was equally important to look beyond this to the reality of the lives of the Palestinian people. He urged that whatever opportunities the withdrawal offered should be acted upon to overcome the misery in which those people had been condemned to live.

He said that it also had to be recognised that Gaza was not the only critical issue because the restrictions had been equally disruptive all over the West Bank. He cited a statistic from the UN Office for the Coordination of Humanitarian Affairs (OCHA) that said while 20–25 per cent of the checkpoints had been removed in the previous months, there had been a 300 per cent increase in flying checkpoints during the same period. Flying checkpoints, normally a few sandbags and armed vehicles in the middle of the road, could occur any time and any place. He pointed out that they were very disruptive of daily life, as people had no way to plan a simple journey to school, work or the market. The UN predicted a gradual worsening of the situation in Gaza and the West Bank during 2006 because there had been no shift in the underlying causes that had led to the crisis, he warned.

Mr Kilcullen pointed out that Trócaire's work in the region supported grassroots organisations in both Palestine and Israel that were seeking a non-violent path to peace based on international humanitarian law. These laws had been constantly flouted, ignored and undermined by the Israeli authorities, he said, and he expressed the hope that the next time he visited Gaza he could gain access.

On 8 March 2006, Trócaire was among a number of organisations that made submissions and recommendations to the Oireachtas Foreign Affairs Committee on the 'separation wall' being built by Israel around Palestinian areas.

EU 'double standards'

In late April 2006, Trócaire accused the Irish government and the EU of applying 'double standards' to Palestine and Israel.

Following a meeting of EU foreign ministers in Luxembourg, the EU threatened to freeze direct assistance to the Palestinian Authority following the victory of Hamas in the general election organised by the Authority. Trócaire then wrote to the Department of Foreign Affairs to seek clarity on the Irish government's position on the suspension of EU funding.

Justin Kilcullen said the threat to suspend aid was another example of how the EU continued to apply double standards towards Israel and the OPT. To ordinary Palestinians, he said, the EU's response was seen as a form of collective punishment for electing, in an internationally recognised free and fair democratic election, a Hamas-led government. At the same time, he continued, the EU had completely failed to apply any real pressure on Israel to abide by its responsibilities, especially to desist from settlement expansion and the construction of the 'separation wall' on Palestinian land, both of which were contrary to international law.

Trócaire urgently called on the Irish government to provide practical details on how it would ensure that the basic needs of the Palestinian people would be met if it suspended aid to the Palestinian Authority. The agency demanded that more stringent steps be taken to ensure that Israel abided by its agreements and responsibilities, Mr Kilcullen said.

In early May 2006, Justin Kilcullen wrote an article in the *Irish Catholic* in which he referred to Israel's 'infamous' separation wall as a 650-kilometre barrier that would separate some 300,000 farmers from their land and isolate almost a quarter of a million people from the rest of the West Bank. He observed that while many political difficulties faced the region following the election, the situation faced by millions of ordinary Palestinians must be seen from a humanitarian perspective.

Men, women and children were facing shortages of basic food supplies such as bread and sugar and were unable to sell the tomatoes and peppers that they grew because the Israelis routinely closed trading points. On top of this, he said, the EU had threatened to withdraw the money that paid civil servants, teachers, doctors and nurses, that kept the clinics running and the schools open. He warned that such a move would compound the suffering of the Palestinians and make it almost impossible for them to meet their basic needs.

Mr Kilcullen pointed out that donor aid to the Palestinian Authority was vital to the social and economic welfare of the Palestinians. It helped to support almost one million, or one in four of the population. The EU had not said how it would continue to meet their basic needs if it withdrew official aid. NGOs or UN agencies were not in a position to fill the gap, he contended, and should not be expected to act as a substitute for a functioning Palestinian Authority.

Late in June 2006, Justin Kilcullen wrote to the newspapers to say that the EU and the Irish government had failed to take firm and clear action to prevent further escalation in the violence in Gaza. The situation for Palestinian civilians inside Gaza had continued to deteriorate. He explained that Israel had been shelling northern Gaza with an intensity of up to three shells per minute over the previous six months, and had closed the main commercial checkpoint into Gaza 41 per cent of the time.

Raji Sourani, director of the Palestinian Centre for Human Rights, a Trócaire partner based in Gaza, told Justin Kilcullen that they were faced with a clear choice: the rule of law or the rule of the jungle. Mr Sourani warned that if the international community continued to allow Israel to undermine international law, then they would be left with the rule of the jungle.

Trócaire called on the Irish government and the EU to condemn clearly all attacks against civilians and to ensure that Israeli and Palestinian militant factions adhered strictly to the principles of international law, Mr Kilcullen said. Trócaire wanted the Irish government and the EU to apply the principles of equality of treatment to both sides so that violations of international humanitarian and human rights law were not rewarded.

Israel's attack on Lebanon in July 2006

As Israel launched an attack on Lebanon in July 2006 to free two of its soldiers captured by Hezbollah, Trócaire stepped up its aid operations in the West Bank and Gaza. It allocated €30,000 to its partner, Caritas Jerusalem, for aid work there. Those funds were used to provide vital specialist medical care and social welfare support for families affected by the conflict. Trócaire also supported the provision of food coupons to help some 10,000 people secure basic food supplies.

Trócaire also swung into action to help its partner in Lebanon, Caritas Lebanon. Launching an appeal for help, the agency asked people to pledge not only their money but also their time to lobby their local politicians to demand an immediate end to the violence. Trócaire organised a peace rally outside the American embassy in Dublin to demand an end to the war. Justin Kilcullen addressed the rally and linked the US to the mounting death toll through Washington's failure to back the UN. He said that allowing the violence to continue showed a cynical disregard for the hundreds of innocent civilians being killed. Trócaire also held a rally on the issue outside Belfast City Hall a week later.

At the beginning of August 2006, Bishop Kirby, in an *Irish Times* article, said that support for a Palestinian state could bring peace and justice to the region. He began by quoting from John Paul II's message for World Peace Day 2002 where he said that the right of a state to defend itself had to be exercised within moral and legal limits and that an entire people must not be punished for the culpability of the few. Bishop Kirby said it was important to keep this message in mind in the context of the conflict in the Middle East, and the conflict could not be untangled from the multiple human rights violations suffered by the Palestinian people.

He said the continued occupation of Palestine by Israel was a source of deep grievance across the Arab world and was the central injustice to which others, rightly or wrongly, attached their flags. He explained that Trócaire and its international Caritas partners were working throughout Palestine and Lebanon to provide immediate humanitarian services for people in the most dire conditions, and that Trócaire and the Irish Catholic Church were also working to build support for human rights in Israel, Palestine and Lebanon, because that was the only way to ensure a just and lasting peace in the region.

Bishop Kirby said the dream of the Palestinian people of realising a Palestinian state had slipped away under the pressure of Israel's expansion of its illegal settlements, the construction of the wall inside the West Bank, the colossal death and casualty toll endured by Palestinian families and the systematic demolition of thousands of homes. He believed that without a real and genuine desire on the part of the governments of the world to realise a Palestinian state, there was little possibility of a just and lasting peace.

Also in early August 2006, Trócaire increased its funding support to its partners in the OPT and Lebanon, and launched a major emergency appeal for funds in Ireland. Eithne McNulty, Trócaire's newly appointed regional manager for Northern Ireland, told the *Irish News* that the agency was providing social welfare support in Gaza and the West Bank where, because of the freeze on aid from the EU and the US since the election of Hamas, 64 per cent of the population was living in poverty.

Trócaire described the Israeli policy of home demolitions as one of the most upsetting human rights violations faced by Palestinians living in East Jerusalem. It referred to one family that had particularly suffered – the Daris. It told how Trócaire, with its partner, Rabbis for Human Rights, struggled for two months to save their home. But early on 11 December 2005, the Jerusalem Municipality, which controlled the eastern Palestinian side of Jerusalem, enforced a demolition order against the Daris. This was the third time that Ahmed Dari, his wife and five children had had their home demolished.

Trócaire's Israeli and Palestinian partners reported that in 2004, 152 homes were demolished by the Israelis in East Jerusalem. In Gaza, since September 2000, 49,979 women, children and men had been made homeless as a result of Israel's home-demolition policy.

Trócaire said the Fourth Geneva Convention governed Israel's occupation of the West Bank and Gaza; under Article 53, any destruction of property not absolutely necessary for military operations was illegal. Further, Article 149 stated that such destruction was considered to be a grave war crime. Ahmed Dari was guilty of nothing but trying to provide shelter and protection for his family, it said. Still, Israel demolished their home.

The Catholic Church and Palestine
At the end of February 2007, a Catholic Church delegation had a meeting with the Minister for Foreign Affairs, Dermot

Ahern, requesting him to call for a review of the EU-Israel association agreement. Mr Ahern rejected the request. The church delegation consisted of Trócaire Chairman Bishop John Kirby, Bishop Ray Field, chairman of the Irish Commission for Justice and Social Affairs (ICJSA), and Fr Eoin Cassidy, chairman of the ICJSA's international subcommittee. The bishops had been members of an international Catholic Church delegation to the Holy Land the previous month.

At a press conference in Dublin before their meeting with Mr Ahern, they launched a position paper, 'Palestine/Israel: Principles for a Just Peace', the culmination of their fact-finding mission to the Holy Land. Bishop Field said that at the very least, the Irish government had a duty to work at EU level to ensure that the existing close commercial and cultural relations with Israel were carried out in a manner that gave priority to promoting the legitimate rights of the Palestinians. The restriction on movement in the OPT was in clear breach of Article 12 of the international covenant on civil and political rights, he said, and he described Gaza as 'little more than a large prison'.

Fr Cassidy agreed with former US president Jimmy Carter's description of the situation of the Palestinians as more oppressive than that of black South Africans during the apartheid era. Israel's 'separation wall' ensured that 10 per cent of the West Bank, taking in the most fertile part, would remain in Israeli hands, he continued, and reduced Palestine to 'a patchwork of municipal cantons or a collection of Bantustans ... thus destroying any hopes of a viable state'.

The three churchmen pointed out that the position paper was a modest contribution to understanding the causes of the conflict and to promoting peace in the region. This conciliatory approach seemed to have been lost on a number of commentators who detected an anti-Israeli slant on the part of the bishops and accused the position paper of being morally compromised in its apparent pro-Palestinian stance.

Speaking to the *Irish Catholic* in mid-March 2007, Bishop Field confessed to being perplexed by this reaction. He said that the position paper was not intended for any one side and pointed to the sections headed 'Hearing the Palestinian Voice' and 'Hearing the Israeli Voice'. He denied that the document was anti-Semitic and said it was unfair for anyone to so claim. All sides – Palestinians, Israelis, Fatah, Hamas, Christians, Muslims – were called in it to work towards achieving peace, he said.

Palestinians in Ireland at Trócaire's invitation

In mid-April 2007, Dr Mona El-Farra, co-founder of the Al Awda Hospital in the Gaza Strip, came to Ireland at the invitation of Trócaire. She spoke to *Woman's Way* magazine about her life and work. She told how, for nearly two years, she slept in her clothes in case she and her fourteen-year-old daughter, Sondos, might have to flee from their flat if shelling started.

The Gaza Strip is an area half the size of Wexford and accommodates almost 1.5 million people. An economic blockade had been imposed by the EU and the US, with movement and trade controlled by Israel in and out of the area. Some 70 per cent of people living there depended on international aid at the time. Dr El-Farra told the magazine that they worked hard to reach people in different parts of the crowded strip where they were imprisoned, in this small area of land with its borders still mainly closed – opened just fourteen times in six months.

She said that anaemia was now prevalent among women, and children under five, as high as 42 per cent for children and 36 per cent for women. The damage was not just to bodies but to minds as well, she continued. Many of the children were found to be suffering from post-traumatic stress and demon - strated it with anxiety, aggression, depression and bed-wetting. As well as specialist referral for this, the health centres for women and children, which Dr El-Farra was involved in running, were places of refuge for those aged six to sixteen to read, play, paint, dance and take part in normal childhood activities in what was a very abnormal environment.

The doctor's day was filled with meetings to discuss what relief supplies, such as food and blankets, were needed; visits to the hospital; whether there was an Israeli incursion into one of the villages; fielding calls day and night from the international media. As soon as the Israeli army withdrew, Dr El-Farra went in with her team to see what needed to be done. Several days of shelling and shooting would leave villagers exhausted. She remembered meeting one woman who had been held up at an Israeli checkpoint for three hours while in labour. She met her again shortly afterwards in her village; she had returned to find that the Israelis had demolished her house while she was away.

Dr El-Farra's patients were seldom able to leave for the specialised treatment they needed, so she had started to bring experts in to do certain operations. Consultants had come from Australia, Sweden and Russia, and two Irish doctors came on the first mission. She said she would welcome more medical expertise and teaching in emergency medicine, orthopaedics and anaesthesia, as well as more nurses.

She said she was coping with the situation with difficulty; she felt she had to be strong for the sake of others but all the time felt vulnerable inside. All she was surrounded by was funerals and death, she remarked. Visiting her eighty-four-year-old mother, who lived only twenty kilometres away, was difficult. The doctor said that, like other Palestinian mothers, she worried about her child's safety when she left for school every day. When she kissed her daughter goodbye, her fear was that she might not get back home safely from school.

On International Women's Day in 2006, Dr El-Farra had started her own blog, 'From Gaza, with Love', to tell the world about the plight of the Palestinian people. As she expressed it: 'I know it is my duty to talk for others who cannot talk.'

During a Trócaire event to mark the fortieth anniversary of the Israeli occupation of Palestine, Patriarch Michel Sabbah, Latin Patriarch of Jerusalem, celebrated Mass with

Dr Patrick Walsh, Bishop of Down and Connor, in St Peter's Cathedral, Belfast on 4 June 2007. He also addressed a public prayer service for peace and reconciliation, hosted by Trócaire and Christian Aid, in the Pro-Cathedral in Dublin the following evening.

In an article in the *Irish Times* that day he said that the situation for the Palestinians since the beginning of the Israeli occupation forty years before had worsened by the day and that people could not remain silent given the manifest injustice visited upon them. He referred to all that the occupation involved – restrictions on Palestinian freedom, the so-called 'security wall', military checkpoints, Israeli soldiers who at any time entered Palestinian cities, killed people, took prisoners, uprooted olive trees and destroyed houses. Added to that, he said, was the lack of vision within Palestinian society and the lack of security, taken advantage of by some who disobeyed the laws and exploited their brothers.

He went on to say that the historical grievances of the Palestinians were now made worse by the existence of the wall. It restricted their ability to make a living, their ability to practise their faith freely and their freedom of movement. He believed it was time to intensify action through negotiation to end the occupation and set up an independent Palestinian state with borders clearly defined (consistent with UN resolutions 242 and 338), giving both Palestinians and Israelis human dignity, security and equal opportunities.

'This Wall Must Fall' and other Trócaire campaigns

At the time of the patriarch's visit, Trócaire launched an online petition, 'This Wall Must Fall', to collect signatures to urge the Israeli government to remove the wall. As part of the same campaign, in July 2007, Trócaire sent twelve young people from all over Ireland to learn more about the human rights situation in the Middle East. They visited Israel and the OPT and met representatives of both Israeli and Palestinian human rights organisations. They visited refugee camps in

Bethlehem and walked through checkpoints in the dividing wall. They saw that this wall separated Palestinian farmers from their land, students from their schools and split families.

In East Jerusalem, they saw how it had been built right through a Palestinian street, separating two neighbouring families. Their houses were no more than five metres apart but, as a result of the wall, could be reached only by a fifteen-kilometre journey through checkpoints and the wall itself.

One of the campaigners, Veronica Keys from Donegal, described meeting an old Palestinian woman who had been displaced in 1948. She had worn the key to the house she had been driven from around her neck since that time, even though there was no hope of returning to her home.

Justin Kilcullen said that Trócaire's campaign was a campaign about people, people suffering from an injustice that had lasted over forty years, people whose daily life had been torn apart by the 'monstrous' structure, which, ultimately, was more to do with annexing Palestinian territory than with protecting the lives of innocent Israelis. In simple terms, he said, Trócaire's campaign was about justice.

Also in July 2007, thirty-four secondary school students from all over Ireland took part in Trócaire's week-long summer school, which focused on conflict, peace and development, explored through the then existing situation in Israel and the OPT from the perspective of international humanitarian law. Representatives from one of Trócaire's partner organisations in Jerusalem, Rabbis for Human Rights, attended the summer school to work with the students. Guest speakers, one from Israel and one from Palestine, addressed the students in an attempt to show the two sides of the conflict. The intention was to support the students in raising awareness of what they had learned and encouraging others to take action.

In August 2007, the *Irish Daily Star* sent a reporter and a photographer to cover Trócaire's work in Palestine. One of the issues the paper focused on was the large number of

Palestinian children killed by the Israeli army – 788 since 2000 according to the Palestinian Centre for Human Rights. Of those, 172 died in blasts but the other 616 died after being shot by Israeli soldiers.

Another issue the *Star* focused on was the infamous wall. Near Ben Gurion Airport in Tel Aviv, the journalists and Trócaire workers passed by Palestinians working on the wall. Trócaire's Palestine programme officer, Eoin Murray, remarked to the *Star* that it could only happen there. Where else, he asked, would the very people whom a wall was designed to oppress end up being the ones to build it.

By the time the wall is finished, the already extremely limited movement the Palestinians have will be curtailed even more. Its route will ensure that some 270,000 Palestinians will be trapped in military zones, effectively doomed to live their lives in enclaves unless they decide to leave for ever. The *Star* reporter regarded this as a high price to pay for Israel's security and remarked that it was also a high price to be paid by the Palestinian workmen outside his car window, trying to make a living by building a wall.

In January 2008, Cardinal Seán Brady visited the Holy Land as part of a fact-finding mission for the Holy Land Coordination Group (a Vatican initiative to support Christians in that region). The visit was part of the ongoing church engagement with the issue of Palestinian rights that Trócaire was encouraging. Afterwards, the cardinal told the *Irish Times*: 'I was shocked and saddened at the sight of the wall. It is with bridges, not walls, that you build peace.' In April/ May of 2008, Cardinal Brady was back in the OPT with an Irish inter-church delegation, which met both Palestinian and Israeli representatives. Trócaire also supported this visit.

A devastating Israeli military incursion into the Gaza Strip in late 2008/early 2009 left between 1,300 and 1,800 Gazans dead, many of them civilians, including a significant number of children. John Ging, an ex-officer with the Irish army, was head of the United Nations Relief and Works Agency

(UNWRA) working for Palestinian refugees in Gaza since February 2006. Although he had been in Rwanda during the genocide and in the Balkans during the worst excesses of the so-called 'ethnic cleansing', he said he had never experienced anything as bad as the humanitarian catastrophe in Gaza in December 2008 and January 2009. Mr Ging delivered the annual Maynooth College/Trócaire Lenten Lecture in March 2009 on the topic of the protection of civilians in conflict.

On 19 January 2009, Trócaire, in conjunction with Amnesty International and Poetry Ireland, organised a reading in St Anne's Church, Dawson Street, Dublin, in response to the situation in Gaza. Some of the foremost writers in Ireland performed at the event, which was an enormous success.

In a recent interview for this book, Eamonn Meehan pointed out that as well as its involvement in actual prog-rammes on the ground, Trócaire also believes it has played and can play a key role as an advocate: an advocate for peace and justice and for identifying the 'grave injustice' that has been done and continues to be done to the Palestinian people. Trócaire, he said, wishes to convey the sense of the apartheid-like situation that exists in the OPT, the sense of deep racism, theft of resources on an ongoing basis and lack of respect for the Palestinians and their just entitlements (to a state, to ownership of their own resources and their own culture).

He said Trócaire has also engaged the Irish Church in the issue, so that a significant number of senior churchmen have visited the area. Mr Meehan regards the work the agency has done as important in terms of mobilising the church and the Irish public around the issue. He acknowledged that it has proved controversial with some commentators and that some Irish politicians reject Trócaire's perspective on the situation existing in the OPT. It has also made Trócaire a target for some pro-Israeli lobbyists and entities, he pointed out.

What he finds extraordinary is how, despite the clear evidence of how much the Palestinians have lost since 1948, so many people can still completely ignore the main facts.

He points to how, over the past sixty years, so much of the land that was once owned by Palestinians has changed hands and how the separate Palestinian entity has almost disappeared. It now exists, he said, in a series of what are effectively little more than 'Bantustans'.

Trócaire continues its work for peace and justice in the OPT.

CHAPTER 21:
Trócaire's Ground-Breaking Work in Development Education

> Abroad, [Trócaire] will give whatever helps lies within its resources to the areas of greatest need among the developing countries. At home, it will try to make us all more aware of the needs of these countries and our duties towards them. These duties are no longer a matter of charity but of simple justice.
>
> Bishops of Ireland on Development, 1973

Background and initial stages

To fulfil its foundation mandate, Trócaire was required to spend its resources in the following way: 70 per cent on long-term development, 10 per cent on emergency relief (outside of special appeals) and 20 per cent on development education. The allocation of 20 per cent of income to develop - ment education was one of the distinguishing characteristics of Trócaire and its perspective on under-development and justice. The agency believed that unless there was public awareness of development and the political will to bring about greater justice, there would be little change in the relationships between rich and poor countries.

Trócaire identified three initial areas for development education. One of those was mass communications, including press, radio, television, publications and public events. Lenten

Campaign materials were an important component as they reached almost every home in the country through schools and parishes. Another area included links with groups such as trade unions, teachers and schools, involving information bulletins and publications and curriculum development activities. The third area was research into issues that affected overseas development. As a result publications covered areas such as Ireland's ODA programme, EEC development policy, free-trade zones and agricultural protectionism.

In the early years, the Press and Information Department focused largely on the media, producing information and education packs on key events and issues in Africa, Asia and Latin America. These information packs were also available to post-primary schools. But Trócaire recognised that while the packs provided worthwhile information, they did not address the needs of teachers and students interested in these issues in a way that was age-appropriate and relevant to the curriculum. As a result, Trócaire produced a series of booklets for senior primary and junior post-primary levels introducing some of the key issues affecting the developing world but which were general and not linked specifically to the curriculum.

Along with Trócaire, the ICJP was campaigning on Ireland's commitment to the UN target of allocating 0.7% of GNP to official development assistance. The ICJP published articles on development and worked with the City of Dublin Vocational Education Committee (CDVEC). The links between the ICJP and Trócaire influenced the appointment of an education officer, Colm Regan, in 1982 to develop this focus of Trócaire's work in partnership. Trócaire also engaged Mary Cole to draft develop - ment materials for the post-primary sector. In 1983, these evolved into 'Dialogue for Development' – the first development education resource for post-primary level.

Development Education: the rationale and understanding
Mary Cole, who wrote 'Dialogue for Development', said in a recent interview for this book that when she was preparing

the books and teachers' handbook for post-primary level, she worked very closely with teachers in schools because she knew they were the people who would be best able to advise her on working out the practicalities of the programme. She found their help and advice invaluable and what mainly emerged from their cooperation with her was a classroom approach that involved team teaching. So, for example, the religious education, geography and English teachers might all work together in presenting a development education module in their school, using her books. It was a process that was very successful, she said, and the demand for books from schools was very high.

Three elements were central to development education: (i) appreciating attitudes and how they are formed; (ii) acquiring knowledge on the political, social, economic and cultural dimensions of development; and (iii) developing skills to assess and analyse information and argument and to acquire a critical approach to information.

Trócaire also saw the benefits of building partnerships with Irish organisations that themselves undertook development educational work designed to highlight the justice agenda and specifically the needs of the world's poorest people. Trócaire strategically supported partners in the introduction of such programmes in the form of financial assistance, personnel, planning and resource support as well as joint initiation and delivery of programmes.

The partnership model was the basis of education projects from the mid-1980s onwards. These included MIC Limerick at primary level, CDVEC at post-primary level, Macra na Feirme in the youth/young adult sector, the ICTU in the trade union sector and Development Education for Youth in the youth sector.

Primary education

The primary sector has been a major focus of Trócaire's education work. As the press and information packs supplied on request did not meet the needs of schools, Trócaire produced the 'Three Worlds' series of booklets for senior primary and junior post-primary. These introduced some of the key issues affecting the developing world but were general and not linked to the curriculum. Trócaire also published teachers' booklets linking the Lenten Campaign to catechetics, and 'Our World' leaflets and posters introduced development issues in cartoon format.

The relationship between MIC, Limerick and Trócaire began in the 1980s. It was clear there was a need for a more strategic approach to integrate development education at primary level than simply producing ad-hoc resources. In 1984, Trócaire commissioned a review of the primary curriculum by MIC to identify opportunities for development education. The first Trócaire primary partnership to engage teachers at in-service and pre-service levels followed with a summer in-service course on development education in MIC in 1986. The course identified a number of teachers who became involved in the partnership over the following two years.

With the 1989 appointment of a full-time education officer to the Primary School Project based in the MIC Curriculum Development Unit, the MIC-Trócaire partnership expanded. Between 1989 and 1992, annual conferences for primary and post-primary teachers were held to build a development education network, the Trócaire Teachers Network. A major focus of the partnership was resource production in environ - mental education. The result was 'Team Planet' (1992–1994), a set of materials on the environment for junior infants to sixth class primary.

The project had a significant impact on the inclusion of development education at pre-service level. Being based in MIC helped promote development education generally, and 'Team Planet' specifically, within the Bachelor of Education (B.Ed.) degree course. Since 1990, there has been an elective 50-hour module on development education for third-year B.Ed. students.

The partnership with MIC originated at the time when Dr Colm Regan was Trócaire's Head of Education. MIC is now the base for a national Centre for Global Development through Education. It is a partner in the Irish-African Partnership for Research Capacity Building and in the Zambia/Ireland Teacher Education Partnership. A large proportion of the MIC staff engage with the development agenda across a range of disciplines and, uniquely, up to 10 per cent of the college's final year B.Ed. students choose to take their teaching practice in an African school.

Lenten materials

Trócaire's Lenten materials go to all schools, and as the development education programme became more focused and strategic, there was a clear need to link those materials to the curriculum to provide practical ideas and classroom activities for teachers. As the range of materials expanded, there was greater involvement by practising teachers to ensure the materials had practical application in the class-room.

From 2003, the Trócaire Better World Award became part of the Lenten primary materials, encouraging exploration of the Lenten theme by teachers and children together. Schools submit their class work, each child receives a certificate and schools that show particular commitment and effort receive a special merit award.

Trocaire's work overseas and at home is above all rights-based. In the mid-1990s, education work took on a strong human rights focus through a partnership with Amnesty International. This sought to explore human rights within development education, building on the work of both organisations. The partnership focused on primary and post-primary schools and included joint teachers' conferences, evening workshops and, in summer 1997, a week-long in-service course for primary teachers. A human rights edu -cation newsletter, 'Cearta Daonna', with primary and post-primary editions, explored children's rights, women's rights, environmental rights and those of refugees and asylum seekers.

Trócaire readily engaged with TV as an additional way to introduce children informally to development. *The Disney Club – Den TV* went out on RTÉ 2 television on Saturday mornings, targeting primary pupils and also engaging children in the studio. Trócaire was involved in two productions: *African Special* (2002) on Zimbabwe and *Filipino Fantastic Far Flung Facts for Fun* (2004), a series of programmes over four weeks. The programmes showed footage of daily life in these countries and engaged children in studio, setting activities to explore development.

Trócaire has continued to produce many more resources for the teaching and learning of development education at primary level. Some of the challenges for Trócaire include where to focus resources. Supporting teachers' pre-service and in-service professional development and materials linked to the curriculum are key to promoting a primary sector development education perspective. Trócaire is also working to develop more first-level contact with teachers and children.

Post-Primary education
The post-primary sector has received most attention from Trócaire's education programme. Since 1973, there have been major changes in curriculum, methodology and teacher support.

Trócaire's approach to post-primary development education was pragmatic, based on the curriculum, the structure of the school day and schools' organisation. While development education is a process, it is also subject-based and some subject areas lend themselves more easily to it than others. Trócaire committed itself to working within the existing structures while at the same time actively supported the introduction of development education to the emerging new curriculum.

In the late 1980s, Junior Certificate curriculum changes in the Republic of Ireland and a review process in Northern Ireland and England presented opportunities to insert development education into the humanities. In the Republic, the National Council for Curriculum and Assessment (NCCA) encouraged cross-curricular linkages with moves towards greater flexibility in content and resources and student-centred, experiential learning.

The Humanities Project was a joint initiative of Trócaire and Birmingham Development Education Centre (BDEC) to focus on the professional development of teachers in development education. A steering group of staff from Trócaire, BDEC, the CDVEC-CDU (Curriculum Development Unit), the Integrated Humanities Association in Britain and individual teachers supported the project. British and Irish teachers worked together identifying innovative curriculum work, making this available to other teachers and sharing ideas on in-service work. There was also a teachers' study visit to Brazil, which produced education materials including 'Colonialism, Conflict and Community'.

From 1990, Trócaire began a partnership project with the CDVEC-CDU, funded by Trócaire and jointly managed by the CDVEC, Trinity College Dublin, the Department of Education and Trócaire. It began at a time of great change in Irish education, with the introduction of the Junior Certificate and a review of the senior cycle. Pilot projects took place in 1990–1991 and the outcomes were compiled in 'A Global Curriculum? Development Education and the Junior Certificate'. The report identified opportunities for development education in each subject area along with teaching guidelines and options.

In the early 1990s, the joint Trócaire/CDVEC-CDU project proposed a subject relating to local and global citizenship, laying the foundations for what became Civic, Social and Political Education (CSPE). The subject was introduced to all schools in 1996–1997 and Trócaire produced several resources: 'Development Matters – a Thematic Approach to Issues of Development; Colonialism, Conflict and Community' and 'Fala Favela', which fed into the NCCA and Department of Education materials.

A number of seminars addressed new thinking in human rights and citizenship education at senior cycle, leading to two publications: 'Towards an Integrated Approach to Human Rights Education' and 'Charting the Future: Social and Political Education in the Senior Cycle of Secondary Schools'. Submissions to the NCCA promoted Leaving Certificate social and political education.

A significant outcome was the publication of 'Citizenship Studies: A Curricular Proposal for Social and Political Education', whose concepts have been the cornerstone for dialogue with the NCCA and other partners. In 2003, the NCCA issued 'Developing Senior Cycle Education – Directions for Development', proposing a new Leaving Certificate course in civic and political education, with a wide range of transition units followed by 'Proposals for the Future Development of Senior Cycle Education in Ireland'.

In 2005, the three-year Trócaire-CDU Citizenship Studies Project began with three overlapping strands: research, curriculum development and policy development, with a view on how to roll out Senior Cycle Social and Political Education. Two 45-hour transition units were prepared: 'Images in the Media' and 'Education for Sustainable Development'. Trócaire has committed to a three-year partnership with the CDU, 2008–2011, focusing on a Trinity College postgraduate diploma programme for in-career teachers, consultations on the draft Politics and Society syllabus with young people and student teachers for submission to the NCCA, and to develop materials for senior cycle citizenship education based on the Politics and Society syllabus.

'Pamoja Kwa Haki' (Swahili for Together for Rights) ran as a pilot programme in twelve schools during 2003–2004. Phase one centred on the 2004 Lenten theme: 'Rwanda, Ten Years After the Genocide'. Trócaire provided training days for a core group of students from each school on research, presentation and campaigning skills. The students shared their knowledge with the wider Pamoja group in their schools. During Lent, each Pamoja group hosted a visitor from Rwanda and ran an action programme in their school and community, which included awareness days, local radio and press interviews, library displays, public meetings, speaking in churches and primary school workshops. The students marked the end of phase one with a national event at which they presented their project work, participated in a celebration and received certificates of achievement. Phase two focused on a Human Rights Summer School attended by students from the Pamoja schools. The Pamoja programme has been developed and extended further in recent years.

Partnership with Macra na Feirme: justice in action

Macra na Feirme describes itself as 'the largest rural, voluntary, non-political, non-sectarian, youth organisation in Ireland'. In 1982 Macra began sending volunteer development workers to Chikuni near Monze in Zambia who acted as advisers to six locally trained staff and the Chikuni coordinator.

The three-year project with Macra began in 1986 and was Trócaire's first development education partnership in the non-formal sector. The broad aim was to promote development education within Macra, focusing on the three central planks of knowledge, attitude and skills and the responses arising from an analysis of issues. The objectives were to inform Macra members about inequality and under-development, highlight Ireland's relations with the Third World and its responsibilities towards those suffering injustice and challenge members to examine their attitudes and motivate them to work for justice.

Fifty-eight Macra members attended the first national conference in Navan, Co. Meath, followed by regional workshops, which agreed four themes: agriculture and rural development, injustice, food and barriers to development. A set of resource materials supported the club, regional and national conferences and seminars throughout 1987-1989, and a newsletter included reflections by members on global issues and project events.

The first national seminar in November 1988 focused on poverty locally and globally, with contributions from Combat Poverty and Trócaire. The second seminar looked at development and different models and theories based on case studies from Brazil, Zambia and Ireland. The last seminar explored the actions Macra members could take arising from involvement in the project.

Macra viewed the Trócaire partnership very positively; it was beneficial and groundbreaking for both organisations. For Trócaire, which had concentrated on public education through the media and the formal sector, the strategic partnership approach involving a youth/young adult organisation in the non-formal sector was innovative. For Macra and its volunteering links with Chikuni, Zambia, it was a new approach to engage in development education while questioning the status quo and encouraging debate which challenged its own structures and working methods.

Partnership with trade unions

In October 1987, Trócaire facilitated a trade unionists' visit to South Africa to establish first-hand links with trade unions there and to report on what they saw. In 1989, Trócaire established the ICTU/Trócaire Education Partnership Project as a response to international equality and injustice issues. The global situation challenged the trade union movement not only because of the issues involved such as jobs, unemployment, multinationals and investment patterns, but also because of the trade unions' role in society.

The ICTU/Trócaire Education Partnership Project aimed to integrate a development education approach with a global perspective, focused on promoting equality and issues already part of ICTU's stance.

The project worked with trade union branches and trades councils to establish core groups of activists through a network of solidarity groups. It also introduced justice and development issues into existing trade union training and education. It sought to support the ICTU Third World Committee to stimulate a more systematic approach to development among trade unions, to educate members and to translate this into effective action through practical solidarity.

A project steering committee comprised representatives from Trócaire and the ICTU and Trócaire provided a half-time education officer and project funding. An extensive programme of workshops, meetings, discussions, seminars and study circles with individual unions, trades councils and union tutors was held.

The ICTU's development education project, Global Solidarity, has offices in Dublin and Belfast and incorporates the work of the International Solidarity Committee (formerly the Third World Committee). Its current work centres on the Campaign for Workers' Rights, based on the International Labour Organisation's 1998 'Declaration on Fundamental Rights in the Workplace'. It highlights child and bonded labour, gender discrimination and the right to form and join trade unions. The project with Trócaire contributed significantly to ICTU's commitment to the integration of global development within union structures and activities.

Research and third-level engagement
From the outset, Trócaire realised that if it was to be a persuasive advocate, it had to have credibility with government and others and that that credibility would have to be built upon a sound evidence and research base. From 1982, a research coordinator, Mary Sutton, assisted by a Research Advisory Group, made up of academics from universities and research institutes, commissioned major studies of key policy issues. An early example was a book by Alan Matthews, *The Common Agricultural Policy and the Less Developed Countries*. The objective of the study was to ensure that in the context of Common Agricultural Policy reform, the interests of developing countries would be articulated and taken into account.

Another early initiative was the *Trócaire Development Review*, first published in 1985 as a vehicle for academics with an interest in development issues to publish and influence debate. At the time there were very few academic courses in development studies and no Irish publications focusing on development. Over time, the *Trócaire Development Review* enabled many young researchers with an interest in development or aspiring to a career in development to submit articles for peer review and publication. The *Review* continues to this day.

The research programme also engaged academics to address political issues. For example, a 1988 study by Dr Brigid Laffan on 'Ireland and South Africa – Irish Government Policy in the 1980s' explored the role of sanctions in addressing apartheid.

A range of other studies throughout the 1980s and 1990s addressed aspects of the 'interface' between economics, trade, finance and politics as viewed from an Irish or EEC/EU perspective and the impact of the resulting policies on the developing countries of Asia, Latin America and particularly Sub-Saharan Africa. While Trócaire could work in developing countries in partnership with local communities to address the day-to-day reality of poverty and injustice, it always recognised that global economic structures and geopolitics were central. Development education, and within it the research programme, sought to shine a light on these aspects of global inter-connectedness and to engage the Irish government, the EEC/EU, the UN and other NGOs in finding solutions that would take full account of the impact of their decisions on those in the developing world with no voice or a very weak voice in the arenas where critical decisions were being made.

Trócaire's commitment to development education
As Trócaire looks to the future and to new areas of engagement within development education, the partnership model provides the opportunity to work with policy decision-makers, those delivering programmes and at grassroots level. Trócaire will continue to employ this model alongside a range of other approaches as its development education prog - ramme evolves in the coming years.

Looking back on her twenty years as an education officer with Trócaire, and as one who has researched this aspect of the agency's work in detail, Sheila Dillon believes that personal engagement was a key element ensuring the success of Trócaire's multifaceted development education work. As well as praising the efficacy of the partnership model, she singled out the Pamoja project as bringing about close engagement with post-primary schools where Trócaire personnel have come to know teachers and students well and have been able to engage with them on an ongoing, closely cooperative basis. She believes development education programmes need that hands-on, personal engagement to achieve as much success as possible.

She has been deeply impressed by the commitment of teachers and the way they have so willingly dedicated themselves to the programmes, giving unselfishly of their spare time and expending so much thought and energy, without any personal material gain. Bringing people on study visits, where they actually see and experience what they have been reading about and researching always has an impact on them, Ms Dillon observed. Direct experience often gives an insight or an understanding that all the research in the world might never give, she believes.

Resources and materials have improved enormously since the 1980s, she maintains, so there is little excuse for people not informing themselves on development issues if they have an interest. However, she believes that there is still much work to be done. She takes hope from the fact that development education has become integrated into both primary and post-primary subjects and is particularly pleased with the existence of CSPE as a compulsory subject at Junior Cert level because it is a subject of huge potential to which young people of all abilities can relate.

POSTSCRIPT: Facing the Challenges of the Future

The ever-changing geopolitical landscape

The previous twenty-one chapters have told the story of Trócaire's work for justice over the past thirty-seven years. They reflect the changes in the global, political and economic context over almost four decades. In the first twenty years, the Cold War divide was the underlying force that shaped the world order. The battles for spheres of influence across Africa, Asia and Latin America, between the capitalist world and the socialist East led to proxy wars being fought in Central America, Ethiopia and Somalia, Vietnam and all too many more. Repressive governments were kept in power, supported by their 'Big Brother' patron as long as they held the line on 'Big Brother's' interests. President Marcos in the Philippines, Mobutu in Zaire, Pinochet in Chile were all patronised by the West. Revolutionary movements in south east Asia and Latin America were actively supported from Moscow and Beijing. The emergence of the national security state, where basic human rights were withheld in the broad interests of security, was a phenomenon of this period. South Korea, the Philippines, even Brazil were typical of these.

The impact of these political forces on the poor was massive. Development took a back seat and powerful vested interests controlled the land and the economy. The army was all powerful. In this context the 'enemy' was all too obvious. In many countries the Catholic Church, being organised across the community, became the most outspoken critic of such regimes. This gave Trócaire a clear context for its work.

The fall of the Berlin wall, the collapse of communism, and then the end of apartheid, all in the early 1990s, changed that context dramatically. The perceived triumph of the capitalist system, the notion of 'the end of history', set in train a whole new set of forces that transformed the global economic order. Globalisation was now in full swing. Increasingly the issue to be addressed was that of growing inequality between nations and within nations.

With no strategic advantage to be gained with the departure of the Soviet Union, Africa was abandoned by the West. Development aid was redirected to the emerging countries from the Soviet empire. The proxy wars descended into bitter civil wars as political factions continued to fight for power. In the mid-1990s you could travel from Angola on Africa's Atlantic coast to Eritrea on the Red Sea and never leave a war zone. Africa essentially dropped out of the global economy. Ravaged by HIV/AIDS, life expectancy plummeted in the 1990s to forty-six years.

In the first years of the new millennium three critical issues emerged. The devastating attacks on New York and Washington in 2001 highlighted the emergence of a new global division between parts of the Islamic world and the West. The war on terrorism had begun, a new kind of war, not now based on enmity between states so much as enmity between radically different ideological viewpoints.

New major economic powers also emerged – China, India and Brazil. This changed the balance of power in the world which had been dominated by the US since the early 1990s. Much of the tensions around this new dispensation surround access to resources – oil and land. The 'arrival' of China and India in Africa, for instance, giving development assistance on very different terms to the traditional donors, often ignoring issues of governance and human rights and focusing

on access to resources, has markedly changed the development environment. The beneficiary countries now have
choices!

An issue even more threatening to the long-term economic and social security of the globe is the phenomenon of
climate change. The voracious appetite of the globalised
economy has resulted in the depletion of the earth's
resources at such a rate that we are now destroying the globe
ourselves. The immediate impact can be seen in those
countries of the global south where erratic rainfall has
increased the incidence of drought and floods, resulting in
crop failure in many areas. It is one of life's cruel ironies that
after almost two decades of unparalleled economic growth,
the number of people now living in hunger has surpassed the
one billion mark for the first time. This represents almost one
in every six people on the planet. There can be no greater
example of the growing inequality of our world than knowing
that those who have done least to create the problem of
climate change, the poorest people on the planet, are those
most affected by it. It is not just that poor people will remain
chronically poor in a world of plenty, but what little they have
is being destroyed by the over-development and greed of the
developed countries.

The failure of the climate summit in Copenhagen in
December 2009 to conclude a binding agreement demon-
strates clearly that the political will to face the current
realities is not there. The wealthy countries seem incapable
of taking the politically difficult decisions necessary to create
a sustainable world.

The economic recession which began with the failure of
major banks in September 2008 has given the world pause
for thought. What was seen, at least, as a part failure of the
capitalist system prompted many to begin to discuss
economic alternatives – a future based on a green economy,
green jobs, more controls of the financial system globally, the
introduction of a tax on currency speculation. Pope Benedict
XVI's long-awaited encyclical on social and economic affairs,

Caritas in Veritate, is challenging on all these and other salient issues. However, as the green shoots of a recovery appear, the tendency to lapse back into old ways has re-emerged. The bonus culture that was at the heart of much of the banking problem is an example, with $75 billion allocated to end-of-year bonuses in 2009.

The new millennium brings fresh hope

All of this is in sharp contrast to the expectations that were raised at the beginning of the new millennium. With a firm purpose of amendment to deal with the continuing scandal of world poverty, the leaders of more than 190 countries issued the Millennium Declaration. The MDGs, derived from the overall objectives of the declaration, set out clear targets against which the fight against world poverty could be measured. The first goal, that global poverty would be halved by the year 2015, set the context for the other major targets – progress to be made on health, education, food security and so on.

The governments of the developing countries undertook to put in place programmes to achieve these goals. The eighth MDG, termed 'a new partnership for development', is the goal that most applies to donor countries. To match the commitments of the poorer countries, the donors undertook to increase aid and to reform debt and trade structures in order to generate the necessary funds to achieve the goals. In addition they undertook to streamline and coordinate the global aid effort to make it more effective and less burdensome on less developed countries.

Progress in implementing the MDGs has, to say the least, been mixed. The Doha Round of the WTO trade talks, heralded as 'the development round', representing a new deal for the world's poor, is now five years overdue with no resolution in sight. The global position on aid and debt relief is little better. The OECD is estimating a $21 billion shortfall between what donors promised in 2005 and their estimates for aid volumes in 2010. Of this shortfall, $17 billion is the result of lower-than-promised giving by the donors and $4 billion is the result of lower-than-expected Gross National Income because of the economic crisis. Even though the major debt cancellation schemes have written off $88 billion in debt so far, the world's poorest countries repay almost $100 million every day to the rich world.

On all of these issues – trade, aid and debt – there is still not the political will to implement the effective and far-reaching reforms that are required to tackle global poverty and achieve the MDGs. For the poorest countries, the result of this lack of political will is that at the present rate of progress the MDGs are behind schedule by over 100 years!

How is Trócaire to respond to these new realities?
Faced with changing circumstances over the past decades, we have revisited our founding mandate to seek inspiration and guidance. The principles it has laid down have stood the test of time. Indeed it is a demonstration of the failure of two generations of politicians that the issues set out in the mandate are as relevant today as when it was written: growing poverty and inequality; the fact that we are rich partly because others are poor; the need to increase development aid to reach the UN agreed target of 0.7% of GNP; the responsibility to establish fair trading relationships and to accept our duties as Christians, in justice, towards the poor people and poor countries.

In responding to these issues, Trócaire established a number of principles that would guide our work. We would work in partnership with local groups and communities, not establishing our own projects and programmes but working with others to enable them to become the 'authors of their own destiny'. We would promote civil society, supporting the training and formation of local and national leadership so that political authorities can be held to account. In this way we can help promote good governance and address the issue of corruption. And we would do this work in a spirit of solidarity, described by Pope John Paul II as 'not a feeling of vague compassion or shallow distress at the misfortunes of so many people [but] a firm and persevering determination to commit oneself to the common good'.

Of all the issues that have emerged over the years that have influenced our work, perhaps the most significant and most challenging is that of gender inequality. Although it is thirty-five years since the UN held the first world conference on women, in Mexico City, there has been a marked reluctance on the part of the international development community to recognise the central nature of gender inequality to the problem of world poverty. This lack of recognition has led to the most simple but often devastating errors in development work. Ninety per cent of the world's food is produced by women farmers, yet training in agriculture, improved farming techniques and so on has been focused largely on men. Women are the traditional water bearers in village society, yet when wells and pumps are installed it is the men who are trained to maintain the equipment. But the problems go much deeper than this. Despite the enormous weight of responsibility placed on women for child welfare, food production, household management, they are constantly denied such basic rights as the right to inherit property from a deceased husband, are the first to be withdrawn from education in hard times and are subject to appalling physical abuse both in the home and in times of war. They are more likely to be poor, have higher levels of illiteracy, be more prone to HIV, and have little or no say in public affairs.

While these issues are widely recognised in theory, there remains obstinacy in addressing them in practice. Deep-seated traditional practices lie at the heart of this problem. Nonetheless, there can be no sustainable solution to poverty and injustice without recognition of these issues and a firm resolve to address them in a real way.

Increasingly over the years we have recognised that the work in developing countries and the work at home in Ireland in raising awareness though education, advocacy and lobbying are inextricably linked.

Mobilising for Justice

Just months before his death in 2005, Pope John Paul II in his message for the World Day of Peace said, 'What is urgently needed now is a moral and economic mobilisation'. In response to this call and in line with the principles outlined above, Trócaire set out its programme for the ten years up to 2016 under the title 'Mobilising for Justice'. In this programme we have decided to focus on three main areas of activity; the promotion of livelihoods, in which communities can tackle the problem of their poverty; governance and human rights, by which communities can participate in the political processes that shape their lives; and emergency prepared-ness and response, by which we can apply the many lessons of past bitter experience in helping the most vulnerable communities to face both the expected and unexpected disasters that are so prevalent in the poorer countries. These three organisational programmes are approached in three distinct ways, recognising that underlying problems of poverty and injustice are the issues of HIV/AIDS, gender inequality and the absence of environmental justice.

In this way we have renewed the mandate given to us at our foundation. The issues may have changed in character and manifest themselves in very different ways, but at the heart of them is the continued marginalisation of poor and vulnerable people.

In his tribute to Trócaire on the occasion of our twenty-fifth anniversary in 1998, the late Fr Niall O'Brien said of Trócaire: 'Trócaire is one of the things that makes me proud to be Irish. It is a church organisation that both feeds the poor and asks the question: "Why are they poor?"' It is a question that remains as valid today as when Trócaire set out thirty-seven years ago. It is a question that demands to be asked daily until it is honestly answered and the issues dealt with. It is a question that Trócaire will continue to pose in all that we do.

JUSTIN KILCULLEN